*World Food*

# MEXICO

Bruce Geddes

**WORLD FOOD Mexico**
1st edition

**Published by**
Lonely Planet Publications Pty Ltd A.C.N. 005 607 983
192 Burwood Rd, Hawthorn, Victoria 3122, Australia

**Lonely Planet Offices**
**Australia** PO Box 617, Hawthorn, Victoria 3122
**USA** 150 Linden Street, Oakland CA 94607
**UK** 10a Spring Place, London NW5 3BH
**France** 1 rue du Dahomey, 75011 Paris

**Photography**
All of the images in this guide are available
for licensing from Lonely Planet Images.
email: lpi@lonelyplanet.com.au

**Published**
March 2000

Although the author and publisher have tried to make the information as accurate as possible, they accept no responsibility for any loss, injury or inconvenience sustained by any person using this book

ISBN 1 86450 023 9

text & maps © Lonely Planet Publications Pty Ltd, 2000
photos © photographers as indicated 2000

**Printed by**
The Bookmaker Pty. Ltd.
Printed in China.

## About the Author

Bruce Geddes was born in Windsor, Canada and educated in Halifax, Guadalajara, Bogota, Kingston and Toronto emerging finally with an MA in Latin American Literature. Prior to this book (the 'Lonely Planet Period') he worked at several jobs culminating with a stint as editor of a horrible failure of a magazine called *MiGente*.

His interest in food & drink came before he developed the faculty of memory but his interest in Latin America is more clear. As an unruly adolescent he spent a year in Brazil which he describes as "like going into detox after a prolonged struggle with uptightedness." Yearning nostalgia kept pulling him back to South America, particularly Mexico where his heart remains. The rest of him lives and works in Toronto.

## About the Photographer

A predilection for playing with knives and fire led Greg Elms to a luke-warm vocation in catering. His life changed when he saw a black & white photograph of a pepper – now others cook while he eats the props.

His Mexican foray was an exercise in over-indulgence but, surprisingly, the highlight was neither alcoholic nor gourmand; it was in Puebla's zocalo, where he drank freshly-squeezed orange juice bought from a vendor who, he figured, had pushed his battered shopping trolley all the way from the orange groves. He's such a romantic at heart. Or so he'd have us think.

## About the Linguist

Paloma Novoa García, Encuentros Comunicacion y Cultura in Morelos, Mexico, and Bruce Geddes put the language section together.

## From the Publisher

This first edition of World Food Mexico was also the first book of the series. Sally Steward, Peter D'Onghia, Brendan Dempsey and Martin Hughes were the gastronomic pioneers who tread where many Lonely Planeteers feared to go.

Martin edited, and Brendan designed. Among the kitchen-hands, Felicity Julian proofed, Renée Otmar and Vicki Webb edited the language section, Charles Rawlings-Way mapped, Andrew Tudor and Tim Uden gave technical advice, and Lara Morcombe indexed. Peter D'Onghia over-saw production of the language section. Kate Ferris and Valerie Tellini from Lonely Planet Images (LPI) co-ordinated the supply of photographs. Sadly, Kate died before the book was produced. She is remembered fondly in all our hearts.

Sally Steward, publisher, developed the series and Martin Hughes is series editor.

## Acknowledgements

The publisher would like to give special thanks to Allison Jones, London, who made helpful suggestions for the series, Guy Mirabella for design concepts, and Richard I'Anson for photographic guidance. Muchas gracias to Paloma Novoa García, who was Greg Elms's guide.

The author wishes to thank Charles Austin, Flor Irene Bautista Carreño, Gustavo Jimenez, William Sosa, Silvia Borbón Zamora (Centro de Información y Documentación at the Museo de las Culturas Populares, Mexico, DF), María Imaculada, Cazzo Family, Ray Craib, Juan de Dios Cruz Bravo, Alicia De'Angeli (El Tajín, Mexico, DF) Jorge De'Angeli (Slow Food, Mexico, DF) Soledad Díaz Altamirano (El Topil, Oaxaca), Señor Erubey, Marco Espinosa, Laura Esquivel, Rachelle & Ian Geddes, Jim Holloway, Erin Iles, Alejandro Mangiola, Tom Lissamen, John Kirk, Rick Lopez, Julio Michaud, Monica (Moreno Travel, Toronto), Ken Norwood, Robert Plowman, Angelina Quiróz Sectur, Penelope Richardson, Claudia Rovelo, Andrew Sackett, Juan Antonio Salívar, Raquel Torres, Delia (UCLA), José Zozaya Agosa, and Aurora Zuñiga.

### Warning & Request

Things change; markets give way to supermarkets, prices go up, good places go bad and not much stays the same. Please tell us if you've discovered changes and help make the next edition even more useful. We value all your feedback, and strive to improve our books accordingly. We have a well-travelled, well-fed team that reads and acknowledges every letter, postcard and email and ensures that every morsel of information finds its way to the appropriate people.

Each correspondent will receive the latest issue of Planet Talk, our quarterly printed newsletter, or Comet, our monthly email newsletter. Subscriptions to both are free. The newsletters might even feature your letter so let us know if you don't want it published.

If you have an interesting anecdote or story to do with your culinary travels, we'd love to hear it. If we publish it in the next edition, we'll send you a free Lonely Planet book of your choice.

Send your correspondence to the nearest Lonely Planet office:
Australia: PO Box 617, Hawthorn, Victoria 3122
UK: 10a Spring Place, London NW5 3BH
USA: 150 Linden St, Oakland CA 94607
France: 1 rue du Dahomey, Paris 75011

Or email us at: talk2us@lonelyplanet.com

# contents

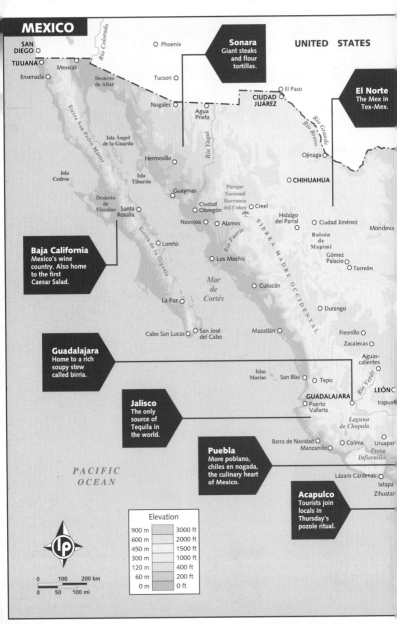

# MEXICO

SAN DIEGO
TIJUANA
Ensenada

**Sonara**
Giant steaks and flour tortillas.

UNITED STATES

**El Norte**
The Mex in Tex-Mex.

Phoenix
Tucson
El Paso
CIUDAD JUÁREZ

Mexicali
Desierto de Altar
Nogales
Agua Prieta
Ojinaga

Sierra San Pedro Mártir
Isla Ángel de la Guarda
Hermosillo
Rio Yaqui
CHIHUAHUA

Isla Cedros
Isla Tiburón
Guaymas
Parque Nacional Barranca del Cobre
Creel
Hidalgo del Parral
Ciudad Jiménez
Monclova

Desierto de Vizcaíno
Santa Rosalía
Ciudad Obregón
Navojoa
Alamos
Rio Fuerte
Bolsón de Mapimí
Gómez Palacio
Torreón

**Baja California**
Mexico's wine country. Also home to the first Caesar Salad.

Loreto
Sierra de la Giganta
Los Mochis
Culiacán
Durango

Mar de Cortés
La Paz
Mazatlán
Fresnillo
Zacatecas

Cabo San Lucas
San José del Cabo

**Guadalajara**
Home to a rich soupy stew called birria.

Aguascalientes
Islas Marías
San Blas
Tepic
GUADALAJARA
LEÓN
Rio Verde
Irapua

**Jalisco**
The only source of Tequila in the world.

Puerto Vallarta
Laguna de Chapala

**Puebla**
More poblano, chiles en nogada, the culinary heart of Mexico.

Barra de Navidad
Colima
Uruapan
Manzanillo
Presa Infiernillo

PACIFIC OCEAN

Lázaro Cárdenas
Ixtapa
Zihuatar

**Acapulco**
Tourists join locals in Thursday's pozole ritual.

## Elevation

| | |
|---|---|
| 900 m | 3000 ft |
| 600 m | 2000 ft |
| 450 m | 1500 ft |
| 300 m | 1000 ft |
| 120 m | 400 ft |
| 60 m | 200 ft |
| 0 m | 0 ft |

LP

0    100    200 km
0    50    100 mi

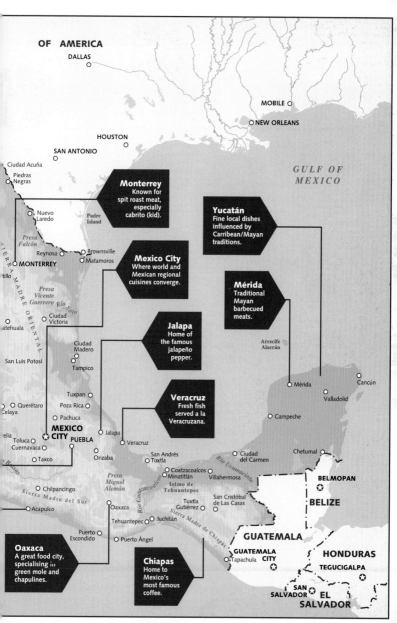

OF AMERICA

DALLAS

MOBILE

NEW ORLEANS

HOUSTON

SAN ANTONIO

Ciudad Acuña

Piedras Negras

GULF OF MEXICO

Nuevo Laredo

Padre Island

Presa Falcón

Reynosa

Brownsville

Matamoros

MONTERREY

**Monterrey**
Known for spit roast meat, especially cabrito (kid).

**Yucatán**
Fine local dishes influenced by Carribean/Mayan traditions.

**Mexico City**
Where world and Mexican regional cuisines converge.

**Mérida**
Traditional Mayan barbecued meats.

SIERRA MADRE ORIENTAL

tillo

Presa Vicente Guerrero

Río Soto

Ciudad Victoria

atehuala

San Luis Potosí

Ciudad Madero

Tampico

**Jalapa**
Home of the famous jalapeño pepper.

Arrecife Alacrán

Tuxpan

Poza Rica

Querétaro

Celaya

Pachuca

**Veracruz**
Fresh fish served a la Veracruzana.

Mérida

Cancún

Valladolid

Campeche

relia

MEXICO CITY

Toluca

PUEBLA

Jalapa

Cuernavaca

Taxco

Veracruz

Orizaba

San Andrés

Tuxtla

Ciudad del Carmen

Chetumal

Río Usumacinta

Chilpancingo

Sierra Madre del Sur

Acapulco

Presa Miguel Alemán

Coatzacoalcos

Minatitlán

Villahermosa

**BELMOPAN**

Istmo de Tehuantepec

San Cristóbal de Las Casas

**BELIZE**

Oaxaca

Río Coatzacoalcos

Tuxtla Gutiérrez

Sierra Madre de Chiapas

Tehuantepec

Juchitán

**GUATEMALA**

Puerto Escondido

Puerto Ángel

**GUATEMALA CITY**

**HONDURAS**

**Oaxaca**
A great food city, specialising in green mole and chapulines.

**Chiapas**
Home to Mexico's most famous coffee.

Tapachula

**TEGUCIGALPA**

**SAN SALVADOR**

**EL SALVADOR**

The cuisine of Mexico is a fiesta; a celebration of the senses, and a window to a past of conquest, colonisation, revolution and reconciliation. It is the rich aroma of a mole simmering on the stove, the light crispiness of a hot-off-the-comal tortilla, the sweat that goes with grinding corn into dough, the harsh fire of a bad tequila and the smooth lingering smokiness of a good one. It is market vendors singing the virtues of this bunch of onions or that basket of tomatoes. It is the bubble and pop of frying flautas at a street stall at night and the chatter of the hungry customers. It is the taste of chiles that are sweet and pleasant and chiles that burn in your mouth long after they have been eaten. It is the mealy corn in tortillas and tamales, the juices of sweet tropical fruits running down your arm, fresh fish grilled to perfection and served with a wedge of lime, and a cold beer or a rich hot soup, filled with the ingredients of this vast and varied land.

To understand Mexico, you must eat here. You must understand that food is a means of communication itself, with a unique discourse that reveals a Mexico not encountered through books and films. The thousands of dishes that are prepared daily – those dating back to pre-Columbian Mexico and those created yesterday – tell their own stories. Each time the dish is made the story changes; it is rewritten, extended and subject to new interpretations. This is much more than simple gastronomy. It's the history of the cooks who make it, the sociology of the families and groups that eat it, the politics of those who control it, the economics of growing it, the ecology that supports it, the anthropology of the peoples who introduced it. In a single bite of a taco, you open an encyclopedia of Mexico.

Whether you're exploring the cuisine in Mexico or your kitchen, treat this book as your jumping off point, from which you will make your own – mostly pleasant, never dull – discoveries about food and drink and Mexico itself.

# the
# culture
## of mexican cuisine

Food in Mexico has a unique significance which transcends mere nourishment. It is a medium of pleasure, a focal point for social gatherings and special celebrations, and a badge of identification. For years, the principal concern of Mexico's greatest thinkers has been a conundrum summed up as **la mexicanidad** (basically, what it is to be Mexican).

Before the 1910–17 Revolution, it seemed clear. Mexicans were descendants of either Spanish or Indians. The division was not entirely a product of skin colour but as much to do with dress, wealth, where you lived and what you ate. The Revolution revealed to Mexicans what should have been evident all along – Mexicans are Spanish *and* Indian, not one or the other. When the Mexican looks to his past, he looks as much to Madrid, Sevilla and Granada as to Tenoctitlán, Chizen Itza and Zempoala. This **mestizaje** (roughly translated as 'mixture') formed **la raza cósmica** (the cosmic race), the children of Cortés and his Aztec wife, la Malinche. They are drinkers of Indian chocolate with Spanish **leche** (milk) and readily pour a chile-based **mole** (speciality sauce, see Mole in the Staples and Specialities chapter) over a **puchuga de pollo** (breast of chicken). These dishes, and many others that combine elements of Spanish and indigenous cooking, have existed for centuries. But it is only since the Revolution that they were truly embraced as part of a national cuisine.

In many ways, the history of Mexico emerges through the foods eaten; how they were produced, purchased, prepared and presented. The story of corn and wheat is particularly revealing about the often uneasy relationship between Spanish and Indian heritage (see History later in this chapter).

Foreign influences, particularly French and American, also impacted on the Mexican diet. Conversely, Mexican food has found its way into the world – sort of. Fast food chains serve a version of Mexican food, loosely based on typical northern dishes. But a toned-down taco topped with sour cream and wrapped in wax paper is no substitute for the real thing. Fortunately, Mexican food uses very basic ingredients and simple methods so reproducing your favourite dishes at home is simple.

The average Mexican's day is centred around the **comida**, the multi-course meal taken between 1:30pm and 4pm. A business person might spend these hours at a restaurant with associates, discussing deals as though they were in a boardroom. In smaller cities and towns, the comida is a time for the whole family to come together, before returning to work or school. The truly civilised among them will carry on one of the most pleasant Mexican traditions, the siesta.

The **fiesta** is another great Mexican institution with food and drink at its foundation. The word translates literally as 'party' and, as such, has snuck into the world lexicon. But in Mexico, a fiesta refers to much more.

The Nobel Prize winning poet, Octavio Paz, wrote that the Mexican fiesta is "any occasion for getting together ... any pretext to stop the flow of time and commemorate men and events with festivals and ceremonies [where] time is no longer succession, and becomes what it originally was and is: the present, in which past and future are reconciled."

Mexico is one of the most celebratory societies in the world and each month, it seems, has its own holiday or fiesta. Some, like the day of the **Día de Nuestra Señora de Guadalupe** (Day of the Virgin of Guadalupe – 12 December), **Día de la Constitución** (Constitution Day – 5 February) and the **Día de la Independencia** (Independence Day – 16 September) are national celebrations but each town and village also has its own day to commemorate local patron saints.

Such fiestas are marked by parades and ceremonies, shouts and cheers, fireworks and pistol shots in the air, singing and dancing. They are times to mourn death and celebrate new life, to end stale romances and begin new ones. Rigid social conventions and the established order are cast aside and chaos reigns for a brief, impossible moment. The prohibited becomes permissible: macho men dress as women, political authority is reduced to a joke, the rich and poor mingle without hierarchical convention, and masks – both real and imagined – are worn everywhere.

In anticipation of a fiesta, women will spend entire days preparing tamales, tortillas and **guisos** (stews). The most humble families will save for years to throw their daughter a proper wedding party. And for those without the cash, an ancient system of bartering exists, where ingredients are swapped or labour is offered in exchange for food.

*Colonial woodwork, Oaxaca City*

Drinking goes on late into the night and delivers the licence necessary for a fiesta to truly become a fiesta. Beer, brandy, **tequila**, **mezcal**, and **pulque** will all be consumed in generous portions and contests break out to see who can drink the most. And when it's all over, everything returns to normal for a year. Memory, tradition and history ensure that the fiestas of a calendar year are repeated every 12 months. Imagine, on every 16 September since 1810, the president of Mexico has stood on a balcony overlooking Mexico City's **zócalo** (city square) to lead the crowd in the **grito**, a collective shout to celebrate Independence from Spain.

Food and drink are also the product of memory, not only for the recipes that were passed down orally through generations of women, but because the stories told around the stove created another layer of history, something beyond the military campaigns and economic experiments.

*Bull fight paraphernalia, La Maestranza Cantina, Guadalajara, Jalisco*

**CULTURE**

## History

When Columbus sailed across the Atlantic Ocean in 1492, he was on a mission to find, among other things, spices. Food and the history of Mexico have been entwined ever since.

Years before Columbus and his brethren began their Conquest of the Americas, Mexico was peopled by several indigenous groups. The Olmecs, Maya, Zapotecs, Totonacs, Toltecs and Aztecs built wondrous cities with huge pyramids, sculpted complex figures (of both real and mythical beings), shaped and painted pottery, and developed agriculture which catered to the local population and provided for trade with other cities.

Anthropologists believe that the first foods to have been cultivated in Mexico were varieties of squash and chiles, planted in the Tehuacán valley around 6500 BC. Corn, which came to hold great spiritual as well as nutritional value, has been traced back to 3500 BC.

By the time the Spanish arrived, farming, hunting and gathering had reached sufficient levels to provide a varied diet of vegetables (chiles, tomatoes, sweet potatoes, squashes, onions and others) fish (white fish, trout, lobster, crab, oyster and octopus), meat (frog, dog, armadillo, deer and turkey), as well as chocolate, honey, beans and corn.

Cooking techniques had also developed and tools such as the **comal** (a flat, clay pan that sat on the fire) and various other forms of clay pottery were in constant use. Corn was milled into **masa** (dough) to make tomales and tortillas. A bitter extract of chocolate was mixed with sweeteners and spices and then melted in water to make a hot drink popular among nobility. Ingredients and recipes differed from region to region but the domination of the Aztec empire and vigorous trade ensured that the best foods from one area would be known to cooks in others.

---

### THE CAESAR SALAD

Contrary to popular belief, the emperor of salads was invented in a Mexican kitchen and is not Italian. Several stories recount its discovery but the most popular traces the Caesar salad to a man called Alex Cardini. In the early 1920s, he was the young owner of the restaurant located in the Hotel Cesar in Tijuana, Baja California, a popular spot for day-tripping Americans and not far from the US-Mexican border. One particularly busy day, a large group of hungry Californians entered the restaurant after its stocks had been almost depleted. All that was left was some romaine lettuce, a few eggs, some stale rolls, garlic, lemon, parmesan cheese and olive oil. The inventive Alex whipped up what became the world's first Caesar salad.

In rituals, food was offered to the gods to ensure that the fields would continue to provide and hunters would continue to find success. Tomales, chocolate and human blood were among the edibles that would be placed on special altars dedicated to specific gods. The Aztecs demanded taxes in the form of food from the people they conquered and Teotihuacán was the site of many lavish banquets featuring dishes from all over the empire. In the court of Montezuma, servants prepared 300 dishes a day for their king and his honoured guests. Neighbours would show their friendship by exchanging **ollas** (pots) of stews and young women were judged by their family and society for their culinary skills.

The colonisation of Mexico threatened all of this. But native cuisines proved resistant and the Spanish eventually incorporated indigenous elements into their own cuisine, although not willingly. In the early days of the colony, King Carlos V populated New Spain with rigid peninsular administrators who hoped for nothing more than to finish their work, get rich and return to Spain. Mexico was not home for them, but rather an outpost and they demanded as much of Spain as they could get, including their favourite foods from the motherland. While some of the most typical Spanish staples – olive oil, wine and wheat bread – were difficult to produce in Mexico and expensive to import, much of what the Spanish introduced became a part of the Mexican diet, including beef and dairy products, pork and pork lard, chicken, and rice.

The fusion of Spanish and indigenous cuisines yielded mixed results. Chocolate was adopted enthusiastically into the Spanish diet and chiles turned up in several Spanish dishes and preparations including **chorizo**, the spicy sausage. Likewise, the natives discovered **manteca** (pork lard) as a cooking agent. Following independence, recipes for **chiles en nogada** (see Central Mexico in the regional Variations chapter) a truly **mestizo** (mixed) dish appeared. But other foods were resisted by both sides. The most famous example is that of wheat bread versus corn tortillas. Wheat bread was essential to the European table while corn tortilla had been a staple in the mesoamerican diet for the previous 2000 years. The Indians offered maize dishes to their gods, while the Spanish remembered theirs by breaking wheat bread. To a Creole, eating bread was a case of asserting identity. The church was adamant about the virtue of wheat and believed that converting pagan souls included converting their taste buds. By the end of the 19th century, the Porfirian positivists who were dominating the intellectual scene, declared that the lack of development among the Indian populations was due in part to a poor diet consisting mainly of corn. It was not until the middle of the 20th century that science finally accepted that eating maize, beans and chiles as a basic diet provided a balanced nutritional intake.

This acceptance of the tortilla paralleled the acceptance of other features of new nationhood. Led by the likes of artists, Diego Rivera and Frida Kahlo (see the boxed text Art & Mexican Food), educator Jose Vasconcelos and President Lazaro Cárdenas, Mexico came into its own as a nation. Indigenous identities were revisited and embraced. Food was no exception.

Mechanisation played a large role in the acceptance of the tortilla. The most labour-intensive part of the process, the milling of the corn, was the first to be supplanted by technology. The first automatic mills came into commercial use in the 1890s and made an immediate impact as tortilla-makers saw their productive capabilities soar. A drawback was that the mechanised masa lacked the same texture as the hand ground variety and purists still resist this development.

## ART & MEXICAN FOOD

Rufino Tamayo (1899–1981) may be the most famous worker ever to come out of Mexico City's Mercado de la Merced. Born in Oaxaca, Tamayo moved to Mexico City (DF) as a boy where he helped run an uncle's fruit stand at the market. This early experience clearly influenced his later work as one of Mexico's leading artists of the 20th century. He is known for his abstract figurative work and bold use of colour. He also produced several pieces featuring watermelon. *Sandías* (Watermelons) and *El Futuro Azul* (The Blue Future) are two of many appetising paintings. The watermelon motif is oft-used in Mexican painting as will be seen on any trip to the Bazaar Sábado in San Angel (in the south-end of Mexico City) or other markets selling paintings and prints.

Diego Rivera and Frida Kahlo, perhaps the art world's most famous couple, were key figures in the emergence of post-revolutionary nationalism. They embraced Aztec culture as any of Frida's self-portraits reveal. This extended to their diets: in one story Diego suggests serving stewed human flesh a la Azteca at a dinner party. Both used food imagery extensively in their work including Kahlo's *Naturaleza Muerta con Sandías* (Still Life with Watermelons) and *Los Cocos* (The Coconuts).

One of the most detailed and vivid food paintings available for public viewing is *Vendedora de Frutas* (The Fruit Seller) by the German-Mexican artist Olga Costa. This large and very detailed work depicts a peasant woman at the market with her products spread from edge to edge.

All of these works can be seen in either the Museo de Arte Moderna in Chapultepec Park or across the street at the Museo Rufino Tamayo.

*Outdoor pastelería (cake shop), Oaxaca City*

Further technological developments like the blender, refrigerator and pressure cooker have also eased the workload of Mexican cooks. Naturally, there is a price to be paid and there is no mistaking the difference in taste between a salsa that has been made with chiles crushed in a molcajete and those whizzed up in an electric blender.

Ironically, the popularity of eating out took off soon after it became easier to eat in. Part of the reason was the rapid growth of Mexican cities. The other was that restaurants were a natural by-product of the boom in Mexican tourism beginning in the 1940s. Mexico is now one of the most popular tourist destinations in the world. Initially, restaurants offered essentially Mexican fare, but today the main tourist areas are packed with American-style chains alongside. Around the same time, Mexico City's Zona Rosa began its reign as the most exclusive, most expensive night spot in the country.

What is most interesting about Mexican cuisine from an historical perspective, is how little has changed. What other national cuisine can point to staples like tortillas or tamales or beans and know that the way they are eaten today is the way they have been eaten for several millennia? Yet, it is still an accommodating cuisine, accepting and adapting to changes with great success. No doubt, it will continue to evolve – there will be new influences, new trends, shifts in the social fabric and in the way people eat – but these essential elements of Mexican cuisine are perhaps more secure than ever.

**CULTURE**

## How Mexicans Eat

The way Mexicans eat has changed a great deal in the past few decades. The rapid economic growth which followed WWII led to massive migration to the industrialised cities which ballooned in size. Infrastructure could not keep up with the growth and streets became congested with trucks, buses and cars which, for the first time, were affordable to the middle class. However, the price of progress meant that residential neighbourhoods were not built as close to the places people worked and Mexicans could no longer easily go home for their main midday meal, the **comida**.

While the comida is still the main meal, workers usually have it in restaurants these days. School-aged children still go home for comida but the main *family* meal is the evening **cena**, often the leftovers of the afternoon meal. It tends to be smaller than the 'suppers' eaten by North Americans or northern Europeans. Cenas become more complicated and lavish in the social context and you are more likely to have a date over cena than comida (unless your date is looking for an excuse to leave after a couple of hours). Restaurants in larger cities stay open until at least 11pm and offer the same menu as lunch minus the **comida corrida**.

*Mariachi in birreria, Guadalajara, Jalisco*

Outside the cities, the comida is still most important. Entire towns shut down from about 2–4pm (the hours vary from place to place); businesses lock their doors, taxis seem to disappear and noise from the street subsides until late afternoon when it all starts up again.

The kind of **desayuno** (breakfast) you eat will also depend on how busy the rest of your day is. For those on the go, it may consist of nothing more than a cup of coffee and a sweet roll or donut. There are even subway advertisements pitching those meal-in-one breakfast bars that allow you to carry on business while you eat. Children will have a more traditional breakfast, sitting down to a bowl of cereal or toast, or perhaps a little **recalentado** (reheated leftovers) from the day before. When there is time or demand, a full breakfast of eggs, cheese, fruit and meat served with freshly squeezed orange juice is prepared for the whole gang. When there is not time, a box is removed from the freezer, popped in the **microondas** (microwave) and the juice comes from a powder and water concoction.

*Pastelería (cake shop) display, Puebla*

For those who did not have enough at breakfast, there is the late morning **almuerzo** (brunch – sometimes translated as lunch). There is nothing formal about this meal, which really amounts to a glorified snack: a quick plate of tacos or a sandwich will do.

A 19th century memoir demonstrates how much has changed. For Guillermo Prieto, the day started with a hot bowl of chocolate made with **leche** (milk) and served with **pan** (bread). At 10am, almuerzo was served and commonly consisted of omelettes, grilled meat or fish, accompanied by beans. As today, the comida began around 2pm when the father returned from work. A soup began the meal, followed by a **sopa seca** (any dish cooked in water or a reduced broth, such as risotto). After the main dish a small, sweet **postre** (dessert) set him up for the afternoon siesta. Another bowl of chocolate with sweet rolls and pastries made up the late-afternoon **merienda**, the equivalent of the English tea, served with friends and family. Cena was served as late as 10pm and consisted of a stew or mole. With five meal occasions a day you have to wonder if he had time for much else.

This is not to say that convenience food belongs exclusively to the modern diet (although it did not originate in cellophane packages with instructions for cooking). **Antojitos** were the original take-anywhere food experience. The word is translated as 'little whimsies' although they are much more than simple snack foods, and include tacos, quesadillas, sopes, totopos, tamales and tortas. You can pick up a couple of tacos from a street stall to bridge the gap between meals, or order a plate of **tacos de pollo** (chicken tacos) at a restaurant, enjoy them

*Drinking from balsa de plastico (plastic bag), Oaxaca City*

with a beer, decide you'd like something else and order **tacos arabes** (tacos made with slightly thicker wheat bread). And if you're still not satisfied, you can choose something else and your 'little whimsy' has turned into a big meal. **Almuerzo**, the disappearing institution of brunch, consists almost invariably of antojitos. But antojitos can be eaten at anytime of the day or night, up to the wee hours of the morning after an evening of music and dancing.

The defining game becomes even more difficult when you consider that every meal usually includes a stack of hot tortillas. Most diners will take whatever is on the main plate – chicken, meat, potatoes, beans – and spoon it into the tortilla to customise the taco. So cena becomes antojito and antojito becomes cena. Definitions aside, they are pleasantly unavoidable and anyone who visits Mexico is bound to become **antojadizo** (used to antojitos).

José Iturriaga, who has written an extensive study on antojitos called *La Cultura del Antojito*, says that the defining ingredient of this most Mexican of foods is the **masa de maíz** (corn dough). It is only when this has been shaped appropriately and stuffed (it doesn't matter with what) that the antojito is created.

*Birria, a Jalisco speciality*

*Some traditional foods of Veracruz. Clockwise from left: Chilpacho (shrimp soup), pulpo en su tinta (octopus in its own ink), mojarra a la Veracruzana (spicy baked fish), salsa, limes, vuelve a la vida (cocktail of shrimp, octopus, snail and crab), camarón (prawns), centre.*

Corn is probably the most pervasive element in Mexican cooking, although staple items such as **frijoles** (beans), **arroz** (rice) and the chile are not far behind. No pantry is complete without these basic ingredients and many may not contain much more than that. When they do it is likely to be **queso** (cheese), **huevos** or **blanquillos** (eggs), **carne** and **pollo** (meat and chicken) and vegetables like **tomate** (green tomato), **jitomate** (red tomato, specifically plum or roma), **cebolla** (onion), **pimentón** (sweet peppers or capsicum), **zanahoría** (carrot), **pepino** (cucumber). The most common spice is **cilantro** (coriander) although chile powders, **oregano**, and **ajo** (garlic) are also important. As cooking agents, **aciete** (oil) is most common although most households will have a container of **manteca** (pork lard) for flavour and in deference to tradition.

Not every kitchen is the same, of course, and differences are especially noticeable between regions. Coastal towns, for example, will rely on fish, caught by people in the community and sold in local markets. Local specialities, a unique bread or a kind of fruit or vegetable grown in the area will also distinguish the Mexican pantry.

## Etiquette

There are no hard and fast rules regarding eating and drinking in Mexico and those that do exist are more about common sense than anything: wash your hands before eating (especially when you expect to have tortillas, which are always finger food, even in the snootiest restaurants). Don't talk with your mouth full. Don't throw food etc. If anything, Mexican meals tend to be pretty casual with lots of conversations carrying on at once. It is acceptable to attract a waiter's attention as he is walking by as opposed to waiting for him to make his rounds to your table. You are expected to eat well and, as a guest, eat a lot.

At home, rules vary from family to family. In big families, meals can be chaotic with children competing for their parents' attention, platters of food being passed in all directions, and lots of lively conversation. The mother runs the whole show, making sure that everyone eats their fill and gets the proper portion of vegetables. The male members of the household will rarely share in meal-time chores, leaving the cooking and cleaning-up to the women. While the mother rushes around making sure the salsa is fresh and the tortillas don't burn, the father will sit in the easy chair, watching television or reading the newspaper. It is an ongoing custom despite the gains women have made outside the home. The machismo extends to the table, where the dominant male will sit at the head of the table, like the chairman of the board.

Food is served in casseroles or on platters and you are expected to serve yourself. Plates are laid out on placemats along with the requisite fork, knife and spoon. A salt and pepper shaker and napkin dispenser may be the only other non-food items on the table. Because many Mexican foods are eaten with the fingers, everyone goes through several napkins in a single sitting. Likewise, drinks – usually water – are served in a jug of some sort and someone may have to get up mid-meal to go for a refill.

*Buffet lunch, Hotel Majestic*

Banquets and other celebrations require a much more detailed approach to dinnerware. A multi-course meal requires several plates and corresponding utensils. Cloth napkins, preferably shaped into some bird-like form, are de rigueur.

Religious homes may say a blessing before diners can begin to eat although Mexico's long and complex history of shaky relations between church-state have mostly eliminated the practice. Most meals begin as soon as you sit down. The mother will usually take her chair last, first ensuring that everything is on the table, and that everybody is happy. If you ever have the chance to eat in a Mexican home, you will be asked several times if everything if fine and if you have enough. We were guests at one home that served a tremendous feast of stewed chicken, rice, tortillas, salads, enchiladas and cooked vegetables. After a good hour of feeding frenzy, the hostess offered us more. When we declined she seemed rather disappointed. "But you haven't eaten anything!" she said. A friend who lived in Mexico as an exchange student had to bring a lunch for some school field trip. His host mother gave him a whole roasted chicken!

There is a certain sloppy quality to eating many dishes because so many begin with a tortilla which is filled with spoonfuls of whatever meat, fish or vegetable is featured. With practice, you will become skilled at knowing just how much your tortilla can take, the ways to fold it so that you don't leave one end open and ready to spill the contents. Until then, make sure there are lots of napkins handy and you're not wearing a white shirt.

Not all meals are at a table. Children often have lunch in the kitchen and most houses will have a small table for that precise purpose. In larger families, these informal occasions allow for rare moments of one-on-one bonding.

Smoking in restaurants is common, but never during an actual meal. It is only after the plates have been cleared that lighting up is acceptable. At home, of course, if the dad wants to smoke, he smokes.

*Eating tacos al pastor, Mexico City*

## Foreign Infusion

There is a tendency in a world obsessed with categorisation to put culture and statehood on the same level, a habit which complicates our understanding of food as a product of a particular place. In Northern Mexico, for instance, the cultural border with Texas is rather blurry. Along the Gulf Coast, from Quintana Roo to Veracruz, food and cooking from Cuba and other parts of the Caribbean is so common that it can't be considered an influence, but a true and traditional part of the culinary culture. Likewise, Chiapan cooking shares several traditions with its southern neighbour, Guatemala.

The original foreign influence on Mexican cuisine was, of course, the Spanish. So great was its impact that today it is impossible to divorce the Spanish from the Indian and vice versa. The Spanish brought wheat, rice, beef and dairy products, pork, wine and such spices as oregano, cilantro (coriander) and saffron.

Spanish cuisine itself evolved after a long series of invasions and occupations that ended only when the Moors were finally driven from the peninsula in 1492, the same year that Columbus discovered America. The Moors had been in Spain for some 700 years and before them the Visigoths, Celts, Vandals and others had their day, bringing new foods and preparations from their homelands. The Romans gave them olive oil (which they, in turn, had taken from the Greeks), the Egyptians brought garlic and the Moors left behind citrus groves, rice fields, eggplants, watermelons and saffron. More importantly, the Moors left a new sensibility about the enjoyment of eating which is reflected today in a typical Spanish **comida** (lunch) which can last up to four hours. One still sees Moorish influence in the names of many common foods: **naranja** (orange), **ajonjoli** (sesame), **ajo** (garlic) and **azafrán** (saffron).

Arab influence has also extended to modern Mexico. One of the better known ways of eating tacos is **al pastor** (shepherd), inspired by the Middle Eastern method of cooking meat on a vertical spit. **Tacos Arabes** are tacos wrapped in **pan arabe**, a wheat bread resembling pita but thinner. In fact, a more appropriate name would be **tortilla arabe**.

## France

Relations between France and Mexico during the 19th century were, to say the least, tumultuous. The French invaded on two occasions, in 1834 and 1864. The second time, Napoleon III installed the Austrian archduke Maximilian and his wife, Carlotta, as emperor and empress. Maximilian and Carlotta brought all the material trappings of French society – architecture, fashion and food – to their court in Chapultepec Castle. The Mexican elite, happy for a break from the years of liberal reform brought by

*Street musician, Oaxaca City*

President Benito Juarez, passionately embraced French culture. Even after the emperor and empress were expelled in 1867 (Maximilian was executed in Querétaro; Carlotta fled back home to Europe and eventually went insane) the **afrancesimiento** (roughly, the Frenchifying) and the taste for things French continued. This naturally included cuisine and Mexico City restaurants caught on to the trend, adding rich sauces and other typically French elements to their menu.

## Argentina

For the **aficionado del carne** (meat lover) there are a number of Argentine **parilladas** (grills) in Mexico City. In Argentina, a parillada is an all-day affair similar to northern Mexico's **asado** (see The Northern Asado in the Celebrating with Food chapter) where copious quantities of red meat are grilled over an open pit and washed down with jugs of red wine. In Mexico, a parillada is a place to enjoy thick cuts of beef. It is a custom that has emerged in the last 30 years, some say because of all the Argentine footballers who came to play in Mexico and stayed. Others attribute it to the fact that during the 1970s, Mexico was seen as a safe haven among Latin America's persecuted left, including those being persecuted by Argentina's military regime.

These restaurants are concentrated in Mexico City's more affluent neighbourhoods like the Zona Rosa and Polanco and tend to be expensive. Steaks are served on wood **tablas** (flat boards) with **chimichurri** (a parsley, tomato and olive oil sauce), fresh bread and French-fried potatoes. Regular servings tend to be enormous, too much for even the most ardent carnivore and many dishes are enough for two.

## United States (US)

The most prominent modern influence is from north of the border. At one time, much of present day US was part of Mexico. This included the states of California and Texas which explains the presence of restaurants on both sides of the border offering cooking styles known as Cal-Mex and Tex-Mex. But US influence extends beyond that, especially in the fast food arena. A **hamburguesa** (hamburger) is a mainstay of nearly every low to mid-price restaurant in the country. Hot dogs are popular street foods. When Mexicans don't feel like cooking they are likely to order a pizza, whether with pepperoni and mushroom or with a Mexican touch of **frijoles** (beans), **chorizo** (spicy sausage) and **chiles jalapeños**. Fast food outlets such as McDonalds and Kentucky Fried Chicken are extremely popular with locals, and, despite being much more expensive than their Mexican equivalents, attract hordes of customers.

**CULTURE**

For the most part, the menus at the international fast food restaurants differs little from country to country. There is, however, the occasional concession to **mexicanidad**. McDonalds, for example, offers a **McMuffin a la mexicana** which includes **frijoles refritos** (refried beans), a folded omelette with tomato, onion and chile jalapeño on a toasted English muffin. You can often tell if a restaurant is American by their insistence on incentive pricing. Instead of 27 pesos, a meal will go for 26.90, which, if truth be known, is less a price incentive than it is an annoyance as the virtually worthless 10 peso coins accumulate in your pockets.

Today it seems that there is no avoiding the foreign presence (but perhaps not influence). Pro-trade economic policies have led to new products being introduced to the Mexican markets. Kiwi fruit from New Zealand, pears from the US, beans from Colombia, lychees from the far east, and many other 'exotic' items are slowly becoming part of the Mexican diet. The trend is likely to continue, though the overall impact is more difficult to predict. Purists can rest easy that tortillas, chiles and tequila will be a part of Mexico for many centuries to come.

---

### THE UN OF FOOD

The Zona Rosa in Mexico City is a concentrated fusion of foreign influences in the Mexican restaurant industry. Catering to the rich and beautiful, the Zona is also home to most of the city's expensive hotels, and foreign business travellers invariably end up here.

There is a Japanese place, on Genova, called *Mr Sushi*. Across the road, *La Parilla Argentina* serves huge steaks in the gaucho tradition. Next door is an Italian restaurant called *La Gondola* followed by the Mexican affiliate of the US *Hooters*. On the next block, *Copenhaguen,* another American joint, *(A place called) Freedom,* serves ribs and burgers with vintage ads for guns and ammo displayed on the walls. Beside it is another meat-eaters' delight, *Angus Butcher House,* where the waitresses are all six-feet tall and look like supermodels. According to a waiter at *El Perro Andaluz,* the Spanish place across the street, the women audition for the role and come from as far away as Cuba to work here. There is a Greek place called *Zorba's,* a Chinese restaurant called *El Dragón,* and a *Chalet Suizo* (Swiss Chalet). Its like a culinary United Nations with all the cultural clichés on show. But eating globally doesn't come cheap: a full meal with drinks in the Zona begins around US$10 and goes up – way up – from there.

## Local Cookbooks

Cookbooks have been helping to spread and maintain Mexican culinary traditions since the middle of the 19th century. With the post-war economic expansion, known as the Mexican miracle, and the increase in literacy brought on by increased social spending, the demand for these books increased. Today, nearly every magazine kiosk carries a selection of low priced magazine-sized books that also serve as advertising vehicles for the product which is most prominently featured (eg flour for tamales, mayonnaise, etc). These magazines are highly specialised and range from single-product titles such as *Thirty ways to cook Nopales*, to recipes for a particular celebration such as a **quinceño** (when a girl turns 15), to collections of economic meals. For information on more expensive and durable cookbooks see the chapter on Recommended Reading.

# staples
## & specialities

Some foods emerge as staples because alternatives are scarce, as with corn, beans and rice in Central America. Mexicans have made these basics their own by shaping the corn into tortillas, tamales and other antojitos, by refrying the beans, by combining dried shrimp with rice, or by adding a salsa made with fresh or dried chiles. It is the destination, the completed work, where cuisines are distinguished, whether between nations, regions or two kitchens on the same street.

# Salsa

Walk into virtually any restaurant in Mexico and you will see a bowl of salsa waiting on each table. It is the most common condiment here, meant to be sprinkled or poured onto every dish on the menu. Most restaurants have their own unique salsa, varying in spiciness and flavour. These are not the same salsas that come in jars. In Mexico, salsas rely more on the flavour of the chile where commercial brands have a barely noticable chile factor, using it to vary the grade of spiciness rather than taste.

A basic salsa includes chile, tomato (green or red), **cebolla** (onion), **ajo** (garlic), **jugo de limón** (lime juice), and **agua** (water). This simple combination gets complicated when you consider that any of the vegetables may be roasted first to bring out a smoky flavour or that there are over 300 kinds of chiles in Mexico and some salsas require many different ones.

The most common are the tomato-based **salsa verde** (green) and **salsa roja** (red). The texture of each will depend on how aggressively they are ground. The best ones are a bit chunky, with cool bits of tomato and onion, bathing in the slight spiciness of a **chile serrano**.

The chunkiest is **salsa bandera**, so-called because its tomatoes, onions, chiles and coriander carry the three colours of the Mexican flag. It is easy to make: chop up equal amounts of the first three ingredients, squeeze in some lime juice or white vinegar, and season with salt and pepper.

Not all salsas are limited to the four or five basic ingredients. In some restaurants, especially Argentinian ones, diners are served a bowl of **chimichurri**, an oily mixture of parsley, onion and lots of garlic. A thin version of **guacamole**, made with mashed **aguacate** (avocado), onion and cilantro will also often make its way onto the table to be served with either bread or **totopos**, deep-fried wedges of stale corn tortillas.

Other salsas have left the realm of accompaniment and graduated to a higher level. **Mole**, which has become one of the keystone dishes in Mexican cuisine, is defined not by its meat (usually chicken or turkey) but by the flavour of the sauce itself. In fact, it's not even considered a member of the salsa family, although it is certainly a sauce. Another national culinary treasure, **chiles en nogada**, features a white almond sauce covering a roasted **chile poblano** stuffed with a ground beef and potato mixture called **picadillo**, and topped with bright red pomegranates. **Enchiladas**, with its chile-based sauce blanketing a trio of corn tortillas stuffed with chicken, is another example of a salsa that defines the dish (see the recipe for Enchiladas later in this section).

In other dishes, such as **Huachinango à la veracruzana**, the salsa and meat are mutually essential. **Huachinago** is red snapper broiled (grilled) and made **à la veracruzana** with a salsa of tomato, onion and green olives.

## Salsa Roja

The most basic and popular of accompaniment salsas, is also very simple to make. The traditional method requires a **molcajete** (thick clay bowl) and **mano** (pestle) but a blender or food processor will do.

### Ingredients
4   plum tomatoes (plum are best because they are
        meatier, but any red, ripe tomato will do)
1   medium onion
    a handful of chiles  (the kind of chile is a matter of
        personal taste but, remember, smaller means spicier)
1   clove garlic
    salt

Boil a pot of water, add a teaspoon of salt, remove from heat. Drop in the tomatoes and let them sit for a minute or two. Drain them and peel. Chop the tomato. Finely chop the onion and pepper. You may wish to remove the seeds from the pepper to reduce the **picante** (heat). Toss all the ingredients into the molcajete and smash them with the mano, using a pounding, twisting motion. When the salsa has reached a smooth consistency, it is done.

For variety, add a couple of tablespoons of cilantro, some freshly ground black pepper, a few teaspoons of lemon juice, a tablespoon of oil (olive preferably). You may also wish to add texture by setting aside some of the chopped ingredients then adding them once the rest have been ground into liquid.

STAPLES

At **desayuno** (breakfast), an order of **huevos rancheros** will get you scrambled eggs topped with a red chile sauce. **Chilaquiles**, another common breakfast meal, consists of day-old tortillas smothered in the same chile sauce and sprinkled with cheese. You may wish to sauce up a **torta** sandwich at **almuerzo** (brunch) or drizzle a spoonful into your soup at **cena** (dinner). It's perfectly acceptable to have salsa with everything, to dip bread into the bowl at the table, or even to spread a spoonful on a fresh tortilla and roll it into a **taquito**. Try it on meat, rice, or mix it with the pool of refried beans.

Chile-based salsas are also widely available in bottled form in grocery stores. They are quite different from homemade salsas yet still delicious as a condiment (and easier to take home). Brand names such as 'Bufalo' are rust-coloured with a smooth, thickish consistency. It's unlikely that you will see bottled salsas in restaurants but they can sometimes be requested. In the streets, you will see them at stands with potato chips and **chicharrón** (fried pork crackling) which are sprinkled with bottled salsa and lime juice.

Foreign contributions available in Mexico include the **salsa de tomate**, sometimes referred to as **catsup**. **Salsa bolangnesa** is a tomato-based sauce used on pasta. **Salsa inglesa** translates as 'English sauce' in order not to torture the Spanish tongue with the word 'Worcestershire', and **salsa china** or **salsa soya** is soy sauce.

## Enchiladas

Enchiladas are a wonderfully versatile food. The only essential ingredients are tortillas, salsa and some sort of filling. The following uses chicken and vegetables but you can use absolutely anything.

**Ingredients**

| | |
|---|---|
| 9 | tortillas (preferably corn but wheat will do) |
| 5 | ounces (150g) white cheese |
| 1 | breast of chicken |
| ½ | small onion |
| 3–6 | chiles (fresh serranos are best but this depends on your tolerance for spice) |
| 1 | cup (250ml) homemade salsa (see recipe for salsa earlier) |
| 1 | tablespoon of oil |

Begin by making a **guiso** (stew) of the chicken, onion, and chiles. Chop finely and sauté in oil until the chicken is cooked and the onion is soft. Heat the tortillas on a flat pan and then roll 2–3 tablespoons into the tortilla. Set in an oven-proof dish, top generously with the salsa and the cheese, then cook under the broiler (grill) until the cheese melts.

# Soup

Much of Mexico is at high altitude and you'll probably need a sweater or a **serape** to stay warm at night. In these conditions a hot **sopa** is the perfect evening meal. Pre-Hispanic cultures knew this method of staying cosy, using vegetable, fish and turkey **caldo** (broth). Most soups today are made from chicken or beef broth and can include an infinite variety of ingredients.

In Mexico City's Mercado de la Merced, there are stacks of **tripa** (tripe), bought in large quantities for use as a flavour base in huge pots of soup. Restaurant chefs and others who cook for a lot of people come in early to buy stacks of the stuff, along with other cuts that don't have so much table appeal: intestines, head, **patas** (hooves) etc.

Perhaps the best known soup is **pozole** which, while made all over the republic, is the pride of the state of Jalisco. There, the pozole is white and includes kernels of **elote** (hominy), chicken, **garbanzos** (chickpeas), shredded cabbage and

*Chilpacho (shrimp soup), a Veracruz speciality*

radish. It can be taken as an appetiser in small bowls or served as a full and hearty meal. In Michoacán, the pozole is made with pork or beef broth. Red chiles add colour and spice. It is possible to get both versions throughout the country and at least one restaurant chain, *Potzollcalli*, specialises in pozole as a meal.

**Sopas secas** is a dry soup and **sopas aguadas** liquid. Sopa seca refers to rice and pasta dishes such as risotto, or anything that was cooked in water or a reduced broth.

Although eaten across classes, soup has traditionally been very important in peasant diets as it provides an excellent source of protein and a means of stretching a little meat a long way. Virtually every comida begins with a sopa and many cenas consist of nothing more than reheated soup with a stack of tortillas.

## Chiles

Put simply and without exaggeration, there would be no Mexican food without the chile. There are very few typical dishes that do not include the chile, whether included in the actual recipe or added later in the form of a sauce. "The chile runs in our veins," wrote Laura Esquivel in a 1993 introduction to *La cocina del chile*. In other parts of the Spanish-speaking world the chile is called **ají**.

The first chiles were cultivated around 3000 BC and have remained a part of Mexican cuisine ever since. They are used as a seasoning with eggs, beans, meats and fish, as a basis for salsas or as a main dish itself, as in **chiles en nogada** or **chiles rellenos**. While most chiles aren't particularly **picoso** (hot), the penetrating spiciness can be the undoing of even the most steel-gutted foreigner. Yet, to a native, the chile is nothing less than the flavour of Mexico.

### Don't You Mean Chillies?

When it comes to this fiery speciality the Mexicans know best. As you're not likely to mistake these powerful pods, and you won't thank us if you do, we've used the local spelling throughout the book.

Natural diversification and biotechnology have given Mexico 300 known varieties. They range from the fist-sized **chile poblano** to the miniature **chile pequín**. They range in colours from orange to red to yellow to green. They can be eaten fresh or preserved by drying in the sun. Cooks will chop or grind the chile raw as an addition to a salsa, or they can be stuffed, dipped in egg batter and fried, roasted or pickled. At the market there is no mistaking their section where the carefully stacked chiles emit a rich, pungent aroma that only hints at the full flavour potential.

*Chiles, Mercado de La Merced, Mexico City*

*Chile stand, Tepoztlan market.*

**STAPLES**

Chiles are grown throughout Mexico although climate and soil conditions dictate which native species will flourish and which varieties must be imported from other parts. Perhaps the world's most famous chile is the **jalapeño**, the stubby, green variety named for the city of Jalapa, capital of the Gulf Coast state of Veracruz. Its fame is due to the enterprising people who decided to pickle it and send it all over the world where it serves as a condiment in Tex-Mex restaurants and the subject of macho dares. The jalapeño in pickled form (sometimes referred to as **en adobo**) is often served in small dishes in Mexican restaurants too, where diners are welcome to garnish their **tortas** or **tacos** with a few thin slices.

The most salient quality of the chile, its spiciness, is down to capsacin, a chemical naturally present in the fruit and concentrated in the seeds and veins. Most dishes call for the removal of both so the flavour of the exterior flesh can be emphasised. A good mole, for example, calls for five different kinds of chiles. Yet, the result is a wonderful balance of many flavours and the spiciness serves to complement each of the others. The impression many foreigners have of Mexican food as a cuisine of firery spice is mostly inaccurate. In fact, it is considered a black mark on the record of the chef who puts too much chile into a dish.

Pre-Hispanic Mexicans believed that the chile contained medicinal qualities. The Aztecs used them to cure respiratory and digestive ailments as well as to alleviate toothaches and earaches. Modern science has confirmed the nutritional value: chiles are high in vitamins A and C and contain vitamins E, B1, B2 and B3.

## THE MOST COMMON CHILES

These are the most common chiles to be found in Mexican markets and on menus. As a general rule, the smaller the chile is, the spicier it will be:

**Chile de arbol.** So named because it grows on short trees while most others are found on shrubs. This chile is small and dark green when fresh but is more often found dried, when it turns a reddish orange. It is very spicy.

**Chile pasilla (chilaca).** Long, thin and deep green when fresh, the pasilla turns even darker, almost black when dried. It is not too spicy and used typically as a garnish for tortilla soup.

**Chile habanero.** Hot things come in small packages. The habanero is also called the scotch bonnet in the English Caribbean and is common in the Yucatán where it is used raw in table salsas. It is about the size of a table tennis ball and comes in several bright colours, each of which is extremely spicy. It should be used with caution, but for those who are prone to throwing caution (and their intestines) to the wind, be sure to have something nearby that will extinguish the fire: a cucumber, slice of tomato or bowl of yoghurt.

**Chile chipotle.** This is a dried and smoked version of the jalapeño which is served in a vinegar **adobo**. It is dark, reddy-brown in colour and spicier than its green cousin. You can buy this canned **en adobo** and use it in your own homemade salsas.

**Chile manzano (cascabel).** Shaped like a small apple, with a yellowish colour, this chile is commonly used in its dried form. Its shell is hard and rattles when shaken, which is why it is sometimes referred to as **cascabel** (rattle).

**Chile poblano.** This is the most common one for making stuffed chiles. It is large, dark green and mild tasting. When dried, it darkens and is called **chile ancho**.

**Chile serrano.** This is a very popular and spicy chile used in moles, soups and stews. Short, thin and green, it is often pickled. When dried it turns bright red and is called **chile japónes**.

**Chile pequín.** The smallest chile of them all is known to many (although not by name) as the fiery base for Tabasco Sauce. The chile pequín is very hot.

# Corn

In their first attempts to create the Mayan people, the gods used clay and wood. But the clay was not strong enough and the wood lacked soul. The perfect balance, according to the *Popol Vuh*, the Mayan holy book, was found in **maíz** (corn). Using both white and yellow corn, raw and ground, the Mayan gods fashioned the great race which has flourished in south-eastern Mexico despite years of attempted assimilation and extermination. To sustain themselves, it was only natural that their diets should be based on corn.

While contemporary scepticism may conclude that corn gained its spiritual meaning because it served as an important nutrient and agricultural crop well before the myth of creation, there is no doubting its importance – both nutritionally and spiritually.

Anthropologists say that the first corn was planted in the Valley of Mexico between 5000 and 3500 BC. At the time, the Indians, who inhabited the region, called it **toconayo** meaning 'our flesh'. Babies were referred to as 'maize blossoms' and young girls were called 'tender green ears'. The 'Lord King Cob' was a strong and able warrior. Corn made the indigenous people what they were and was treated with due respect. Not a kernel was wasted and many societies used corn as the principal offering to their gods.

*Tamales & tamales dulce, Puebla*

Much of the economic activity of the country centred around the cultivation and consumption of corn. Men would tend to the crops while women were charged with converting it into an edible form. This process began with soaking the kernels over night in a mixture of warm water and lime stone in order to soften the hard shells to the point where they could be milled. In the morning, the milling process began, using a metate and mano to grind small portions of kernels into a smooth **masa** or dough.

Over the years, experimentation propelled the many uses for corn: from movie-house popped, to the dough used in tamales and atole, and to corn roasted on the cob and served on a stick. According to historian Eusebio Davalos Hurtado, there are over 700 different dishes that use corn as a base including the very common tacos and quesadillas, but also the rare and exotic such as tamales stuffed with pickled fruits or pockets of corn masa filled with various viscera then fried and smothered in salsa. But by far and away, the most popular use of corn is the tortilla which serves as the basis for the ample selection of antojitos.

*Corn seller, Mexico City*

# Tortillas

There may be nothing better (or more Mexican) than the taste of a hot corn tortilla, straight from the comal, almost too hot to touch. A fresh tortilla, cooked until slightly crisp on the outside, almost melts in your mouth, filling it with the taste of corn.

The tortilla is a hugely important food in Mexico. It is a symbol of a link with a past that stretches back 2,500 years. It is the main source of nourishment for many Mexicans, especially those in rural regions. Simultaneously a food and a utensil, it serves as a receptacle for stews, grilled meats, vegetables, guacamole, potatoes, rice – virtually anything that will fit in the cradle it forms when folded in two.

The origin of this simple flat bread is thought to be in the central highlands of Mexico and, while the method for making them has changed considerably with the arrival of new technology, the ingredients have not. Until the beginning of the 20th century, the daily life of the Mexican woman revolved around the preparation of the stacks of tortillas that would feed her family. For generations of farmers the need to grow corn for tortillas provided their source of income. This history is the reason why the tortilla is such a strong symbol of what José Vasconcelos called **mexicanidad**.

In traditional tortilla making, kernels of corn are cut from the husk and then soaked in a mixture of warm (but not boiling) water and cal or mineral lime. (In markets across the country you can still buy chunks of this white, chalky stone.) The corn must soak for at least 5–7 hours, usually overnight.

The next morning the corn is rinsed and drained and is now referred to as **nixtamal**. It is then ground into a masa using a **metate** and **mano**. The metate is a heavy clay grinding stone with a flat surface and three legs. Like the **molcajete**, the surface is textured to aid the milling process. The mano is a long round roller of sorts, made slightly wider than the metate but of the same textured material.

The process of turning corn into masa is very laborious, requiring the cook to kneel in front of the metate using the mano to grind and roll. The masa has to go through the whole process three times to achieve the proper consistency for making tortillas.

Once done, the cook can begin shaping the tortillas by hand. A hunk of masa, the size of a golf ball, is first pressed flat and then passed from palm to palm with each stroke making the tortilla a little flatter until, after 30–40 slaps, the tortilla is the right thickness. It is then placed on the **comal**, a flat, iron pan which has no rims, allowing the cook to get close to the surface. The tortilla cannot be dropped as any air trapped underneath will create pockets that can lead to uneven cooking. After about a minute or so, the tortilla is flipped and cooked on the other side. Vigilance is important, for burning a tortilla is considered bad luck. The result is a slightly crisp yet chewy tortilla that is best eaten right away.

Today, most tortillas are not made in the home but in commercial bakeries. The biggest plants employ several hundred workers and distribute their product throughout the country. But you can still buy your daily supply at **tortillerías** located in the neighbourhood. According to a 1992 study, there are some 18,000 such independent establishments in Mexico.

One place is the *Tortellería Alex*, located in Jalapa, Veracruz. The bakery is dominated by a huge tortilla machine that stretches the 5m length of the shop. With it, Alex produces some 600kg of tortillas each day, and with about 35 tortillas to the kilo, that means about 21,000 per day. The stream of customers is as constant as the flow of tortillas and so it is rare that the product ever waits on a shelf, which is good because there is no extra space here.

It is possible to combine some of the traditional way of tortilla-making with modern technology. Masa is widely available in just-add-water versions eliminating the time-consuming and back-breaking milling process. You can also buy a heavy iron **prensa** (press) which quickly turns a ball of dough into a perfectly round tortilla, ready for the comal. *Maseca* is a commercial brand of instant masa widely available outside Mexico in Latin American speciality food shops. The press is harder to find and you may have to purchase it in Mexico. A regular rolling pin will also work, although achieving the perfect roundness becomes trickier.

*Tortillería, Cuernavaca*

Tortillas come in all sizes, from 5cm, doubled up for plates of tacos, to the giant **tlayuda** from Oaxaca. They come in different colours and flavours depending on the type of corn used.

Tortillas need not only be made from corn flour. The northern tortilla is white, made from wheat, softer in texture and larger than the corn variety (see El Norte in the Regional Variations chapter).

## The Basic Tortilla

For corn tortillas you can buy *Maseca* at any good Latin American store and add water. Wheat tortillas can be made from scratch with the following recipe.

**Ingredients**
- 9 cups flour
- 2 teaspoon salt
- 6 tablespoons vegetable shortening (be exact)
- 1 cup (250ml) of warm water

Mix the first three ingredients until the flour has a grainy consistency. Add the water slowly, continually mixing the dough until you have a somewhat elastic, shiny mass. Cover with a damp towel and let it sit for 45 minutes.

To make the tortillas, pull off a golf ball-sized hunk of the dough and work it gently in your hands to form a round ball. Pat it down gently then use a tortilla press or a roller to flatten it to the proper thickness (2–3 mm). Cook on a hot flat pan turning once after about one minute or until the edges begin to brown. Serve immediately and keep warm in towels or a **tortillera** (a thermal container for tortillas). Hint: when rolling it, you may want to use two sheets of wax paper to prevent sticking.

The tortilla has been used in Mexican cooking for over 2,500 years and continues to be one of the most versatile and utilitarian foods in the world. Whether camping or supplied with a fully-equipped kitchen, the tortilla can be used to wrap anything and everything.

Make your own guiso by stewing meat and finely chopped vegetables (include tomatoes to create a bit of a sauce). Fold the results in a warm tortilla and enjoy a fork-free, plate-free meal or create your own fusion foods using tortillas to hold foods from other cultures: curries from India, stir fries from Asia, even mashed potatoes with onion and garlic.

## Tamales

The **tamal** is not the most common dish on menus here but it is nevertheless a key element in the nation's gastronomic fabric. Someone from Campeche may brag about a tamal made there with a salsa of guajillo chiles, **axiote** (a regional spice), jitomate, garlic, onion, pepper, clove, cumin, oregano and mixed with pork, olives, almonds, **chile dulce** (sweet chile) and wrapped up in tightly packed masa. Meanwhile the Sonoran can take pride in the **nacatamal**, the regional speciality made with pork, olives and raisins. The two of them can then get together and show their national tamal pride before the other tamales made in the Americas, from the Mississippi Valley to Colombia.

The word tamal (plural: tamales) comes from the nahuatl word **tamalli** and refers to anything wrapped up. The design is pragmatic, with the **hoja de platano** (plantain leaves) serving as plate and insulator, keeping the contents warm. They may have been the Americas very first take away food.

But the tamal has also gained great ceremonial and ritualistic importance. It was used regularly as an offering to the gods. Even to the present day, women will spend hours preparing tamales for family celebrations like weddings and **quinceños** (when a girl turns 15) or for national and regional fiestas. On the **Dia de los Muertos** (Day of the Dead) relatives of the deceased will build an altar and leave their loved one's favourite tamal (see the Celebrating with Food chapter for details of these occasions).

A tamal essentially consists of three elements: the leaf, the masa and the **relleno** (filling). The leaf is generally the massive hoja de platano which is wrapped around the filled masa, chile sauces and even mole. Sometimes the relleno must be cooked first, sometimes the ingredients are cooked within the tamal. The only kind of meat never used is the **chivo** (goat) which has given rise to an expression, 'hagan de chivo los tamales' (make tamales of goat) which refers somehow to a spouse's infidelity.

The most common cooking method is **a vapor** (steamed) using a large double-boiler with the tamales sitting atop a **tapesco**, or bed of plantain leaves. They can also be cooked underground, in the same sort of apparatus used for softening maguey plants for **mezcal**. Others are roasted on a comal or fried in fat.

The tamal is one of the dishes being reclaimed by nueva cocina mexicana (new Mexican cuisine, see the boxed text in the Where to Eat and Drink chapter). In restaurants in Mexico City, chefs are experimenting with new ways of cooking and presenting this ancient dish. One place uses a mould to give definition to the normally shapeless tamal. Another place we visited in the federal district, *El Tajín*, makes a tamal without masa, in the tradition of the mixiotes, another kind that is small and eaten as a **botana** (snack).

*Tamales & Tamales Oaxaquenos (in banana leaves)*

## Manteca

It may be difficult for some to accept pork lard as a national speciality, but such is the case with **manteca**. It is not so much that manteca from Mexico is any greasier or lower in cholestoral than manteca in other parts of the world, but rather that Mexicans use it a great deal and it does bring a distinctive flavour to many dishes.

There was a time when manteca was used as the sole cooking agent. Olive oil was available as an import and was, therefore, only affordable to the very rich. Likewise, butter was just too expensive for most. And so, in the true spirit of frugality, manteca became the fat of choice.

Today, it is still widely used, but cooks conscious about the ill-effects of too much saturated fat use it with vegetable-based oils to preserve the special **toque** (touch) of a dish traditionally made with more manteca.

## Cheese

A wide variety of cheeses are available at supermarkets and speciality shops in municipal markets but Mexicans mainly use just two varieties in their cooking: **quesillo**, a stringy goat's milk cheese from Oaxaca and **queso fresco**, made with cow's milk. In the north, the Mennonite communities produce several varieties which are stamped with a seal of authenticity and are renowned throughout the country.

Cheese is used as a stuffing for antojitos or as a covering for dishes such as **chilaquiles** and grilled meats. It can also be eaten as a **botana** either before a meal or with cocktails.

Mexican cheeses are mostly mild in taste and do not have the heavy creaminess associated with high fat-content cheeses. One exception is **queso añejo** a hard, aged variety with a sharp flavour similar to parmesan.

*Woman selling Oaxacan cheeses, Mercado Juarez, Oaxaca City*

Beans & Rice 45

Beans and rice are listed together because they serve as a staple food for many Mexican diets – beans provide the protein and rice the carbohydrates. In higher altitudes, dried beans are better cooked using an **olla de presión** (pressure cooker). Without one, your pot of beans will have to boil for hours before they are ready to be eaten.

The most common way to eat rice is steamed. It can serve as a side dish or be mixed with meat and vegetables to make a casserole. Beans are most often eaten **refritos**, first cooked then crushed or pureed then refried with manteca and spice. Virtually every **entrada** (appetiser) in a Mexican restaurant will come accompanied by a large spoonful of this brown paste, sometimes topped with crumbled queso fresco and a few totopos. Refried beans are generally made with the red kidney variety. Black beans are also used widely and a popular Veracruz dish includes them with onion, bacon, jalapeño chiles and cheese. There is even a tasty dish made in the Yucatán and on the Gulf Coasts which combines white rice with black beans and goes by the decidedly tasteless name **moros y cristianos** (Moors and Christians).

*Beans, Tepoztlan market*

# Mole Verde (Green Mole)

This most Mexican of recipes is also one of the most time-consuming and laborious. That said, there is probably no greater sense of culinary accomplishment than creating your own mole. The most famous among them is the mole poblano which can be found in paste form in many Latin American food stores. **Mole verde** is a personal favourite. It is very good yet relatively simple compared to some common moles which may include dozens of ingredients and require half your day in the kitchen.

## Ingredients

### Meat
2    large chicken breasts
1    small onion, diced
     salt

### Sauce
2    small cloves of garlic              pinch cumin
1    can plum tomatoes                   pinch black pepper
½    medium onion, chopped               salt
1    clove
½    cup cilantro (coriander)
1    teaspoon vegetable oil
½    cup pumpkin seeds
1    small chile jalapeño, stems and seeds removed
2    chile serranos, stems and seeds removed
6    boston lettuce leaves (or 3 romaine leaves)
½    teaspoon ground cinnamon

Cook the chicken and diced onion in 6 cups of boiling water, skimming the scum from the top. Cook until the breasts are nearly done. Remove the chicken and strain the broth. Toast the pumpkin seeds on a flat pan stirring occasionally to prevent burning. This should only take four to five minutes. Cool and then mash in a blender until powdery. Mix in one cup of the broth. Remove from blender. Drain the canned tomatoes and toss them in the empty blender with the chiles (remove the seeds to reduce the heat). Add lettuce, onion, garlic, coriander, ground cloves, cinnamon, pepper and cumin. Blend until smooth. Heat oil in the pan then heat the pumpkin/broth sauce for about five minutes, stirring constantly until thick and dark. Add the vegetables and stir. Gradually add about 2 cups of chicken broth (depending on thickness), and simmer for 25–30 minutes. Season with salt. Just before serving, return the chicken to the sauce until it heats through.

# Mole

Mole is one of the national dishes that defines Mexican cuisine. It is used on all festive occasions and each region, even each family, has their own variation, from the very simple to a very complex combination of ingredients and precise preparation (some recipes call for up to 100 ingredients!). The first mole is said to have come out of the city of Puebla, to the south-east of Mexico City. There, a Dominican nun, Sor Andrea de la Asunción, discovered the magical, indescribable flavour that the addition of chocolate gave to her **guiso** (stew) of puréed roasted chile, clove, cinnamon, pepper, cilantro, sesame seeds and turkey broth. Another legend attributes mole to a certain Fray Pascual, who stumbled upon the recipe when he spilled an entire spice tray into his cooking pot. Others attribute the development of the sauce to the 17th century taste for the baroque in arts and culture. If a building could be composed of as many decorative and lavish ornaments as could possibly fit, they reasoned, then why not a dish? Contemporary researchers believe that the mole is a result of a long development process that began in pre-Hispanic Mexico. The name is derived from the Nahuatl *molli* for sauce and not, as many assume, from the Spanish *moler*, to grind.

A mole is worth having at least once, as it is truly a unique experience. It tends to sit heavily in your stomach afterwards so you might decide one experience is enough. Unfortunately, because of the complexity of creating a mole, many restaurants simply don't bother. You can, however, buy moles in powder form or in a thick concentrated paste which is reconstituted using broth or water.

What makes the mole so important to the Mexican identity is its reliance on the fusion of the native and the Spanish ingredients to make a single, homogeneous sauce to be served with turkey or chicken or even fish. It is a truly mestizo dish and has therefore been embraced by patriotic Mexican foodies for centuries.

*Mole and salsa roja, two Mexican specialities*

STAPLES

*Meat on a spit, Tepoztlan*

## Meat

When an Aztec noble really wanted to live it up, he'd request a stew made with the meat of dog. And not just any mutt either, but the **izcuintli**, a breed that today is all but extinct (perhaps the nobles lived it up a bit too much). Failing izcuintli, he might have a tasty frog, or the succulent white meat of snake, a roasted armadillo, even the gamey meat of deer if it was available.

The Spanish weren't keen on the wild carnivorous tastes of their conquered race and immediately began breeding cows and pigs for meat consumption.

Mexicans are big meat eaters, especially when dining out. The most popular tacos are **bistec** or **al pastor**. Bistec is thinly sliced beef which is chopped and fried before being stuffed into a hot tortilla shell. Tacos al pastor is an all-day preparation, where a pile of beef is stacked with onions and seasoning on a vertical spit and then slow roasted, rotating before a hot element. The idea is that the meat cooks at the same rate as customers demand it so everyone gets juicy meat in their taco but often you'll end up with overdone, dry meat – another reason to stick to busy places.

If truth be known, the best beef is to be found in the gargantuan portions of tender rib-eye, sirloin and veal offered by one of the Argentinian restaurants in Mexico City. Kid is very big up north, and is the most important ingredient in **birria**, a Jalisco speciality.

# Poultry

**Pollo** is very popular in Mexico and is prepared and eaten in a variety of ways, the delectable greasiness of a **roticieria**, where flocks of birds roast on a spit and are served by the quarter, half or whole, to the **mole poblano** which calls for a chicken breast or leg, although in this case, the chicken is secondary to the rich chile-chocolate sauce in which it is smothered.

**Pato** (duck) is a delicacy although a man who lives near the airport in Mexico City claims that, in his neighbourhood, duck is a common dish. At the time of the Aztecs, Mexico City was as much water as it was solid land and one such body of water attracted ducks migrating south from their summer habitat in the marshes of Canada and the US. The locals naturally took advantage of this opportunity and duck became a seasonal mainstay in the neighbourhood. Even after the lake dried up and the ducks fell under the protection of environmental laws, the habits of the **barrio** (neighbourhood) continued and to this day, it is known (although not by many) as an area with a penchant for duck.

The first poultry to be a part of the Mexican diet was **pavo** (turkey). In the pre-Hispanic kitchen, it made its way into many **guisos** (stews) which survive in some variety today.

*Chicken seller, Mercado Juarez, Oaxaca City*

# Fruit & Vegetables

The colours of a municipal market are testament to the abundance of fruits and vegetables available. Blackberry, spinach, broccoli, carrot, raspberry, strawberry, grapefruit, apple, pineapple, chayote, eggplant (aubergine), onion (green, purple and white), beet, potato, green pepper (capsicum), pumpkin, cabbage, mango, grape, orange, papaya, passionfruit, melon, pear, prickly pear, lettuce, purple onion, radish, squash, tomatoes (both green and red), white onion, zapote negro and many others, are piled high.

You will also see piles of **nopales** (the flat leaves of a cactus plant). Nopales grow everywhere in Mexico as any bus ride will show. They are prepared for sale by removing the spikes and peeling thin strips from the edge then eaten like any other vegetable.

Strangely, cooking here does not include as many vegetables and fruit as you might think, given all that is available. But that shouldn't stop you from trying them. A selection of fruits can make a refreshing salad, perhaps a welcome change from the more common meat and tortilla-based meals.

While eating whole fruits is not a universal practice, drinking fresh juice is. At **puestos** (street stalls) all over the country you can purchase a cup of fruit juice made to order.

Vegetables such as onions, tomatoes and chiles are commonly used as additions to salsas or stews. Less common are lettuce-based salads, although shredded lettuce is a common topping for **tostadas** or **huaraches** (fried, thick corn masa) where they might be joined by radishes and carrots. Again, if you have access to somewhere where you can cut vegetables, you may wish to make a trip to a market, buy your favourite salad fixings and make your own. Fruits and vegetables should be thoroughly washed in purified or bottled water before eaten (see Water in the Fit & Healthy chapter).

*Nopales, Mercado de La Merced, Mexico City*

# Herbs & Spices

When you live in a land of 300 chiles, other spices take a back seat.
Indeed, in most typical Mexican dishes, the chile (whether ground, in dry
powder or fresh) provides the undertones that distinguish the good from
the sublime. Actually, there are other seasonings, besides salt and pepper,
which are used in the Mexican kitchen.

Cilantro (coriander) is the most common flavouring agent after the
chile. It is used fresh only in salsas, soups and stews. In the south,
particularly on the Yucatán peninsula, a similar herb called **epazote** is used
in place of cilantro although the flavour is distinct. You may also
occasionally taste oregano, parsley or thyme in certain dishes and spices
such as cumin, cinnamon (particularly in chocolates and sweets) and cloves.
**Laurel** (bay) is also essential for use in soups and long-cooking stews.

STAPLES

*Top: Eating huauzontles – the buds are pulled off
the stem by running thumb and forefinger along it*

*Spice ingredients for cooking birria*

## Bread & Baked Goods

Bread, or **pan**, made from wheat flour, was introduced to Mexico by the Spanish. Because wheat was so much harder and more expensive to grow in Mexico, it became a symbol of elitism among the Spanish and Creole population. Young men, even those who in reality were too poor to afford bread, reportedly sprinkled crumbs on their jackets and collars to feign prosperity. Today there is still an air of elitism to eating wheat bread. The best restaurants will serve a basket of it with butter prior to a meal while the more modest ones will serve a container of tortillas.

Bread is an important breakfast food – whether in the form of freshly baked **cuernos** (croissants), **banderillas** (long flaky pastries) or **conchas de vanilla** (a mini-loaf topped with a vanilla icing). Other families will eat toasted slices of **Bimbo**, a brand modelled after Wonder Bread which stays fresh for an unnaturally long time. **Donas** (doughnuts) are popular in many splendid varieties: chocolate, cinnamon and multi-coloured sprinkles on white icing.

French-style baguettes are widely available and although not as long as the European variety, serve well as the basis for tortas. Smaller french rolls, called **zeplines**, are also made into sandwiches.

Another popular variety is the **pan de yema**, a yellowy, rich, almost heavy bread made with egg yolks. A similarly heavy bread is the glazed **pan de muerto** (bread of the dead).

*Panadería, Mexico City*

*Veracruz fish market*

## Seafood

Mexico's two coasts are blessed with a wide variety of **pescado** (fish) and **mariscos** (shellfish). The lakes and rivers of the interior also provide many fresh-water species, although increased levels of pollution have raised questions about the safety of eating these.

The most common variety of fish is **huachinango** (red snapper) and **rabálo** (sea bass). On menus, when you see the word 'fillet' under the pescado section, you can assume that you will be served some sort of white fish. Dried, salted cod, called **bacalao**, is a popular fish when chopped and added to soups.

Shell fish is for the most part a delicacy although **ceviche** is common. This is a sort of cocktail with shrimp, oysters or crab mixed with **escabeche**, a sauce made with lime, onion, salt, tomatoes and bottled salsa.

# drinks

Mexico's warm climate has inspired a wealth of alcoholic and non-alcoholic drinks. Tequila is a source of national pride and its harsher tasting cousins, mezcal and pulque, are used as tools to test male machismo. Beer is also an ambassador to the drinking world with brands like *Corona* and *Dos Equis* exported to all corners of the globe and the red *Tecate* logo has become a mainstay on the world racing car circuit. With all the hype about alcohol, it is easy to forget – at least until the morning after – the dozens of juices available and the ancient drink known simply as 'chocolate'.

## Alcoholic Drinks
### Tequila

There was a time in Mexico when tequila was the exclusive tipple of testosterone-driven machos. Elsewhere, it was known only to American frat boys as an instant intoxicator during college hazing rituals or to tourists who drowned it in syrupy margarita mixes. Tequila has grown up considerably and is now regarded as a more refined drink. On a wine list (so called even if there is no wine on the list) the price of a shot of tequila can rival that of an imported single malt whiskey and is taken much the same way: neat in a small glass, enjoyed with decadent pleasure in tiny sips.

The turn back to tequila is being led by young people, who are abandoning cocktails with brandy or rum in favour of a nice **reposado** or **añejo**. Their enthusiasm has given rise to a new breed of mixed drinks to join the margarita. A Bloody María, for example, substitutes tequila for the vodka of a Bloody Mary. A tequila martini, with a drop or two of dry vermouth, is available at trendy bars in Mexico City.

But the most popular tequila technique is still to drink it straight from one of three glass sizes: **cañita**, **caballito** and **medida**. The time-honoured tradition of using salt and lime remains but more frequently tequila served in restaurants comes accompanied by an equal portion of **sangrita**. This thickish, bright-red drink is made with orange juice, grenadine, chile and salt and is available in bottles wherever tequila is sold but is also made in restaurants with far better results (see the Sangrita recipe later in this section). Sangrita prepares your mouth for the tequila with a tartness that complements the smoky bite of the shot.

*Planting blue agave for tequila, Jalisco*

*Cutting Agave plants for mezcal*

Lime and salt are also eschewed by the macho tequila drinker but for those willing to forego their manhood for the sake of taste, this combination is best when sangrita is not available. As tradition dictates, salt is sprinkled on the flat part of an upturned fist and then, in almost one fluid motion, licked off, followed immediately by a good suck at a lime wedge. The mouth is now conditioned and ready for the tequila, which can go in by sips or all at once.

In bars you may be coerced into a tequila popper (or slammer), where a member of the waiting staff mixes tequila and Sprite in a glass, smacks it on the table to cause a carbonated eruption, then helps you throw it down by shaking your head. It's good for a few laughs, mostly at your expense.

All tequila sold throughout the world comes from the state of Jalisco where the arid climate and highland soil provide perfect conditions for the blue agave cactus, from which tequila is derived. **El Consejo Regulador de Tequila** (the Tequila Regulating Council) ensures that any tequila produced outside of the state doesn't call itself tequila.

Legend has it that a bolt of lightning struck a blue agave plant, releasing the pungent nectar found in this cacti's heart. The natives learned to boil the hearts then mash the plant to release juices which were then fermented. The drink was ritually used to induce euphoria in warriors, priests and shamans.

**DRINKS**

The Spanish brought more sophisticated distilling techniques and the modern tequila industry was born. The same basic process is used to this day: the **jimador**, the man responsible for the initial stages of the tequila-making process, first prepares the **piña** (heart) of the mature blue agave (only the blue agave is used) by removing the leaves and stock. The plant is then steamed for up to 36 hours to soften the fibres and release the **aguamiel** (must). The next stage, mashing, separates the fibre from the thick, dark juice with the liquid funnelled into large tanks for fermentation. It is then distilled, sometimes twice, and pumped into barrels for aging.

The length of the aging process determines the colour, taste, quality and price of the tequila. The basic, common **blanco** is aged least, followed by **reposado**, left to age for 2–12 months, and **añejo** which has a dark, whiskey-like colour and undertones of wood. The most common fine tequila, Don Julio, named for the founder of the Tres Magueyís tequileria is aged well over a year. Some añejos remain in their barrel for up to 12 years and sell for over US$200 a bottle.

The first mass production plant was founded by Don Pedro Sánchez de Tagle in 1600. Today there are dozens of distilleries and the best known, *Jose Cuervo* and *Sauza*, dominate the Mexican market and export their product worldwide. Most offer tours and all are located within day-trip distance of Guadalajara.

**DRINKS**

## Sangrita

This non-alcoholic drink makes a great accompaniment to any of the better tequilas. You can either drink it following the tequila or take it in alternating sips. There are bottled versions available but it is much better made fresh.

**Ingredients**
1      cup (250ml) fresh orange juice (the fresher the better)
1      tablespoon (15ml) grenadine
       pinch of dried chile powder (depending on your tolerance
              for spice, ground white pepper can be substituted)
       salt to taste
1/2    teaspoon (2ml) of lime juice (or the juice of a quarter of
              a small lime)

Mix all ingredients well, preferably using an electric mixer or blender. Chill for at least two hours before serving and serve only cold. Yields about four servings.

*Tequila selection, Guadalajara, Jalisco*

## Mezcal & Pulque

The antecedents of these two drinks may have been something the Aztecs called **octli**. It was made from a combination of the juices from different agave plants. However, drunkenness was frowned upon in pre-conquest Teotihuacan and nobles favoured the sweet, frothy taste of chocolate for their liquid indulgence. Octli was, for the most part, strictly reserved for feasts and other celebrations. But even then, excess was not permitted and those that had one-too-many were punished by being put to death.

The modern versions of mezcal and pulque are the poorer cousins of tequila. They are made from any one of a variety of **maguey** plants in small, independent distilleries dotted across the country. Mezcal is the drink made famous by the worm that appears at the bottom of some bottles. The idea is to eat the worm after finishing the bottle, a ritual that foreigners are particularly encouraged to participate in. But in actual fact, the worm is a bit of pasta, placed there to symbolise that the mezcal is flavoured with the dried and ground remains of the **gusano maguey**, a worm that lives in the plant.

Pulque is cheaper, less potent but much harder on the palate than mezcal or tequila. It is somewhat thick and foamy, with a cloudy colour. Traditionally, it's produced and consumed at bars called **pulquerías** and is difficult to find commercially (see the boxed text, Pulquerias – The Original Mexican Watering Hole, in the Where to Eat & Drink chapter).

*Tequila & Mezcal shop, Jalisco*

DRINKS

## Cerveza (Beer)

Mexican beer seems to have been precisely engineered to go with Mexican food. With a few exceptions, it is light and well-carbonated, perfect for dousing the spiciness of a chile sauce and cutting through the grease of a **cabrito asado**. Alcohol content is only specified by the phrase 'menos que 6°' (less than 6%) but is likely to be more.

The Aztecs had a kind of beer called **sendecho**, which was made with corn as opposed to barley and flavoured with **tepozán**, a vegetable with curative qualities. The Mayans also had a brew made with juice extracted from corn stalks. The Spanish introduced European-style beer to the Americas soon after the conquest, but it wasn't until the end of the 19th century that brewing really took off in Mexico. It's no coincidence that this was around the same time as improvements in refrigeration made it possible to keep beer cold.

There are two major breweries in Mexico. Modelo, based in Mexico City, makes Corona, Negra Modelo, Montejo, Modelo Especial, Modelo Light, and Victoria. Cuauhtemoc Moctezuma, the Monterrey-based brewery, is responsible for Dos Equis (the XX beer), Sol, Bohemia, Tecate, and Carta Blanca. Many brands began as independents but were swallowed up along the way by the two giants. Competition is fierce and both breweries spend millions every year trying to win over the beer-drinking public. Television commercials are incessant, you can't walk down a street without seeing a billboard and at football games two enormous inflatable cans stand behind each goal. Small restaurants and food stores leverage deals on signs and furniture by including the logo of one brand or another. Beer companies are universal sponsors and have floats at **carnaval**, bullfights, wrestling matches, rock concerts and wherever else people congregate. The names and logos have become part of the urban landscape and are rivalled only by the Coca-Cola wave.

At the home of the Cuauhtemoc Moctezuma brewery in Monterrey, Nuevo Leon, the cultural significance of beer is hammered home. The plant is not only the base for a major national icon, but also an art museum featuring the work of the likes of Roy Lichenstein, the American pop artist who took comic strips to a new level. In another building (but all part of the same free tour) the Mexican Baseball Hall of Fame displays memorabilia from the stars of Mexico's second most popular sport. Afterwards, you can enjoy a complementary cerveza **a barril** (draught beer) in the open-air beer garden, where a line of trees blocks your view of the surrounding factories and rail cars.

Naturally, every beer has its niche market. Corona and Sol seem to go after the football market and have their logos emblazoned on the jerseys of many first division teams. Bohemia and Negra Modelo, with their gold foil wrapping around the neck of the bottle, targets the connoisseur. Victoria, identifying itself as neither a dark nor a light beer, targets those suffering from a crisis of identity. And, tellingly, there are no Mexican non-alcoholic beers. Light beers include low-calorie (and low-taste) versions of brands like Corona and Modelo. Imported beers, mostly from the US, are available in supermarkets and convenience stores and include non and low alcoholic varieties.

The time-honoured practice of plunking a wedge of lime in the mouth of a bottle of Mexican beer is not as common in Mexico as it is in foreign bars serving Mexican beer. Legend has it that the practice began as a means of keeping the flies out of the beer and developed into an essential part of the beer drinking experience. It is much more common to receive a small plate of lime wedges with your order, leaving the decision, to squeeze or not to squeeze, up to you. With the lighter, crisper beers like Corona or Montejo, the squeeze option may actually improve the taste, but the best Mexican beers require nothing more than a bottle opener.

*Bohemia beer & birria*

### Buying Beer

Beer is available in virtually every store that sells food, from the closet-sized neighbourhood kiosks to the colossal grocery stores. There are special shops which devote themselves to selling cold beer at lower prices, but they are mostly designed for larger purchases and are neither numerous nor conveniently located.

You can buy beer in bottles or cans, as singles, in six-packs and in cases of 24. However, bottles require a deposit and deposits are store-specific, meaning that if you want your money back, you have to return the empties to the same place you bought them. We ran into one shop that was even trickier than that. They wouldn't let us buy a beer without returning an empty for every new one purchased. Furthermore, the proprietor required that we buy the brand of beer that corresponded to the empty, a sort of forced brand loyalty of which marketing types can only dream.

## CERVEZA (BEER)

The following is a highly subjective rating of Mexican beers. My own taste tends to run somewhere between light American lagers and hoppy British bitters. For the most part, Mexican beers tend to be on the **clara** (light) side of the beer spectrum following the German lager tradition as opposed to the darker ales of the UK.

**Bohemia** – with its gold foil wrapping and simple label, Bohemia is marketed as *the* premium Mexican beer. In fact, it's also the best tasting, being slightly bolder than the rest, yet not so heavy as to ruin it as a refreshing accompaniment to Mexican food.

**Dos Equis Obscura** – Obscura (dark) is harder to find than its Lager cousin, but well worth a try if it comes your way. The dark is more a description of its colour, but the taste leans ever-so-slightly toward malty.

**Dos Equis Lager** – one of Mexico's most popular brands, this familiar green bottle contains a balanced lager, the perfect accompaniment to food, especially larger meals like comida.

**Montejo** – once only available in the Yucatán, where it was named for a local hero, Montejo is still very popular in the south but now available in many other parts of Mexico. A straight-ahead lager, it stands up well to Dos XX.

**Negra Modelo** – Mexico's only true dark beer. Don't expect a soupy Guinness, but dark beer lovers will get a measure of satisfaction from this ale.

**Pacifico** – as the name suggests, this beer is most common on the Pacific coast of Mexico. An adequate lager, perhaps a bit light.

**Victoria** – advertised as something between a light and a dark, this copper brew is available everywhere.

**Indio** – another dark-in-colour, light-in-taste attempt at an ale but a bit sweet for my liking.

**Tecate** – I only ever saw Tecate in cans, which to me is an unfortunate way to drink a beer.

**Corona** – despite its world-wide popularity, Corona is not among my favourites. It does the job on a hot day at the beach, but falls short as a complement to food.

**Carta Blanca** – Monterrey's favourite brew. Carta Blanca is the beer of choice with cabrito and if that's all there is available then it will do. Otherwise, it's a bit light and tasteless.

**Sol** – Sol is not a good beer. Although one of the most aggressively marketed, it is very light, very bland and very unsatisfying.

**DRINKS**

## Wine

Mexicans don't drink much **vino** but they have had little choice. The conquistador, Hernán Cortés, brought the first vines from Spain in 1524, making Mexico the first wine-producing region in the Americas. In fact, such was Cortés' passion for the preferred drink of his homeland that he issued an edict ordering all new settlers to plant vines on their lands. At the time, New Spain included Northern California, one of the finest wine-producing lands in the world. Production in Mexico, however, went into decline and the remaining vineyards used their grapes for brandy. America's wine-making legacy was left to Chile, Argentina and California.

In the 1940s the industry was revived and 10 states, led by Baja California with its temperate climate, began to once again grow grapes for wine. But in a country where traditions of eating and drinking were well established, the return of wine was not met with open arms and the evolution was a slow process.

Furthermore, the majority of the grapes grown went to make brandy which gained popularity as a cocktail drink and continues to be among Mexico's best selling alcoholic beverages. This is a situation the wine growers would no doubt like to see change, with an eye to the enormous commercial success the Chilean and Argentinian wine industries have had exporting their product all over the world.

Julio Michaud, a food writer with *El Universal* and author of a book on wine in Mexico, believes that drinking habits among Mexicans are changing, albeit slowly.

"Thirty years ago, it was rare to see wine on a table, but today in the finest restaurants it is rare not to see a bottle of wine on the table ... people who go to Europe and the US and get exposed to other wine drinking cultures are coming back and demanding wine here." Michaud also cited the emergence of several wine clubs as proof of a growing appreciation for table wine in Mexico.

Be that as it may, wine is by no means a popular drink. With the exception of a very few labels, it is priced out of the range of even middle-class Mexicans and is much more expensive than other drinks like beer or tequila. There may be some hope that free trade agreements with wine-producing countries like the US, Canada and Chile will bring better wines into Mexico at more reasonable prices, but for now, you can either pay a lot or drink something else.

Pedro Domecq is the undisputed champion of the wine industry in Mexico and shelves in stores are dominated by the name. Others include Cetto, Bodegas de Santo Tomás, Casa Madero (Coahuila) and Bodegas Balmar.

## Sparkling Wines

Champagne is, of course, exclusive to that area in France for which the drink is named. Sparkling wine, however, can come from anywhere, including the state of Querétaro in Mexico. Both drinks are out of the price range of most Mexicans and even those who can afford it drink it only on special occasions. There is only one such vintner in Mexico, Sala Vivé, which also has the license to make Freixenet, the famous black-bottled sparkling wine from Spain which produces some 100 million bottles per year worldwide. The Querétaro location accounts for a mere 350,000 of those bottles.

Sala Vivé is located in a beautifully maintained hacienda outside the small town of Ezequiel Montes, about three hours north of Mexico City or an hour east of Querétaro. The hacienda is surrounded by relatively small fields of grape vines, supported by neat rows of white poles. Freixenet chose this area for its soil conditions and climate. Launched in the early 1980s, it is only the second branch outside Europe (the other is the Sonoma Valley, California, US). Tours are available and make a nice afternoon trip from picturesque Tequisquiapan, a nearby town.

## Brandy

Part of the reason for the slow development of the wine industry in Mexico is that most of the grapes grown in the country go to producing brandy. They share the same history and, today, the same companies that produce wine also produce brandy and the Pedro Domecq label dominates the market. Brandy grapes are grown mostly in the north in the states of Sonora and Baja California.

As a drink, brandy rose in popularity in the 1960s contributing to a period of rapid expansion for the industry. During the 1970s the amount of acreage devoted to grape growing doubled. In addition to the stodgy snifter-and-cigar method of taking brandy, it is used as a cocktail in place of many hard liquors. A **cuba libre**, for example, is just as likely to be cola with brandy as with rum.

As with tequila, the price range for brandy is very wide, from a few dollars a bottle to a few dollars an ounce.

## More Licores

In shops selling liquor you will usually find an impressive variety of bottles from around the world. There is **ron** (rum) from the Caribbean, **vodka** from Russia and Scandinavia and various sweet liqueurs and fortified wines. One notable absence is gin (although tonic is available). **Whiskey** (sometimes spelled **güisqui** – but never on the label) whether Scotch, Irish, Canadian or bourbon, is all grouped under one banner. In restaurants you will have to specify, although the generic term refers to Scotch.

## Non-Alcoholic Drinks
### Aguas & Aguas Frescas

Everyone, Mexicans and visitors alike, are warned off drinking **agua de llave** (tap water). There is a concentrated television and poster campaign with instructions on boiling water for at least five minutes before storing it in a sealed container. Without treatment, bad water can cause a number of medical problems, from minor diarrhoea to cholera and more serious maladies like dengue fever. In larger cities, toxins from industry that seep into the water supply are also a cause for concern. In restaurants where water is served from a jug, be sure to ask if it is **purificado**. If you are still concerned, ask for **agua en botella** or **enbotellada** or see the Fit & Healthy chapter for more details.

Bottled water is available everywhere. Most hotels will either include a few bottles in your room or have a large container in the hall on each floor. Every store and corner kiosk will offer water, sometimes on ice, other times **a clima** (at room temperature). When you request bottled water in a restaurant, you may be asked if you'd like it **con gas** (soda water) or **sin gas**, with or without gas. In either case, you may wish to specify whether or not you want ice, **con hielo** or **sin hielo**. Remember, there is no guarantee that the ice is made with purified water. It's best to ask or avoid the worry by having your drink without.

Bottled water is either treated or comes from a spring. The difference in taste is noticeable. Look for the word **manantial** on the label to ensure you are getting the good stuff.

A number of restaurants and **puestos** (street stalls) also have **aguas frescas** (fresh water) a sort of tea that comes in several flavours. In the Yucatán, **agua de jamaica** is a popular drink made by steeping the red flower of the Jamaica plant in warm water and then serving it chilled (see the recipe). **Agua de arroz** (rice water) a Jalisco tradition, is a starchy liquid spiced with **canela** (cinnamon) and **clavo** (cloves) and served over ice in large clay mugs. While most aguas frescas are boiled during preparation, they are cooled with enormous blocks of ice that may or may not have been made with purified water.

*Refreshment, Tepoztlan*

### Chocolate
See the Chocolate chapter.

## Agua de Jamaica (Jamaica Flower Cooler)

In markets and on street stalls, you will see large jugs of this deep red, refreshing-looking drink. You will be tempted to try a cup, but may be put off by concerns about the water or the chunks of ice used to keep it cool. Now you can use this recipe to make it for yourself.

**Ingredients**

2     cups Jamaica flowers (available at markets and supermarkets)
½     cup of sugar (or to taste)
5     cups of water

Bring the water to a boil (best to use bottled water to begin with). Add the flowers and sugar and stir while the mixture returns to a boil. Remove from heat, pour into a jug and let it steep for at least two hours. Strain the drink and chill. Serve over ice.

## Refrescos

The world's best known soft drink, Coca-Cola, sometimes referred to by Latin American radicals as 'the black waters of Yankee imperialism', has been a fixture in Mexico since the pre-revolutionary days of Porfirio Diaz.

*Drinking horchata con turia (rice & cactus fruit drink), Mercado Juarez, Oaxaca City*

**DRINKS**

Its main competitor, Pepsi, has yet to establish itself to the same degree as Coke but still finds its way into every city and town in the country. In one town, San Juan Chamula in the state of Chiapas, a type of Pepsi fanaticism emerged when the local distributor encouraged residents to use Pepsi for ritual occasions, as bride's dowries, and in place of wine at Mass, with the belief that the bubbles would help release the demons trapped in their soul. These two brands dominate the market. Other American brands: Sprite, 7UP, Fanta Orange, follow these and are much more common than Mexican brands like Boing! which offers exotic fruit flavours like mango and pineapple, or Manzana, a carbonated apple juice.

Refrescos are available in every restaurant. You may have a choice of **frio** (cold) or **a clima** (at room temperature) so you should specify.

*Coca Cola and shade, Guelavia, Oaxaca State*

DRINKS

*Pouring cafe lechero at La Parroquia, Veracruz*

## Coffee & Tea

In this age of speciality coffees, Mexico remains refreshingly simple. Your basic choice will be **café americano** or **espresso**, served hot at your table. Cappuccino is also widely available in cafes. Mexicans tend to put a lot of milk or cream in their own coffee but this is strictly a matter of taste.

Coffee is an important export product for the Mexican economy and the state of Chiapas is virtually dependent on the little red bean to pep up its economy. Veracruz is also known for its homegrown and also for **café de olla**, a special coffee sweetened with **piloncillo**, a raw brown sugar.

Cafe culture is quite highly developed in places that grow coffee, particularly in Veracruz where a trip to the Gran Café de la Parroquia is a mandatory excursion for coffee lovers. You will enter a crowded room to a cacophonous symphony of spoons clinking against glasses, the way the customers attract the attention of the wandering waiters who pour steaming hot coffee into glasses from precarious heights. It is a treat for the eyes as much as for the palate.

Tea drinkers may be a little bit disappointed by the flavour of those brews available in Mexico. Camomile seems to be the house tea of choice although some places offer **té negro** (black tea) and **limón** (lime). Hardened tea fanatics may wish to pack their own before leaving home.

## Jugos (Fresh Juices)

There are many restaurants devoted to the provision of **jugos** and they are worth checking out on a hot day. They are usually small with short menus of fresh juices served alone or in combination. Some will also serve **crepas** (crepes) or other snack foods, but their principal raison d'être is juice. For the visitor trying to jam as much of Mexico into a short day as possible, these make wonderful stops for re-energising. Juices have recently gained popularity among the health-conscious for their rich vitamin content. They come at around US$1 each and in many flavours; papaya, guayaba, mango, kiwi, strawberry and of course orange. Our favourite is the exotic **zapote negro**, a black mushy fruit that combines beautifully with **mandarina** (mandarin orange).

*Orange juice stand, Tepoztlan market*

## DR JUGO

Juice as a health drink is slowly catching on in Mexico, fuelled by dubbed info-mercials featuring octogenarian men in track suits running around a sound stage demonstrating the recipes for the juices that keep them so young and virile. Dr Jugo (Dr Juice) runs such a place in Mexico City. He spent several years in Buffalo, New York, better known perhaps as the founding city of the chicken wing as bar food, than its healthful juices.

Upon returning to Mexico City, he set up Dr Jugo, a small store-front operation that also makes traditional tortas with a healthy touch of alfalfa sprouts. It is located in MA Quevedo in Coyoacan, Mexico City's tiny residential neighbourhood that is also known for its famous former residents, among them Hernán Cortes, Frida Kahlo and Leon Trotsky.

On the menu, each juice is listed by what ailment it cures: for liver problems, a combination of carrot, apple, beet and cranberry; for the heart, carrot, apple and celery. Others cure maladies of the kidneys, intestines, or help memory and aid digestion.

Dr Jugo wears a white lab-coat and makes his juice with a small blender or a juicer that whizzes through a dozen carrots in less than a minute. With a muscular build and bleached blond hair against a school-break tan, he looks the picture of the health his juices claim to promote. But whatever your reason for visiting the good doctor, you are assured, at the very least, a thick cup of cool, fresh juice for about US$1.

You may also see a section of the menu devoted to **licuados**, which are blender drinks whipped into a froth and featuring fruits like bananas, raspberry, blackberry and milk or water.

**Malteadas** (milkshakes) may also be available although you are more likely to get them at places that also sell ice cream.

# chocolate

The world has the Americas, and Mexico in particular, to thank for the gift of chocolate. The first to discover the process of extracting the dark rich substance from the cacao beans were the Olmecs, who lived on the Gulf Coast (in the present-day state of Veracruz) from about 1500 BC to 400 BC, and took their chocolate in liquid form. In fact, it was drunk for almost 3000 years before it occurred to anyone to eat it.

Since then, vast fortunes have been made by those who have found the right combinations of sugar, nuts, cream or caramel that compel us to sneak a bar between meals or greedily polish off a litre of chocolate ice cream in a single sitting.

Chocolate as we know it today, whether a drink, tablets for baking, or as the main element of countless tempting sweets, is a product of the cacao bean. In fact, these are not beans but seeds that grow within a large, bulbous, sweet and pulpy fruit on trees of the same name. The cacao plant is a fickle tree that will not produce fruit outside of tropical climates. It also requires high temperatures, plenty of moisture and is susceptible to myriad diseases.

When the fruit is ripe, the beans are extracted from the pulp and undergo a process of fermentation (when the seeds begin to germinate – necessary to give the 'chocolate' flavour), drying, roasting and finally winnowing, when the skins of the beans are discarded. The final product is called the nib and is ready to be ground into what we happily know as chocolate.

*Chocolate cigarettes sign, Puebla*

# History

Chocolate is but one of the legacies of the Olmec people, the other being those enormous heads they fashioned out of stone (which leaves the chocolate lover to fantasise fruitlessly about what they could have achieved if they had discovered solid chocolate). As Olmec civilisation faded (by 400 BC) the Mayans took up the tradition. Cacao appears in the Popol Vuh, the Mayan creation myth where it is said to be one of the key ingredients (besides corn) the gods used to fashion the Mayan race. As the classical Mayan period ended and the Aztecs began expanding their empire, the use and value of chocolate increased and wars were waged over control of cacao-rich lands. The Aztecs enthusiastically embraced chocolate, a tendency which worried the intelligentsia, although their dire warnings of its addictive qualities were ignored.

Among the inhabitants of Teotihuacán (present day Mexico City), it was regarded as the 'Drink of the Gods' and was offered in the hope of maintaining amicable relations (not unlike our own Valentine's Day rituals). But chocolate was more than a pleasant drink: the cacao bean, from which chocolate is derived, was also a form of currency. The emperor Montezuma, said to be among the most ardent of chocolate lovers, would demonstrate his power and wealth by having his 'money' converted into a hot, frothy drink to be served to honoured guests.

When the Aztecs ventured forth to conquer neighbouring and distant lands, they collected 'taxes' in the form of cacao beans from regions where the plant flourished. Enormous warehouses were constructed to store the beans for the wealthy of each city who, in turn, used them to buy food (a small rabbit would go for 30 beans while a large axolotl – the larval salamander considered a delicacy – cost four beans) and pay the salaries or their hired help. Forgers even made counterfeit beans from ash, chalk, avocado pits, wax or dough, and these were sometimes mixed in with a batch of real ones.

The first European to encounter chocolate was Christopher Columbus himself. During his fourth (and final) voyage, his crew intercepted and captured a long dug-out canoe piloted by Mayan traders somewhere off the coast of present-day Honduras. Its cargo included roots and grains, a fermented corn drink and, the cacao beans, described later by Columbus' son Fernando as almonds. Columbus himself never tasted chocolate, but had a good idea of the worth of the bean by the way the traders kept their eyes fixed on the captured bags.

Subsequent expeditions of conquistadors discovered the true value of chocolate, both as coin and drink. At the court of Monctezuma in 1519, Hernán Cortés was served his first steaming cup of chocolate. While the Spanish invaders were intrigued by the drink, they rejected the bitter

*Pan de yema (yolk bread) & chocolate milk*

Aztec version and added cane sugar and milk to create the sweet, creamy beverage similar to what we know today. They also added cinnamon, black pepper and anise. Finally, they made the preparation easier by introducing the **molinillo**. This mixing stick has a textured knob at one end that, when spun between two palms rubbing furiously together, whips the chocolate into an irresistible froth.

No one can say for sure who first brought chocolate to Europe, although most seem to think it went back with one of Cortés' expeditions. The first time it appears in print, however, was as part of the gifts presented to King Philip II of Spain by a delegation of Kekchi (part of the Mayan nation) nobles. However it may have got there, history seems to agree that chocolate was in general consumption in the Spanish court by the beginning of the 17th century. The drink even invaded the ritualistic bullfight when spectators were served huge cups as they watched the action below.

The word about chocolate, both as a medicine and a drink, spread through Europe, first to Portugal and then throughout the Italian peninsula and north to France, Germany and England. New recipes were concocted for using chocolate as a flavouring or in sorbet and baroque designers created special vessels for preparing and cooking the drink.

CHOCOLATE

Meanwhile, in Mexico, consumption reached addictive proportions among the new arrivals, often to the chagrin of church authorities. One unfortunate friar was brought before the Holy Office of the Inquisition in 1650 on charges of drinking chocolate before Mass. Among the native populations, chocolate remained a currency thoughout the colonial era and in the decades following independence from Spain. Even Creoles used it for small transactions with the natives.

The high demand for chocolate in Europe propelled large parts of Mexico's colonial economy. Indians were pressed into labour as virtual slaves on plantations owned by Creoles. Independent farmers were forced to pay a tribute in the form of cacao beans to the Spanish crown and several other petty officials in between.

Solid chocolate did not come along until much later, probably not until the 19th century (although some say that Mexican nuns figured out the process much earlier). The real breakthrough, that which brought it from the elite to the masses, occurred in 1828 when a Dutch chemist named Coenraad Johannes Van Houten invented a process that removed half the cocoa butter fat from the mixture. After some more adjustments, the world's first chocolate bar came out in 1847. Over 150 years later, it remains the world's favourite confection.

Yet, you have to wonder what Montezuma would think of seeing today's chocolate, sweetened beyond recognition and mixed with gooey foreign substances. And one can only imagine his rage at seeing this revered drink, reserved for special occasions, reduced to 'a little something to tide you over 'til dinner.'

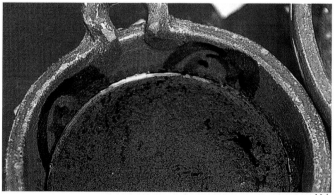

*Mole*

# How Chocolate is Made

The Aztecs made their **tlaquetzalli** (Nahuatl for 'precious thing') by grinding the dried cacao beans into a paste and then slowly adding hot water. The liquid was then poured from one vessel to another several times in order to raise the foam. Some drank it without adding anything, while others flavoured their drink with ingredients such as spicy chiles, sweet honeys, edible flowers, or fruit juices. It was served at the end of a meal like a cognac and, at feasts, the after-dinner cup was the host's way of impressing guests. Outside this privileged class, only warriors in the service of the emperor were permitted to taste the treasured liquid with regularity.

Today, chocolate shops permit a tidy mixture of tradition and modern technology. While the chocolate is processed into a soluble powder or blocks by large metal machines, the consumer still has the choice of exactly what proportion of chocolate bean, cinnamon, almonds and sugar will be used to produce the final product.

Once the recipe is determined, the chocolate beans are fed into a large metal mill. The dark brown paste produced has a horrible, bitter taste. The workers delight in giving tourists a sample and watching their faces screw up in disgust. This paste is mixed with the ingredients specified by the customer and the combination is put through a mixing machine to ensure that all the flavours are properly distributed. The resulting powder is either bagged or pressed into moulds. When chocolate is bought commercially, it can come in either form, although the moulds are more common.

Preparation of chocolate is a simple yet precise method. You must be very vigilant, allowing the chocolate to come to a gentle boil before using the molinillo to whip up a froth. This step is repeated three times until the volume of the liquid has substantially increased. The more foam the better (flat chocolate is a failure as it can't bring the pleasure of delicate bubbles tickling your lips as they pass over them).

Chocolate can also be made at home. You can buy it already formed into **tablillas** (tablets) or make it from scratch. To make your own, the cacao beans are first toasted on a hot **comal** (flat pan). The skins are removed and the softened beans are crushed in a **molcajete** (preferably one devoted only to the purpose) until it forms a paste. Cinnamon, powdered almonds and sugar are added and mixed over low heat. The resulting paste is formed into whatever shape suits your fancy and stored in a cool place.

When it is time to make the chocolate, the tablillas are melted in a mixture of milk, heated to the verge of boiling and then beaten using a molinillo. The knob goes in the chocolate and is then twisted rapidly between the palms of the hands to bring air into the mixture and create the froth. In proper recipes, the boiling and beating process should be done three times before the chocolate is ready to serve.

*Pollo (chicken) in Mole Negro, Oaxaca City*

**CHOCOLATE**

## Chocolate in Modern Mexico

In Mexico, chocolate is used mostly for the hot drink known simply as 'chocolate' not all of it is sweetened and drunk. Mole poblano, perhaps the most Mexican of all dishes, could not exist without that special, bitter touch of chocolate. There are also several varieties of chocolate candies although fine chocolates, the kind we might be used to as treats, or those using different degrees of sweetness or gentle flavourings such as mint or orange, are quite rare. We visited one candy shop in Puebla that had wonderful varieties of salt-water taffy but no chocolate whatsoever! Any pastry shop worth its name will stock a few shelves with delectable samples of cookies, breads and shortcakes dipped with a thin layer of chocolate.

But, to the average Mexican, chocolate is the drink. A large cup of frothy chocolate, served with fresh bread, makes for a great breakfast, especially on chilly mornings. If you approach the corner of Mercado 20 de noviembre and JC Mina in Oaxaca City, you will be overwhelmed by the smell of chocolate – rich, sweet and warm – emanating from the dozen or so **comedores** (cheap restaurants) vying for the chocolate-drinking trade. Each morning, their counter-side stools are packed with workers sipping away at their breakfasts. For a little added substance, ask for an order of **pan de yema** (egg yolk bread), a heavy, soft crusted bread that serves as a wonderful, edible sponge for drinking chocolate that is too hot to take directly.

Chocolate is also served cool (not cold). In Oaxaca, a popular recipe called **tejate** calls for the addition of mamey seeds, cocoa flowers and corn dough. Another variety, **tescalate**, is popular in Chiapas, and is made by grinding the cacao beans with toasted corn and achiote (a deep red spice used frequently in the south).

# home cooking
# & traditions

Home, wherever it may be, is where our relationship with food begins. In Mexico the kitchen is the centre of the house, both figuratively and, quite often, literally. In pre-Hispanic Mexico, houses were built around the kitchen. While modern architecture tends to place the kitchen further back in a home's layout, it remains the metaphorical heart of the Mexican family dwelling.

Until recently, the kitchen was the exclusive domain of the female members of the household. From pre-Hispanic times to the middle of the 20th century, women drew much of their identity – and in certain respects their sense of self-worth – from their skills in food preparation. Mexican wedding ceremonies included the mother of the groom feeding her new daughter-in-law four mouthfuls of tamal. The bride, in turn, fed tamales to her new husband in a ritual designed to symbolise the role of the

## DINNER WITH FLOR

Dinner with Flor began with a trip to the Mercado 20 de noviembre in downtown Oaxaca. It was just after dark, around 6:30pm when most workers were heading home. The narrow aisles of the market were packed with people like us, shopping for the evening meal.

Flor was all business, knowing exactly what she wanted. "We'll make an Oaxacan speciality," she said. And so we stopped by a woman who sold **tlayudas**, very large and crisp flour tortillas. She bought six of them and, from the woman sitting alongside, a black plastic bag for one peso. We stopped next at the cheese counter where Flor bought a grapefruit-sized hunk of **queso oaxaqueño** or **quesillo**, a stringy cheese made from goat's milk. We picked up onions, chiles, avocado, **jitomates** (red tomatoes) and **col** (cabbage). After weaving from stand to stand, we arrived in front of an old woman displaying a pile of reddish pellets which, upon closer inspection, turned out to be fried **chapulines** (grasshoppers). The large variety were about an inch long and slightly thicker than a pencil, the small ones no larger than rice grains.

Flor picked up one of the big ones and popped it in her mouth. "Here, try," she said, holding one out for me. I reminded myself that I was being paid for this and popped it in my mouth and crunched down on the hardened body of the insect. Chapulines taste of the chile powder and lime juice in which they are fried before eating. They are cheap (no more than US$1 for a small bag) and people eat them like snacks. At a party you may see a bowl which appears to be filled with some sort of dark red nut which is actually filled with grasshoppers. They are very popular in Oaxaca and are sold by several women in the market who sit before small mounds of them waiting for customers. I asked one of them how they are gathered. "In plastic bags," she said.

Once out of the market, we visited a chocolate shop, one of many in the immediate vicinity. Flor explained the procedure, the special order where the customer chooses exactly what proportion of chocolate, sugar and spice will go in, the milling, mixing and bagging. After the woman in making sure her family ate well. Midwives forewarned baby girls about what their future would bring: "thou wilt become fatigued, thou wilt become tired; thou art to provide water, to grind maize, to drudge." As late as the 1940s small-town Mexican women had to prove their abilities at tortilla-making before they were considered eligible for marriage. Until technology relieved much of the labour associated with grinding corn, most Mexican women spent their days in the kitchen.

second step, the cocao beans are ground into a thick, oily paste. Flor took a small spoon and dipped it in. "Try this," she said. I took the spoon and tasted. Now I knew from getting into my mother's baking cupboard as a child that not all chocolate was like a sugar-laden bar, but this was such that my entire face convulsed involuntarily. "Bitter, eh?"

Flor lives in a typical middle class house with her younger brother, not far from the city centre. There are two levels and a semi-private apartment out back where Flor takes in borders. The kitchen is a pleasant balance between rustic and high tech, with a late 1970s fridge and stove set, a table with six chairs, a water cooler and a single sink. The dry goods – beans, rice, canned goods, cooking oil – are kept in an **alacena**, a simple cupboard covered with a curtain.

Flor prepares the food as she lectures about eating in the Mexican home (a family production, where the mother is director), about the things she makes to honour her father's memory on the Dia de los Muertos (tamales, she says, lots of tamales) about the difficulties the modern woman faces when having to juggle professional and domestic duties: "If I don't cook for my brother, he doesn't eat," she says. She repeats everything twice, like a teacher.

She calls this evening's dish **pizza oaxaqueña**. The tlayuda serves as the crust and is first topped with aciento, a by-product of pork lard, then slathered with **frijoles molidos** (ground beans) and sprinkled liberally with chopped onion, tomato, avocado slices, cabbage and cheese. It is heated stove-top on a comal, and then folded like a taco before eating. At this point it becomes tricky. The size of the pizza is awkward and the toppings tend to fall out before reaching your mouth. Eating it becomes a two-phase process with the initial attack followed by salvaging the fallen toppings off the plate below.

The smell of the cooking pizzas attracts her brother, who to this point has been upstairs. He introduces himself, then sits and waits. Flor serves him a pizza which he folds before launching in. Flor looks at me with an I-told-you-so expression of resignation, then throws the next tlayuda onto the comal, ready to make the next pizza.

While cooking is definitely hard work, Mexican culture has been enriched by the importance of home cooking and everything associated with it. A sub-culture – incorporating the history of individual families, neighbourhoods and towns – is shared among the women of the household. In the kitchen, knowledge passes from generation to generation – and not just gastronomic know-how. Sor Juana Ines de la Cruz, the 17th century Mexican poet who anticipated feminism by 300 years, once commented that if Aristotle had cooked, he would have written much more.

When space allows, there will be a small table where light meals are eaten and around which the family may sit when a meal is being prepared. The mother in the house is the undisputed chief in the kitchen and it is very rare that the male members of the household will do anything there except eat. The sense of maternalism is strong: when a child comes home from school the first question they're is asked is if they'd like something to eat.

While the role of women has been broadened in recent times, men still don't cook and lifestyle and opportunities for a Mexican woman still lag behind, say, her North American counterpart.

Another interesting aspect of Mexican home cooking is the impact it has had on restaurant food. In some countries, restaurants exist to offer diners something different than they would normally receive. Especially creative chefs scour markets for unique and exotic ingredients and experiment with new styles and methods in a never-ending effort to be the most original. In Mexico, the most intense growth in the restaurant industry occurred when urban expansion made going home for **comida** (the day's main meal) a logistical impossibility. Most restaurants attempt to mimic a typical meal with set menus featuring all the mainstays of home cooking: soup, tortillas, and a main dish of meat, chicken or fish with beans, vegetables and rice. With the exception of high-priced restaurants that affiliate themselves with a particular national style, it is only recently that professional chefs have departed from the culinary canon to create new dishes – although even these may have traceable links to home cooking.

## BARBACOA

The barbecue has become an institution in summery climates around the globe. If a method of cookery can be considered a cultural institution, it is the barbecue. While humans have been putting meat to fire since shortly after fire was discovered, the word barbecue (or in Spanish **barbacoa**) has its origins in the Americas. In fact, it is one of the first words Columbus brought back to Europe with him. Columbus found it in the Caribbean, first spoken by the Arawaks.

**HOME COOKING**

## Appliances & Utensils

A typical Mexican kitchen will not be overwhelmed with dozens of electric gadgets or long-forgotten gifts from well-meaning mothers-in-law (rubber garlic peelers, power can openers or two-pronged corn-on-the-cob holders, for example). There are, however, some features which are both useful and common.

### Alacena (Cupboard)

The walls of a Mexican kitchen won't usually have cabinets. Instead, dry items such as beans, rice, pastas and canned goods, as well as those vegetables and fruits that do not require refrigeration, are kept in an **alacena**. Standing from floor to ceiling, the alacena is built into the wall allowing for plenty of shelf space. Sometimes, it will be covered with a colourful curtain.

### Botellón de Agua

Virtually every kitchen will have a large, blue bottle of purified drinking water. In some it will stand alone, to be poured into pitchers cooled in the fridge, while others will be inverted and popped into a stand-alone cooler. Because it is so essential, delivery trucks pass on a daily basis, driving slowly up and down streets calling 'Aaaaagua' from a loud speaker as boys jump from the truck to deliver the new bottles and take away the empties.

*El bistec (steak) & chorizo (sausages) cooking, Oaxaca City*

## Molcajete

The **molcajete** is a bowl of thick clay, baked to hardness and enamelled which stands solidly on three stubby legs. The surface is heavily textured, some with engraved multi-directional lines, others with a sort of stucco. The texture allows salsa ingredients to be mashed and mixed with greater ease. The **chimolera** is a textured pestle. It comes in a variety of shapes, all with a round head. In some families, molcajetes are passed down from generation to generation and it is said that, with use, they become seasoned and the salsas made in them are better for it. In other families, the molcajete serves as nothing more than a heavy kitchen ornament, and the blender is used to make the salsa. If you want to get a molcajete and chimolera you can find them in virtually any market. However, they tend to be very heavy so if you want one, wait until the end of your trip.

## Molinillo

You need a molinillo to make chocolate perfectly smooth and frothy. The basic molinillo will consist of a stick with a carved bulb on one end. The bulb can be quite ornate – an assortment of grooves and ridges and added wooden rings. The details help to whip air into the chocolate for the desired frothiness. To get there, you hold the stick between both palms and rub your hands together as fast as possible until the chocolate begins to bubble.

### TONALÁ & TLAQUEPAQUE

If you're interested in refurbishing your kitchen with a Mexican flavour, visit Tlaquepaque and Tonalá, both located within bus or taxi distance of Guadalajara (they are really suburbs of the city). Tlaquepaque, the larger and more expensive, has a great selection of kitchenware coveted as much for its beauty as its usefulness. Tonalá is more popular with the locals and has a more utilitarian approach. Pottery is decorated with simple patterns without much attention to aesthetic details.

Take an afternoon to wander through the main market areas in both. You will pass storefronts with rust-coloured oblong plates stacked by the dozens, **cacerolas** (casserole dishes) of every size, wooden utensils, spatulas, sauce spoons and **molinillos** for making the perfect chocolate.

In Tlaquepaque, you will also find hand-painted dish sets and serving platters, silver utensils with intricate decorations, and blue-rimmed glassware from tequila shot-size, to wine glasses to brandy snifters.

Many of these items are fragile so leave the shopping until you're almost heading home if possible and be sure to wrap them well to avoid fragmentary disappointment once you get home.

*Mole Poblano with molcajete and chimolera*

### Estufas (Stove)

The **estufa** is used much more than the **horno** (oven) in the kitchens of Mexico. In fact, in some homes, the oven serves as nothing more than a space to store stove-top pots and pans.

Most are gas powered and gas is delivered to the home in cylinders that arrive in huge, lumbering trucks manned by a couple of young boys who lug these containers from door to door.

In houses with enough space, there is likely to be a **brasero**, a charcoal-burning barbecue for grilling meats and giving roasted chiles a special, smoky flavour.

### Olla de Presión (Pressure Cooker)

This is a must for cooking beans and legumes at high altitudes where water boils at a lower temperature (lower boiling temperature means less heat and if there's less heat the cooking takes longer). Even at sea level, the pressure cooker cuts the cooking time, an important consideration when gas is expensive.

### Licuadora (Blender)

The electric blender is the time-pressed Mexican cook's best friend and turns dozens of laborious tasks – like salsas, juices, nixtamal and crushed ice for a margarita – into the press of a button.

### Juice Presser

These come in several shapes and sizes, from the simple conical shaped press-and-twist version to the electric juicers, either the kind that pulverise anything you feed them or those made especially for citrus with a spinning cone powered to extract the juice at several hundred RPM.

The most common juice press, however, is a cast iron instrument with a lever that presses the half orange against the ribbed cone and allows the juice to flow out through a funnel below. You'll see these used by streetside vendors throughout Mexico.

### Comal

A comal is a flat pan that sits atop a stove element. Natives once made them from earthenware but today they are made of metal.

It is not only used for making tortillas but many other antojitos which don't require oil. There are no real sides to the pan, only a ridge that might serve to prevent leaking – a design which allows you to carefully place a tortilla on the surface without creating air pockets that can lead to uneven cooking.

### Prensa Para Tortillas (Tortillas Press)

Tortillas taste best when they are made fresh and cooked immediately. Having a prensa para tortillas helps. It is a simple utensil consisting of two hinged metal plates. Dough is rolled into a **testal** (ball), flattened slightly by hand and placed between two sheets of wax paper before being pressed flat and cooked on the comal.

### Cuchillos (Knives)

A sharp cuchillo for chopping vegetables, peeling fruit and slicing meat is a must. To keep knives **afilado** (sharp), a mobile tinker circulates every few days ringing a bell to attract his customers.

### Metate & Mano

The metate and mano can be traced back to some of the country's earliest settlements. Both are very heavy and made of clay which is moulded, enamelled and baked to rock hardness. The metate stands on three stubby legs with a flat surface where the corn is ground. The mano is an oblong roller used to grind the corn against the rough surface of the metate. Today, the metate has mostly been replaced by a blender or commercial brands of just-add-water nixtamal mix.

The switch to technology was a slow process which met with much passionate resistance, despite the enormous effort that goes into providing a family 's daily supply of tortillas and other corn-based dishes. The first large-scale mills appeared in the latter half of the 19th century and the first mass tortilla machines, using conveyor belts to take the tortillas through special ovens, were introduced in 1919. Still, rural women resisted. Part of the reason was the change in the flavour and texture of mechanised tortillas. But more than this, automation – despite its progressive intentions – represented a true threat to a way of life. For *un*progressive rural men, discarding the metate and mano also meant that women no longer had to spend most of their days in the kitchen.

Today the metate and mano are are mostly relegated to kitchen corners where they serve as ornaments and reminders to a very different past. Tortillas are either bought from a **tortillería** or made using already milled flour and a press.

### Cazuela

Cazuelas were also handed down from Mexico's indigenous past. Basically, these are earthenware pots used to make any kind of **guiso** (stew) or **salsa** (sauce). Local artisans often turn basic cazuelas into beautiful pieces of art which many Mexicans hang on their kitchen walls.

## Other Pottery

The pre-Hispanic Mexicans were excellent potters. They developed both the skill and the technique to create durable, functional and beautiful platters, pitchers and comals. The use of clay pot cooking vessels corresponded with the food they ate which, after all, also came from the earth. Today such work is mostly used as decoration but is no less a part of the Mexican kitchen.

The states of Jalisco, Guanajuato, Michoacan, Tlaxcala, Puebla and Oaxaca are renowned for their pottery. Each has a distinctive, identifying pattern – abstract geometric patterns or actual drawings of the regional specialities, plants and animals – which does not change in any dramatic way from workshop to workshop in the same area.

# laura
# esquivel
## author & tortilla maker

Coyoacán is rich with history. Cortés settled here after defeating the last Aztec emperor. In 1847, an invading American army defeated a Mexican garrison in a decisive battle of the Mexican-American war. Frida Kahlo and Diego Rivera lived here, as did Leon Trotsky before he was bludgeoned to death in 1940. It is appropriate then, that Laura Esquivel, who has awakened in many Mexicans a sense of their own culinary history, should live in Coyoacán.

*Laura Esquivel*

Her house is not far from Churrubusco, in a quiet street shadowed by trees that break through the sidewalk pavement. From the outside, her house is nondescript. The interior is accented in dark wood furnishings and a number of oil paintings – mostly figurative, mostly of women, and mostly contemporary with the notable exception of a portrait of the Virgin of Guadalupe which hangs in the corner of the dining room where Laura Esquivel sits, reading.

It was late afternoon, the hour when Mexicans who follow such traditions have finished their comida, taken their siesta and begin the second half of their work day. She wore a shin-length white cotton shirt, in the style of Nehru, with embroidery at the shoulders and accessorised by a multi-strand necklace of coffee-coloured beads. Her youthful looks belie her 49 years – her face is virtually wrinkle-free, and her long hair, curled with the disorder of a bird's nest, has but a few grey strands. We chatted for an hour about food: food and the Mexican identity, food and sex, food and art, food and spirit, food and the environment, food and memory.

Esquivel's first novel, *Como Agua para Chocolate (Like Water for Chocolate)* has sold over 3 million copies and has been translated into 30 languages. The film of the same name, released in 1992, won countless awards locally and internationally.

The novel deals with Tita, a woman coming of age, just prior to the revolution in small-town Northern Mexico. As the youngest daughter, she is bound by tradition to remain unmarried and take care of her onerous mother until she dies. To make matters worse, her one and only true love, Pedro, marries her oldest sister, a woman whose relationship to food is marked by indigestion and chronic flatulence.

*Like Water for Chocolate* is subtitled 'A Novel in Monthly Installments with Recipes, Romances and Home Remedies.' Each installment begins with a recipe for a dish which plays a role in the ensuing action. Each dish, prepared by Tita in her kitchen, serves as a means of expression for a woman who has had every natural emotion repressed by her mother and by society at large. The kitchen, acting as both prison cell and seat of power, is her private domain and she finds solace in the grinding of corn or the slow process of preparing a mole. For Tita, a cook whose talents are known throughout the area, food and cooking become her voice, her totalising discourse.

As such, *Like Water for Chocolate* is not a book wholly about Mexican food. It is a simple love story, where food serves as the medium for communication of a range of emotions from anger to lust. There is a sensuality attached to the food, one that allows the reader/eater to understand the complex machinations of each character, without being burdened by words.

"Food is our first pleasurable contact with the world," says Esquivel. "And in the moment you feel pleasure, whether in touch, smell or taste, you stop suffering. In this moment you know perfectly your place in the world. Your existence is very clear and that consciousness of existence gives you peace. And so a minute dedicated to pleasure multiplies into hours of peace. Shared pleasure encourages peace."

The use of food in this manner explains, in part, the international popularity of the novel. Esquivel discovered this for herself when she travelled to places like Japan and Finland, where tortillas and moles are simply strange foreign foods. Yet people still identified with the cooking process. "What they understood was the sensual relationship with the land, with the aromas and with all that progress has made distant in one way or another." she says. "I think I found a large hole in these souls and once they read the book, they were able to recuperate the aromas of the kitchens of their childhood and youth."

The idea of 'recuperation' is key. Even after the death of her jail-keeper mother, Tita remains closely attached to the kitchen. Cooking was an integral part of her essence as a human being, of her identity.

Likewise, food and identity are closely linked in Mexico. The old expression 'You are what you eat' takes on new meaning here where the cuisine is, above all, **mestizaje** (literally, a mixture). Like the nation itself, it was born of the fusion of native and Spanish cuisines. This element fascinates Esquivel.

"What is interesting about the mestizaje is that to achieve it, you have to have a congruence between at least two cultures. A balance was found in the religion (the Christian image of the Virgin of Guadalupe appeared with Indian features), the same is to be found in Mexican cuisine. For example, before, chocolate was mixed with water because there were no cows. It was only since the arrival of the Spanish that we began to take it with milk. **Sopes** (antojitos topped in a variety of ways) were not fried because we did not have pork lard. There was no cheese, no cream. The mestizo then, is one who has grown accustomed to taking foods from other cultures and assimilating them to make them his own."

The assimilation was not always an easy process. In her book, *Intimas Suculencias*, a collection of food-related articles, essays, speeches and other work written between 1988 and 1998, is a telling piece called *Arriba Dios! Abajo el Diablo* (Up with God! Down with the devil!). In it, she takes the voice of a young convent resident living in Mexico during the early days of the colony. After interpreting a particularly cryptic phrase uttered by the convent's chaplain she comes to the realisation that in fact, Indians and Spanish are the same. She is crushed because "Indians, as their name indicates, are plebes, ugly, sacrilegious, vile, sinners, dark, dirty and heretical ... what do I," she wonders, "daughter of one of the best families in New Spain, have to do with the pagan Indians buried beneath my house?"

Yet her rejection of all things Aztec hits a stumbling block when it comes to food. Her stomach is now **antojadizo** (used to antojitos). Like a penitent soul, she does her best to avoid the fruits brought by the Indians to market. She tries to avoid the aromas of cooking corn, beans, squash and tomatoes. Her breaking point, however, comes when she drinks a big bowl of foamy chocolate. With it, she undergoes a dreamy journey through Tenoctitlán and realises, and appreciates, the points of convergence between Spanish and Indian. Ironically, we are told at the end of the story that the narrator speaks to us while awaiting an appearance before the inquisition, indicating that such thought was not welcome by the church authorities. And so it was for many years in Mexico: while the Spanish and Creoles held strongly to the appearance of being continental, they were, in fact, slowly becoming assimilated to Mexico through the integration of Mexican ingredients into their pantries.

At this point, she calls after her maid, Nati – a short, middle aged woman with Indian features. Nati has recently taught her how to make tortillas, and Esquivel wants to know if the corn is ready to be ground. It is and Nati gets the metate ready.

One of the reasons tortilla-making came so late in Esquivel's life is that her mother was born in the north and therefore ate wheat tortillas which are made from already milled flour. But more than this, as a teenager and young woman, she saw the kitchen as a symbol of oppression. The kitchen was a stagnant place; no wealth ever came from the molcajete, no revolutions could be lauched with a comal.

"I belong to the generation that believed firmly that to be in the kitchen was the worst kind of slavery, that the action, knowledge and life was outside. Things worth fighting for were outside the kitchen. Inside there was nothing but death. And with the passing of time I have realised that life is in the kitchen and that the recuperation of the soul is there and if one doesn't recover this it becomes impossible to confront a totally materialist world – a world that is destroying us, a world that doesn't care about the destruction of the people, of nature, all in the name of obtaining more material goods."

The key to her realising that the kitchen was a central part of her life was leaving it. It's an observation that can be applied in analogy to those of us who have ventured outside our own country for any significant length of time. When you are away from your own country, you gain a new appreciation for it, and the role your own national culture has played in shaping your life – whether you like it or not.

One of Esquivel's first forays back into the kitchen is described in another piece included *Intimas Suculencias.* At the time the story takes place, she is living in New York with a group of students and, feeling homesick for the mole her mother used to prepare, decides to cook up a batch herself. The result is disastrous – the mole burns, the fire alarm is triggered and the sprinkler system dumps litres of water into her preparation. At the end, a less-than-pleased room-mate suggests that if she misses her mother's cooking so much she should go back to Mexico – which, of course, is sort of what she was trying to do in the first place.

Yet most Mexicans will rarely leave Mexico and, as a result, will miss out on what it means to be Mexican. Cookbooks offer another example: most kiosks will have a stack of cookbooks and they seem as popular in Mexico as anywhere else. Yet, says Esquivel, very few Mexican cookbooks contain the basic information that Mexican cooks must understand to make Mexican food: the roasting of a chile, the grinding of pumpkin seeds, the wrapping of a tomal, even how to make tortillas from scratch.

And so we make tortillas. From scratch.

Her kitchen is an ultra-modern, all-white room with a double-door fridge, five-element gas range, microwave and conventional oven and two long shelves, jammed packed with cook books and collections of recipes. Yet in the middle of the floor sits the ancient metate, grey with slavish curves in direct contrast with the sleek lines of the appliances made in factories. On the counter in the corner sits a bulky molcajete, one handed down to Esquivel by her grandmother.

Nati begins the process by taking a handful of corn and moving it to the rough surface of the metate. Kneeling on a cushion with a Charlie Chaplin print, she begins to mill the corn with the mano, twisting and rolling, adding a few drops of water, until the corn is turned into a paste. It is a procedure that must be repeated three times, the second time being my turn. Handling the mano is no easy task. It is heavy and hard to control against a pile of wet corn mush. On my attempt, the corn spills over the side of the metate and much of what should have been crushed under was simply pushed. In short, a total failure. Esquivel herself finishes the job, narrating as she grinds.

It is an incredible amount of work and yet nothing compared to what was done each and every day in every Mexican household before the introduction of milling technology in the late 19th century. It was work that was classified as unproductive because it served to feed families and did not directly boost the GDP. Today, the same task completed in a bakery is considered productive while making tortillas from scratch at home is a time unwisely wasted. Esquivel disagrees with this common notion: "I don't think that this is time lost but rather a recuperation of time that is now spent on this absurd struggle to accumulate material goods. For me, the kitchen is a magical space which gives us the opportunity to enter into a common balance. The tortilla bought in a tortilleria will never be the same as that made in the house. Not spiritually, not nutritionally, not socially."

Back at the metate, the resulting masa is turned into a pile of fresh tortillas by the skilled hands of Nati. We eat them hot off the comal with a slathering of mole. Tortillas are like new cars, they lose a great deal of their value as soon as they are driven off the lot. There can be no better way than eating them like this, with the light texture of ground corn, a slight crispiness and spicy-chocolatey mole. For Esquivel, the moment is equally pleasurable.

"For me, the tortilla is sensational. In the moment you eat a tortilla, you make contact with all the previous generations that have eaten this tortilla. When we eat maize, it no longer becomes a question of biology but rather a question of entering in communion through the tortilla with our past, a past that gives us our character. And that has great meaning."

A week or two later, back home in Toronto, I stop by a store which sells Latin American products: pirated Cantinflas films, sugary soft drink from Colombia and Peru, and illegally imported compact discs from across the Americas. They also sell *Maseca*, a commercial brand of corn flour used, as the package says, for tortillas, tomales, empanadas and other Central American and Mexican specialities. I buy a kilogram, take it home, mix it with the proper amount of water then pound out a half-dozen misshapen tortillas which I cook in a cast-iron pan and top with President's Choice brand Volcano Salsa. One bite later, the entire batch and the bag of Maseca is in the garbage as, for now, I prefer to go without tortillas, rather than desecrate the memory of what I had in Mexico.

# celebrating
## with food

Whenever you visit Mexico you're likely to get pleasantly caught up in some kind of celebration. Be it a personal, local or national occasion, you'll be swept along by the verve of the people and the zest it gives to life here. The food and drink associated with each event provides much more than mere sustenance: recipes and customs are passed down through generations and help preserve the traditions which provide the link between Mexico past and present.

# The Mexican Fiesta

The Mexican calendar is full of fiestas, each with its own origin. Many of the occasions are religious, such as **Dia de la Virgen de Guadalupe**, **Corpus Cristi**, **los santos reyes** (Holy Kings) and **Pascua** (Easter). Others are embraced by every Mexican. National days include **Dia de la Independencia**, celebrating independence from Spain, **El 5 de mayo**, celebrating a 1863 victory in battle over the invading French army, and the **Dia de la Constitución** which marks the passage of the 1917 constitution.

Each town, village and sometimes neighbourhood, will also have the day of its patron **santo** (see Local Fiesta: El Grande Veracruz later in this chapter). Cities on the coast have their pre-Lenten carnivals (see Carnaval!) while individuals celebrate birthdays, weddings, and events like the **quinceño**, which marks a young woman's entrance into society, held some time around her 15th birthday.

A quinceño is a very formal occasion where lots of money is spent on new clothes, renting a hall, hiring a caterer and feeding as many of the girl's friends and relatives as can be accommodated. There are formalities: a church service, speeches about the girl, a special dance between daughter and father and various presentations. Before childhood was mercifully extended, the quinceño marked the point in a girl's life when she was considered ready for marriage. Her suitors would begin their courtships at this party by presenting gifts and signing her dance card. Gifts and dancing are still the norm but, for the majority of these girls, marriage is still several years away. There may be a sit-down dinner or simply tables of snack foods. The next day, remaining relatives will gather for a late breakfast of seso (cow's brain) soup (or whatever hangover remedy is preferred) and gossip about the previous night's scandals: who was seen doing what with whom, and the rest of it.

The Christmas season also offers ample opportunity for partying. Each of the nine days preceding 25 December and the 12 days following (the days are called **posadas**) is marked with gatherings, parties or religious services. Gifts are presented to children on 6 January (**Dia de los Santos Reyes**).

Eating, drinking and the smashing of **piñatas** (animal-shaped dolls made of clay and filled with sweets) goes on throughout the Christmas period. One particular dish, the **rosco de reyes**, a sort of large donut, has a small plastic baby baked into it and if you get the piece with the prize, you get to throw a party at your *own* house two weeks later! The most traditional food at any Mexican fiesta is **mole**. Tamales and other antojitos are also common but a party is not a party without a large pot of steaming mole ready on the stove.

## Dia de Muertos

On the surface, Dia de Muertos celebrations are not remarkably different from other national parties: there is mole, drink, music and general revelry. But when you consider that Dia de Muertos translates to Day of the Dead, the festivities take on a decidedly ironic edge.

The origins of the holiday reach back to the Aztec month of Miccailhuitontli which was named for the goddess Mictecacihuatl, the 'Lady of the Dead'. It originally fell in July or August but was changed by the Spanish to fall on 2 November, the day following 'All Saints' Day' because the Spanish hoped to assimilate the heathen holiday – yet another example of cultural **mestizaje** (mixing). Offerings of food and drink were left to supply the departed on their journey through the nine tunnels which conducted them to the world beyond.

Sociologists have sought a unique dynamic between the living and the dead which exists where a day that commemorates an ostensibly sad occasion – the passing of relatives and loved ones – takes on a celebratory air. Some say it is a celebration of the cycle of life and death, others that it's a means of avoiding the anxiety that comes with contemplating the unknown horrors of the afterlife, and others think that the spirits of the living and dead co-exist on the same plain on this day.

Or perhaps it is another form of existential machismo, a chance to stare death in the face and laugh. Octavio Paz, the Nobel prize winner, once wrote, "the Mexican's indifference towards death is nourished by his indifference towards life." The irony has been helped along by artist Jose Guadalupe Posada, whose comical etchings of **calaveras** (skeletons wearing enormous feathered hats or with belts of bullets strapped across their rib cage) have been a mainstay at Dia de Muertos celebrations since the end of the 19th century.

Celebrations – and they *are* celebrations – also include food and drink. Candies made with marzipan and shaped into skulls with hideous, toothy grins are gobbled up by children. Women spend 1 November making the favourite dishes of the recently deceased. When there has been a death in the house in the previous year, the day is especially important and relatives and friends gather to eat and drink with the visiting spirits.

An altar to the dead, decorated with bright flowers, ribbons and coloured candles, is erected in one corner of the house. Plates of tamales, **pan de muerto** (bread of the dead), a heavy loaf made with egg yolks, fruits and tequila or mezcal are left so that the dead feel welcome on their return.

Outside, vendors pass among the crowds selling candies and sweetbreads as memorial processions make their way to cemeteries, where people leave bunches of marigolds on the graves of their loved ones.

**CELEBRATING**

# The Northern Asado

In Northern Mexico, celebrations – birthdays, anniversaries, graduations, family reunions – are marked by **asados**, whole-day, whole-family occasions. The word asado is loosely translated as barbecue.

Any good asado begins with the **leña** (wood for cooking) which must be mesquite in order to infuse the meat with the distinctive flavour. Also, the mesquite must be from the north as it's said to have a special quality due to the composition of the region's soil and dry climate. The meat is either beef or **cabrito** (kid or baby goat), prepared with a simple combination of salt, pepper and lime (in measures dictated by the family recipe.)

Predictably, men prepare the leña and the grill while the women season the meat and prepare the **salsa bandera** (flag sauce) named for the red of the tomato, the white of the onion and green of the chile. Generations come together, with the old ones teaching young ones the secrets of the great asado: preparing the **leña**, selecting and seasoning the meat etc.

Meat is the star of the show, but the asado also includes guacamole, vegetables, potatoes and wheat tortillas. Kids (the goat variety) are grilled virtually whole, split at the ribs and spread like giant butterflies over the grill. The drippings from this fatty meat cause frequent flare-ups that burn the skin crisp. In the north of Mexico, where goat and cattle herding were a fundamental part of the region's economy, the asado has special, sentimental meaning. Even the most urban families will discuss the quality of the meat as though they had been raised on a ranch.

There is little formality to an asado, especially the large ones. People eat when enough of the meat is ready. They sit wherever they can – outside by the grill, in the dining room or in the kitchen. An asado will probably last the whole afternoon, and many will sneak off to one of the bedrooms for a little siesta. Needless to say, no one leaves hungry.

*Tuba player, Easter parade, Tepoztlan*

# Carnaval!

It's mid-February, carnaval time in Mexico. As in New Orleans and Rio de Janeiro, Carnaval erupts here during the nine days leading up to Ash Wednesday and the beginning of Lent. It is not a national ritual, although most Mexicans will tell you they've been to at least one in their lifetime. Some of the most popular take place in Campeche and Mazatlán but the most famous is in Veracruz where they've been crowning the **reina** (queen) and the **rey feo** (ugly king), dancing in the streets, watching parades and entertaining visitors since 1924.

The heart of carnaval is the weekend and the Monday and Tuesday preceding Ash Wednesday. In Veracruz, bleachers are set up for a 10km stretch along the seafront Camacho Boulevard. There are six parades in total, two during the day and four at night.

Each float has its theme, taken from movies, songs and dances in popular culture. Some have bands, dancers, or a collection of young women dressed in matching spandex who wave from their perches and throw sweets into the reaching crowd. Each also has its own 3m-stack of speakers, pumping out salsa, meringue, soca, even a camp version of the already camp American folk classic Oh Susannah! The Brazilian-inspired samba schools march and drum in perfect synchronicity, their flag-bearers swaying from the top and jiggling from below.

The parades are about being seen as much as seeing. Spectators regularly jump out of the stands to dance with paraders, sometimes at a distance, sometimes closely and suggestively, with hip grinding and a concluding kiss of anonymous and very public passion.

To cool said passion, vendors pass the stands selling beer, water and soft drink at double its normal price. Behind the stands, **puestos** do a brisk business selling barbecued chicken, tacos and grilled chorizo. Lines form outside convenience stores serving beer by the litre in huge plastic cups. Boys from the country conduct their mule-driven carts, overflowing with peanuts or pistachios, playing looped tape through a very bad sound system where only the words **cacahuete**, **pistacho** and **ricos** (delicious) are clearly audible through the fuzz.

The party continues after the parade, spilling into the nightclubs, discos and restaurants downtown. The music doesn't stop. Marimba bands set up on side walks and plug in huge speakers which send the sounds down several city blocks. Old women stand in front of huge pots of steaming corn. The combination of a mango vendor and a sharp knife results in a flower-shaped treat on a stick. The patios are packed with eaters and drinkers, some still fully in party mode, others winding down, resting up for the following day.

## Local Fiesta – El Grande, Veracruz

Every city, town and village in Mexico is protected by a patron saint, for whom a church is named and to whom prayers are directed when the future of the town depends on the sort of circumstances best handled by divine managers. Every saint has its day which gives the people an opportunity to celebrate their patron with an all-day fiesta. In smaller communities, these days are the highlight of the calendar.

Nuestra Señora de Lourdes is the patron saint of El Grande and her day is celebrated on 11 February. El Grande, which means 'the big one' is a village of about 400 some 15 minutes outside of Jalapa in the state of Veracruz. It's not far from a town called El Chico, 'the little one' (which is actually more populated).

Food plays an important role in the fiesta and **mole** is the most popular choice. The best cooks in the village begin their preparations early in the day, and then open their kitchens and dining tables for several **tangas** (sittings) to which the whole village and out-of-town friends and relatives are invited. In the Jalapa area, there are two principal moles prepared, the slightly sweet **xico** and the spicier **naolinco**.(See the Staples & Specialities chapter for more information on mole).

While mole dominates the menu, other dishes, such as **chile relleno**, (stuffed with chopped chicken and chile), rice dishes and, of course, fresh tortillas, are also served in abundance. The food has to last at least two days and sometimes longer, depending upon how many guests have come and how long they end up staying.

It's a truly communal party and no one is excluded. For the cooks, a house full of eaters is an auspicious sign that will bring luck for the rest of the year.

One popular drink of choice in El Grande is **aguardiente**, made from the sugar cane that grows in the lower lying areas of the state of Veracruz. It is often made in small non-commercial distilleries in the village but can also be bought at frighteningly low prices (about US$.60 a litre). For those who would rather avoid this very strong drink (and the vicious hangover it can produce) there is cold beer.

As night falls, the highlight of the fiesta begins. Five bulls have been fashioned out of papier maché and equipped with a rudimentary scaffolding that carries a large collection of fireworks. These **toros cohetes**, or 'firework bulls' as they are called, fit onto the heads and shoulders of five volunteers.

One by one, the bulls head into the village's one main street, and kneel before a priest to be blessed. A fuse of indeterminable length is then lit. Around the town square, huge speakers begin to blare the traditional music of the **corrida**, with its ominous trumpet growing louder and raising the tension.

CELEBRATING

*Roman soldier, Good Friday procession, Taxco*

The machos, with the same bravado seen at Pamplona's running of the bulls, taunt these toros, approaching them, teasing the rockets, bearing their chests as a sort of dare. The bull weaves through the crowd, charging, turning and charging again. Then, always surprisingly but never unexpectedly, the fireworks begin to shoot in all directions. Children run giggling into their houses, adolescent boyfriends shield their adolescent girlfriends and the machos scatter. The danger is real and the next day a few will emerge with stitches or burns.

The glow of a single firework, strategically placed up the bull's behind, signals the end of that bull's life. The children emerge from their houses, girlfriends kiss their heroic boyfriends and the machos head back into the street, ready to take on the next one.

# regional
## variations

While some ingredients – beans, corn and chiles in particular –
are found in kitchens from Tijuana to Tuxtla Gutiérrez, Mexico's
cuisine remains highly regionalised. The country's geography is
rugged, marked by two mountain ranges that cut it in three parts
from north to south. Before the advent of air travel, going from
one state to another was a major journey. As a result, regional
cuisine developed in relative isolation, using what was readily and
locally available.

**REGIONS**

UNITED STATES OF AMERICA

MEXICO

GULF OF MEXICO

PACIFIC OCEAN

✪ MEXICO CITY

BELIZE

GUATEMALA

Central Pacific Coast
El Norte
Yucatán Peninsula
Gulf Coast
El Bajio
Mexico City
Central Mexico
Southern Pacific Coast

Climate also shaped Mexico's regional cuisine and almost every climatic condition is represented. The dry north offers little in the way of edible vegetation. In the subtropical south, lush forests characterise the landscape. In the centre, temperate highlands get enough rainfall to sustain a family farm, and the temperature of low-lying coastal plains delight beach-goers and provide a large variety of tropical fruits.

With so much climatic variation, naturally the soil composition varies. Some areas also benefit from the mineral rich volcanic soil left by millions of years of eruptions. As a result, according to purists, a chile serrano grown in Jalisco will not taste the same as one grown in Oaxaca.

Some native groups were nomadic and warlike such as the Chichimec in the north. Others, like the Aztecs in the Valley of Mexico, the Zapotecs in Oaxaca, or the Mayans on the Yucatán, developed permanent cities and agricultural economies. Their own cuisines naturally differed according to climate and availability but distinctions between them became blurred with centuries of trade, war and domination.

Foreign influence also helped shape regional diets. In the Yucatán and along the Gulf Coast, there is a definite Caribbean flair to many dishes, while cooking in Nuevo Leon and its northern neighbour Texas can mirror each other. Mexico City, with its worldliness, has been subject to foreign influences from as far away as Asia and Europe.

# El Norte
**(including Baja California, Baja California Sur, Sonora, Chihuahua, Durango, Coahuila, Nuevo León, and Tamaulipas)**

There is a saying among Mexico City snobs claiming that the north is 'Donde se acaba la cultura y empieza la carne asada' (where culture ends and grilled meat begins). It is meant as an insult but somehow loses its sting when you taste a perfect **cabrito asado** (roast kid) or a **carne asado** (roast meat), chopped and wrapped in a wheat tortilla with salsa bandera. The north has provided what most people beyond Mexico consider to be 'Mexican' food: fajitas, quesadillas, nachos, burritos – food that has inspired Taco Bell and countless other fast food outlets. It is a food described by cookbook author Patricia Quintana as "austere, filling, and without pretensions."

Geographically, the north is Mexico's largest region. It is also one of the more sparsely populated. It stretches along the US border from Baja California in the west to the Gulf Coast. The southern border is a bit harder to define but probably stops by the time you get to San Luis Potosi and Zacatecas on the east side or Sinaloa and Jalisco on the west. The climate is extremely dry and the map is marked by two large deserts, the Sonorense and Chihuahuaense. A large marsh, called Cuatrociénagas breaks up the sand and dirt. But the north is also marked by snow-capped mountains and the impressive Copper Canyon.

Baja California is a bit of an anomaly in the north. Its geographic isolation and dependence on the sea means local cooking is dominated by **pescado** (fish) and **mariscos** (seafood), as opposed to beef or kid, as is the case with the rest of the area. In place of dry deserts, Baja boasts fertile valleys, which have helped the peninsula develop as the centre of Mexico's small wine industry, as its climate best mimics that of the Mediterranean.

The north also differs from the rest of the country in that the indigenous people who lived there were nomadic and so the magnificent pyramids and huge sculptures found in central and southern Mexico are nowhere to be seen. Their means of sustenance was limited to what they hunted and gathered. They were also able to successfully resist the expansion of the Aztec empire and so were never introduced to the diet of the south.

The Spanish were late in arriving north and when they got there (in the 16th and 17th century) they found nothing that made them want to stay. Agriculture was underdeveloped and the area was poor and isolated from the rest of the country. The situation began to change in the middle of the 16th century when the governor began offering huge tracts of land to Creoles to stimulate development. Migrants began to arrive from the south, bringing with them their culinary traditions, and cattle farming flourished.

## BUSTAMANTE: BREAD & MEZCAL

Bustamante is a sleepy little town halfway between Monterrey and the Texas border. At one time, the town thrived as a centre for the area's agricultural production. But better roads and bigger scales of production have left Bustamante with no alternative but to seek a slice of the tourist cake. As such, guides published by the state tourism office list it as a place famous for its breads and **mezcal**.

I caught a mid-morning bus out of Monterrey and arrived in Bustamante about noon following a two hour drive through a valley flanked by green-brown mountains and dry fields of mesquite and assorted cacti.

Everyone in Bustamante knows the bakery known as Panaderia Hermanitas Cazzo. The **hermanitas** (sisters) in question are six spinsters, Dolores, Irma, Yolanda, Gloria, Magdalena and Olivia who now run the bakery which their grandmother founded so her girls would not have to leave home to work. "There isn't any work in Bustamante," explains Maria de Socorro, their mother, "Ya no hay cabra, ya no hay res" (no more goats, no more cattle).

The Panaderia is less a bakery than a collection of shacks, topped by heavy canvas and corrugated iron. The main building, which may be the only one with permanent walls, serves as a kitchen where all the dough is prepared. The baking is done behind this building, in two clay ovens – white washed mounds with small openings where mesquite burns down to hot embers, ready to receive the bread. I have arrived early, too early to get pictures of the bread being baked. No matter though – one of the sisters pulls out the giant wooden spatula used to pull the bread in and out of the oven. She poses with a loaf of raw dough and then with an already baked loaf – like one of those cooking shows where the host puts a dish into one oven and then, in a miraculous instant, pulls the same dish out of the next one, cooked to perfection.

The Hermanitas speciality is **semita de nuez**, a round bread with a slightly heavy texture and chopped pistachios. They also prepare baked **empanadas**, including one stuffed with the delicious **flor de calabaza** (squash flower). Another table displays various pecan-based sweets covered in **miel de caña** (a sugar cane extract), while a fourth has a collection of pottery: plates, casseroles and dishes. Everything is sold from the front of the bakery, which is open to the street and where a hand-painted sign announces "the best bread made by traditional means."

As I left, I asked one of the sisters for directions to La Guadalupa, where Bustamante's famous mezcal is made. "Oh, Rancho Vino" she said, referring to mezcal as many rural Mexicans still refer to any alcoholic drink, as wine. "It's too far to walk and there aren't any taxi's in Bustamante. Go to the police station and get one of them to take you. Tell them you're from *turismo*."

The police station is located behind the Palacio Municipal. Bustamante's finest on this day consisted of one officer, an ample-bellied man in his late 30s, with a red VW bug. I explained my situation and he said he'd have to ask the *comandante*, who was out now and should be back *en un* which didn't sound very promising. I commented to him on how nice and quiet the town seemed, meaning it as a compliment from one who had only ever spent time in Mexico's biggest cities. He took it as an insult and insisted that on weekends, the place erupts with dances that attract people from the surrounding towns, requiring all ten officers in the Bustamante police force to be on duty to break up fights and haul off the drunks.

The comandante didn't actually take too long and after some introductions, the officer was dispatched to take me to La Guadalupa. On the way, I asked him if he liked mezcal. "Not much," he said, "the hangovers are terrible. But every once in a while on a cool evening I'll have a bit to warm me up."

We arrived at La Guadalupa in a very short time. As a distillery, it's not much, a single building, half of which is devoted to making the product, while the other half serves as a warehouse and business office. Throughout, there is an acrid stench of fermentation, although I seemed to be the only one that noticed.

Mezcal begins with maguey plants which are grown in the area. Once the long spiney leaves have been removed, the hearts are heated using a large underground pit in order to soften them and weaken the cell walls. They are then pressed in a mill powered by two mules who are strapped to the machine via a long pole. The mules walk in continuous circles as a worker feeds the maguey into the metal presses. The tobacco-coloured juice then flows into a fermenting chamber, a truly foul-smelling room of half a dozen open barrels. From there, the product is filtered, purified and bottled. La Guadalupa sells its products on the premises as well as in stores in the area. (For information on mezcal, see the Drinks chapter.)

Leaving La Guadalupa, my police escort showed me the main attraction in the area, the canyon campground where a spring-source stream sends fresh water into man-made pools before continuing its path. He pointed out the cliff with an overhang known as *la nariz* (the nose) which seemed to be ready to drop onto the highway. He explained how on the weekends, the place was full of people from Monterrey and even the US, which was but a two hour drive. On a number of occasions he kindly reminded me to "say nice things about Bustamante."

Led by this agricultural wealth and buoyed by its proximity to the rich US market, the north began to industrialise in the latter half of the 19th century. The economic capital, Monterrey, was home to a number of families who built factories that today manufacture everything from telephone equipment to beer. Brewery giant, Cerveceria Cuauhtemoc, maker of Dos Equis, Carta Blanca, Bohemia and Tecate is based here.

The proximity to the US is evident by the number of fast food chains here. Not that they are unwelcome. At lunch hour, a Kentucky Fried Chicken will have a line-up almost out the door. Shopping habits have also been influenced by US supermarkets and convenience stores with their walls of fridges and wide bright aisles.

*Wild nopales*

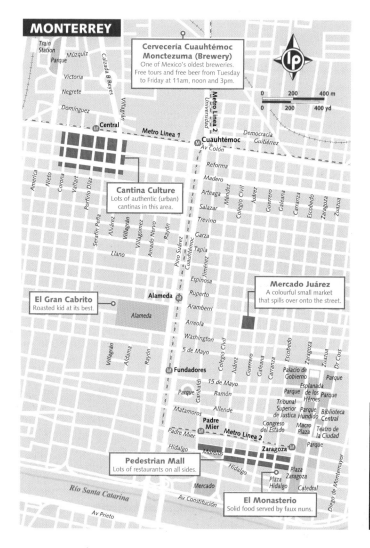

**MONTERREY**

Train Station
Parque
Múzquiz
Victoria
Negrete
Domínguez

Calzada B Reyes
Villagrán

Central

**Cervecería Cuauhtémoc Moctezuma (Brewery)**
One of Mexico's oldest breweries. Free tours and free beer from Tuesday to Friday at 11am, noon and 3pm.

Metro Linea 1

Metro Linea 2
Universidad

Cuauhtémoc
Av Colón

Democracia
Guitiérrez

0   200   400 m
0   200   400 yd

America
Nieto
Corona
Vallart
Porfirio Díaz

Serafín Peña
Alvárez
Villagonez
Villagonez
Amado Nervo
Rayón

Llano

**Cantina Culture**
Lots of authentic (urban) cantinas in this area.

Reforma
Madero
Arteaga
Salazar
Trevino
Garza
Tapia

Méndez
Colegio Civil
Juárez
Guerrero
Galeana
Carranza
Escobedo
Zaragoza
Zuazua

Pino Suárez
Cuauhtémoc

Jiménez
Espinosa
Ruperto
Aramberri
Arreola
Washington
5 de Mayo

Alameda

**El Gran Cabrito**
Roasted kid at its best.

Alameda

**Mercado Juárez**
A colourful small market that spills over onto the street.

Villagrán
Aldama
Rayón

Fundadores

Garibaldi

Parque
Ramón
Matamoros

15 de Mayo

Allende

Colegio Civil
Juárez
Guerrero
Galeana
Carranza
Escobedo
Zaragoza
Zuazua
Dr Coss

Palacio de Gobierno
Esplanada
Parque de los Héroes
Parque

Tribunal Superior de Justica
Congreso del Estado
Parque Hundido
Macro Plaza

Biblioteca Central
Teatro de la Ciudad

Padre Mier
Padre Mier
Metro Linea 2

Zaragoza

Parque

Hidalgo
Moretos

**Pedestrian Mall**
Lots of restaurants on all sides.

Hidalgo

Mercado

Plaza Zaragoza
Plaza Hidalgo
Catedral

Río Santa Catarina

Av Constitución

Av Prieto

**El Monasterio**
Solid food served by faux nuns.

Diego de Montemayor

## Regional Specialities
### Tortillas de Harina de Trigo

Tortillas are as important in the north as they are in the rest of the country but here they're made with wheat flour instead of corn. The change makes all the difference. Wheat tortillas are made with flour, vegetable shortening and water, and rolled with a pin when made at home instead of being pressed. They are more pliable than corn tortillas and have less flavour, yet with a lightly seasoned **carne asado** or **queso fundido** (cheese fondue), wheat tortillas simply go better than their corn counterparts. You can make wheat tortillas at home or buy them commercially (although they are more expensive than corn tortillas).

### DON'T MISS

- Spanish seafood soups of Baja California
- thick, juicy steaks missing elsewhere in Mexico
- wheat flour tortillas
- **asado cabrito** (roast kid) and **frijoles borrachos** (drunken beans) in Monterrey
- the wines and brandies of Mexico's best grape-growing region of Baja

### Meat

The distinguishing meat of the north is, of course, **cabrito** (kid). A little like lamb, only greasier, cabrito is a mainstay in Nuevo Leon. In Monterrey, there are several restaurants devoted to serving it, fresh from the barbeque pit, where it roasts whole on a spit for hours, the skin turning golden crisp in the from the heat of the mesquite embers. These restaurants are all huge and cavernous, made for serving parties of six or more as eating cabrito takes on a sense of ritual, where **norteños** (northerners) remind themselves of who they are. It's pretty heavy, though, and you may feel like you're anchored to your seat after you've eaten. Portions come large, so be prepared to gorge. As though it weren't enough on its own, cabrito comes accompanied by guacamole, roasted onions, salsa and **totopos** (crisp tortilla chips).

Cabrito isn't the only meat served in the north. The states of Sonora and Chihuahua are well-known for their steaks and northern **chorizo** is a milder version of the national sausage. **Machaca** is a dried beef developed before the arrival of refrigeration by the Tlaxcaltecas from the south. It is very popular at breakfast, served diced with eggs and a mild chile salsa. It's also eaten as a **botana**, shredded and served hot with a sprinkling of lime juice.

# Central Pacific Coast
## (including: Sinaloa, Nayarit, Jalisco, Colima)

Tourism has put this region on the map – Mazatlán, Puerto Vallarta, and Manzanillo are all located here – but within Mexico, it's also known for its agricultural traditions. Fruit, vegetables, meat and fish from here find their way to local, national, and even international markets. Sinaloa is particularly known for its rice, sugar cane and greens. Nayarit is equally blessed with rich, nutritious soil and a coastline famous for its seafood. Colima – home of Pedro Paramo, perhaps Mexican literature's best known character – also counts on the sea for food. But it is Jalisco that defines the region.

Jalisco and its capital city, Guadalajara (second largest in the republic), have contributed much of what the rest of the world sees as Mexican. Tequila was first distilled from the area's blue agave plants, mariachi's began strolling the streets of Guadalajara before anywhere else, the **charro**, a sort of cowboy that has passed into the nation's folklore, is another Jalisco original. Writers Juan Rulfo, Agustin Yáñez and Elena Garro were born here, as was composer Agustín Lara, silver-screen vamp María Félix, and outspoken muralist José Clemente Orozco.

The area is geographically diverse with the low lying coastal planes leading up to the Sierra Madre Occidental with its snow-capped mountains and volcanoes (live and extinct). Climate is also conducive to agriculture with long, dry

*Tequila monument, Tequila, Jalisco*

growing seasons punctuated by a short but intense rainy season from June to September. The Indian groups that lived here before the conquest were both sedentary and nomadic but did not lack for edible plants and animals including **chapulines** (grasshoppers), ants, **chicharras** (crickets) maguey worms, wild turkey, deer, armadillos, corn and chile. Although they escaped Aztec domination, they traded with the Valley of Mexico. It is said that Moctezuma was especially fond of the chocolate from what is now the state of Jalisco.

In the colony, Guadalajara became a point of transit between the capital and the silver mines in Zacatecas, one state to the north. It developed as a trading and financial centre which continued to grow long after the mines in Zacatecas had been exhausted. Artisan activity has also played a large role in the region's economy, the legacy of which can be seen today in Tonalá and Tlaquepaque, two towns near Guadalajara (see the boxed text Tonalá and Tlaquepaque in the Home Cooking & Traditions chapter).

The dish which evokes the most regional pride is **birria**, a sort of soupy stew, made with meat (traditionally goat) and a chile-based, and heavily spiced, broth thickened after a long cooking process. Tapatíos, as people

**GUADALAJARA**

Avenida Juarez
The downtown dining district

Mercado Libertad
Four levels of food & merchandise

Plaza de los Mariachis
A pleasant place for a drink and mariachi music

Restaurant La Chata
The best place for Agua de Arroz (rice water) in Guadalajara

from the city are called, are also fond of their special version of **pozole**, a hearty soup with pork, hominy, garlic and topped with raw cabbage, radish and onion. Both **birrias** and **pozoles** are often accompanied by **charales**, a tiny fish from Lake Chapala which is breaded, fried and served with salt and lime.

Jalisco is also the exclusive home of Tequila (see Tequila in the Drinks chapter) and all production is centred within a few hours of Guadalajara. Although tequila is available throughout the country, you should sample some of the finer **añejos** and **reposados** if you find yourself around here. A bar called La Riconada, on Avenida Morelos, just west of the Plaza Tapatía, offers a wide selection of tequilas served with a homemade sangrita. The waiters are quite knowledgeable about what they serve and can tell you the differences between brands and make solid recommendations.

In general, Guadalajara's downtown is a pleasant place to stroll, beginning at the Parque Revolución and ending at the Plaza de los Mariachis, where you can sit in a closed street and order a beer and botanas from any one of the several restaurants operating on either side of the plaza. By dusk, groups of mariachis, those strolling groups of musicians that appear in every bad movie about Mexico, begin work, soliciting diners to have them play songs.

One of the treats of Guadalajara is the Mercado Libertad which takes up an entire city block at Avenida Javier Mina and Calzada Independencia Sur. This multi-level market has a bit of everything. There is even an entire aisle devoted entirely to batteries of every shape and size. And of

*Mercado Libertad, Guadalajara, Jalisco*

## DON'T MISS

- sampling some fine drams in Jalisco, the home of Tequila
- **birria**, a soupy stew which is the culinary pride of Guadalajara
- **camarones rellenos** (stuffed shrimp) and **huachinango a la naranja** (red snapper in orange sauce) of Sinaloa
- regional **pozoles**, accompanied by **charales**, a tiny fish from Lake Chapala
- **sopa de coco** (coconut soup) of Colima the atmosphere of Mercado Libertad in Guadalajara
- shopping for kitchenware in Tonala and Tlaquepaque

course, there is food. The lower level is devoted to fruit and vegetables, meat, dry chiles and spices. Directly above, on a balcony overlooking the fruit market, are some of the best market comedores in the country. Each offers a hearty meal specialising in tacos, **ceviche** (seafood cocktail), birria or other antojitos. While Guadalajara may be a bit too far inland to completely trust the seafood, the meat-oriented comedores shouldn't present a problem as long as you're a carnivore. Toward noon they become crowded with shoppers who have made the trek downtown to pick up shopping and enjoy a hot meal. Even if you decide not to eat, it is worth a wander through this section to take in the aromas of the fresh tortillas on the comal, **guisados** stewing in enormous clay pots, and chile sauces simmering on the stoves. The comedor-types are aggressive and you will be invited to sit down at every place you pass with a persuasive "**Que va a comer?**" (what will you eat?).

The coastal cities are mostly tourism-oriented and the Carlos O'Brien chains (Carlos & Charlie's, Guadalajara Grill ) are well represented in the more popular spots. These mix Mexican and US traditions to ensure that both adventurous and timid diners will be satisfied. But there are also many excellent seafood restaurants popular with locals and Mexican tourists. In Sinaloa, look for **camarones rellenos** (stuffed shrimp). In Manzanillo, **robalo** (bass), caught fresh by teenage boys who stand on rocks and cast their lines continuously into the sea until landing a saleable catch, are served. There are even tamales made from shrimp.

*Mercado Libertad, Guadalajara, Jalisco*

## Southern Pacific Coast
### (including Guerrero, Oaxaca, Chiapas)

The south of Mexico is colour, just colour. Huge bouquets of balloons – red hearts, yellow happy faces and metallic circles that read '**Feliz Cupleaños**' (happy birthday) – float among canopies of leafy trees. Beautiful young Zapotec girls, dressed in cotton dresses trimmed with intricate embroidery and green, red and gold ribbons, pose for pictures with tourists. Smaller children and old women wander without direction, offering hammocks, rucksacks, bookmarks, roses and other bright items for sale. The colonial buildings surrounding the zòcalo are mostly brown and grey but, on the patios below, tables with plaid patterned tablecloths in crimson and violet sit in the sun, waiting for customers. Even a small protest seems to whet the appetite with colourful hand-painted signs denouncing some injustice. Mercado 20 de Noviembre is awash with ice cream stands, advertising some 30 flavours, from the basic: chocolate and **fresa** (strawberry); to the odd **queso** (cheese), **elote** (young corn); to the risky, tequila and mezcal.

While the region is considered ethnically diverse, it holds strong to its indigenous roots. The Zapotec language is commonly heard in the streets of Oaxaca and native costumes constitute everyday fashion in many areas. This geography of the region made transportation and colonization difficult, helping to preserve the region's unique identity. Until the middle of the 20th century, a journey to Mexico City from Oaxaca took up to three days. Today, with superhighways, that time has been cut to five hours. A flight takes less than an hour. The isolation was even greater for those living in Guerrero and in the subtropical Chiapas.

*Highway collectors eating paleta helada (ice cream), near Guadalajara*

## Pozole

This hearty soup is loved all over Mexico and is often taken as an entire meal. In the state of Guerrero, it is an institution and Thursday has somehow been declared Pozole day. With so many ingredients, it is possible to substitute, so don't be put off by the long list.

### Ingredients

| | | | |
|---|---|---|---|
| 1 | can hominy | 1 | small onion, chopped |
| 1/4 | cup (50ml) cilantro | 2 | cloves garlic, chopped |
| 3 | bay leaves | 1 | tablespoon vegetable oil |
| 4 | limes, wedged | | |
| 1 | avocado | | |
| 1/2 | teaspoon (1ml) oregano | | |
| 5 | ounces (150g) lean pork shoulder, chopped | | |
| 1/4 | chicken (either white or dark meat), julienned | | |
| 1 | can peeled, stewed, diced tomatoes | | |
| 2 | chilli jalapeños, chopped | | |
| 3 | cups (750ml) chicken broth | | |

Sauté the onions and garlic in oil (lard would be more authentic). Add the pork then chicken until just browned. Toss in the jalapeños and let cook for a minute or two. Add the tomatoes and the broth, the cilantro, hominy and bay leaves, cover and allow to simmer for about 45 minutes or until the meat is completely cooked. Meanwhile, dice the avocado. When the soup is done, serve in bowls and plunk the avocado in along with a squeeze of lime juice.

Guerrero is home to Acapulco, which became Mexico's first true resort town in the 1950s. Visitors (mostly North American) have been flocking to its beaches ever since for one week escapes from the dark winters of the north. Restaurants cater to their tastes and, as a result, food along that part of the coast has developed a decidedly gringo character. The one exception is **pozole** which has become a Thursday tradition in Acapulco for locals and tourists alike. Naturally, the Pacific Ocean provides many of the main dishes for coastal residents in both Guerrero and Oaxaca.

But most of the area is unknown to mass market tourism and culinary authenticity is not hard to find. And you can't get much more authentic than **chapulines**, grasshoppers fried in lime and dried chile powder and eaten as a botana. These crunchy snacks are available in all the markets in Oaxaca and have a very subtle flavour that is all but snuffed out by the chile and lime.

REGIONAL VARIATIONS

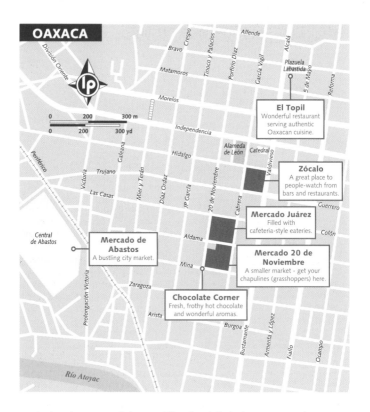

**OAXACA**

0  200  300 m
0  200  300 yd

División Oriente
Allende
Crespo
Bravo
Tinoco y Palacios
Matamoros
Porfirio Díaz
García Vigil
Alcalá
Plazuela Labastida
5 de Mayo
Reforma
Morelos
Independencia
Galeana
Hidalgo
Alameda de León
Catedral
Valdivieso
Periférico
Victoria
Trujano
Las Casas
Mier y Terán
Díaz Ordaz
JP García
20 de Noviembre
Cabrera
Guerrero
Colón
Aldama
Mina
Zaragoza
Prolongación Victoria
Arista
Burgoa
Bustamante
Armenta y López
Fiallo
Ocampo
Río Atoyac
Central de Abastos

**El Topil**
Wonderful restaurant serving authentic Oaxacan cuisine.

**Zócalo**
A great place to people-watch from bars and restaurants.

**Mercado Juárez**
Filled with cafeteria-style eateries.

**Mercado de Abastos**
A bustling city market.

**Mercado 20 de Noviembre**
A smaller market - get your chapulines (grasshoppers) here.

**Chocolate Corner**
Fresh, frothy hot chocolate and wonderful aromas.

As in other parts of the republic, the chile is the strongest element in the region's cuisine and the fertile soil of the south allows for the cultivation of a wide variety. Edible flowers such as the **flor de frijol** and **flor de calabaza** are also used extensively and help give southern dishes a distinctive flavour.

Cooking is taken very seriously in Oaxaca which is known to food-lovers as 'lugar de siete moles' (the place of seven moles). These range from **amarillo** (yellow) a soupy, subtlety spiced sauce with chayote squash, avocado leaf and several varieties of chile, to **estofado** (stew) served with pork and accented by almonds, capers and black olives.

Markets like the **Abastos** in Oaxaca are packed everyday with shoppers gathering ingredients. These often include unhealthy amounts of **manteca** (lard) which is falling quickly out of favour in other parts of the country, but is still used regularly as a cooking and flavouring agent in the south.

There is no real organisation to markets in the south. Vendors stake out their place along aisles so narrow that two people can barely pass thorough with comfort. Food and non-food items seem to be separate, and meat is sold in its own section, set apart from the rest. You will hear Spanish, but you are also likely to hear one of the many native languages that still survive in the region.

*Chapulines (grasshoppers), Oaxaca City*

**REGIONAL VARIATIONS**

## The Yucatán Peninsula
### (including Yucatán, Campeche and Quintana Roo)

In the bars and restaurants in Merida, the largest city on the Yucatán peninsula, they seem to keep their fridges at a lower temperature and the beer is cold enough to cut your throat with refreshment – a small detail but one you'll appreciate on a typically scorching day in Merida.

The Yucatán peninsula is Maya country, a land of white beaches, crystalline waters and spectacular architecture from the classical period. Today, the Mayan community and sense of identity remains strong, having successfully resisted the near-total assimilation that saw the heritage of so many other indigenous peoples diluted.

The land is mostly flat, with gently rolling hills rising inland. It is soaked in a strong Caribbean sun making it a popular destination for tourists from the north (Cancun is located here). There is a strong sense of Caribbean influence in the Yucatán. Men, from labourers to executives, sport **guayaberas**, the ornamented, untucked shirts that served as an unofficial uniform throughout the Caribbean basin. Baseball is more popular than soccer as it is in the Dominican Republic, Puerto Rico and Cuba. The hard liquor of choice is **ron** (rum), sometimes referred to simply as Bacardi, the famous former Cuban label.

Historically, relations between the Yucatán and the Caribbean have been tight. In 1850, for example, a posse of Cuban nationalists launched an unsuccessful invasion from the Yucatán in an effort to free the island from Spanish colonial rule, an event which is celebrated with a mural in the Palacio del Gobierno in Merida.

The food of the Yucatán (a word which is derived from yucca, the fibrous plant common to many Caribbean cuisines) has benefited from this mixture of Mayan and Caribbean-filtered Spanish influence. It is quite distinct from the food found in the distant centre of Mexico, both for its ingredients and its preparation. The porous soil in the region requires irrigation, but the Mayans managed to figure out how to cultivate corn and beans and also hunted the abundant wildlife (deer, wild turkey, armadillo etc).

The chile of choice here is the **habanero**, the hottest chile known to humanity whose Mexican home is the Yucatán. The heat of the habanero is incessant. Once it gets inside your mouth, no amount of drink of any sort seems to douse it. Water, in fact, makes it worse, spreading the flames to deeper parts of your mouth and around your lips. It is like a forest fire, with no identifiable source, but rather several different small, yet potent hot spots that combine to go out of control and cause incalculable destruction. Well, that's how it feels.

*Habanero chiles, Tepoztlan market*

The Yucatecan **recado** (marinade) helps to give meat dishes flavour and texture. Recados are made from a variety of chiles, garlic and spices, including the rare and valuable saffron, cumin, cinnamon, oregano, and achiote seeds, a condiment which adds a deep red colour to the meat. The liquid portion of the marinade comes from lime, grapefruit, orange or **naranja agria** (bitter orange).

## Regional Specialities
### Meat

Throughout the country, when people think of the Yucatán, their minds automatically turn to **cochinita pibil**. The word **pibil** means to 'roast in a hole'. Luckily, modern cooks have devised a method that requires no shovel. The dish is most typically made with pork, but any meat can be cooked using this method and called 'al pibil'. The first step is the recado which is how many Yucatecan meat dishes begin. The marinade is made from citric fruit juices, garlic, chiles and spices (see Recado recipe earlier in this section). The meat is then wrapped in platano (plantain) leaves with onions and steamed, or roasted, and served with **cebolla en escabeche** (onions marinated in a vinaigrette). Another regional speciality is **Poc Chuc**, a thin slice of pork, cooked on a grill and then served on a sizzling plate with a bitter orange sauce. **Pavo** (turkey), an important part of Mayan cooking tradition also finds its way into many typical dishes.

## Recado

When Yucatecans cook meat **al pibil** (on a barbecue) it is often prepared using a recado as in the dish, Cochinita Pibil, below. These are marinades that penetrate the flesh and spread the flavour. The following is recommended for beef but can also be used for pork and chicken (just shorten the marinating time).

### Ingredients
¼ cup (50ml) fresh ground black pepper
1 teaspoon (15ml) cinnamon
1 teaspoon (15ml) cumin seeds
2 teaspoons (30ml) dried oregano
6–8 cloves of garlic
¼ cup (50ml) vinegar (balsamic is good here)

Mix all the dry ingredients, making sure the garlic is well chopped and distributed evenly. Add the vinegar to get a paste. Rub the mixture into the meat and let it sit at least an hour for thin cuts, longer for thicker cuts. Cook the meat to taste.

## THE MERCADO LUCAS DE GALVES

At the centre of the Mercado Lucas de Galves, Merida's main market, the merchants have built a small shrine to the Virgin of Guadalupe. Decorated with Mexican flags, coloured paper and scattered candles which will remain lit until they melt entirely, it's the only thing in the whole place that is not for sale.

The Merida market occupies an entire city block although, as in other cities, booths have found their way onto the street meaning that the market is much larger than municipal records show. The produce is simple: citrus fruits, papaya, mango and vegetables like onion, tomato, sweet peppers, carrot, cabbage and the **habanero**, the world's hottest pepper. Meat is sold in two sections, one for fresh and one for cooked where items like thinly sliced grilled meat, **chicharron** (fried pork rinds, mostly fat) and **manteca** (lard) are available. The booths that surround the central area sell anything and everything: belts, shoes, tools, kitchen supplies, cassette tapes, sunglasses, watches and watch batteries, pornographic comic books and old magazines. Emaciated stray cats creep between stands sniffing for a bite to eat.

What is absent from the Merida market is, well, the marketing. In the (stereo)typical Caribbean sense of work, vendors don't sing out prices, consumers wander freely without the constant requests to have a look at this bunch of onions or these lovely oranges. Bartering still takes place but the tone verges on tranquility.

There are a number of comedores on the upper level, with long tables extending from open kitchens. One place is *El Matador* (the killer) – perhaps not the wisest choice for a foreigner with a delicate stomach. A sign suggests the place is 'El Very Good'. Another says (in Spanish) 'We have no competition. We are the competition.' El Matador himself stands in the walkway, beckoning customers to look at his menu, to take a seat, to look at the menu some more, to please take a seat.

The diners are mostly old men, their Mayan faces wrinkled under battered straw hats or baseball caps with English slogans written in iron-on bubble letters across the front.

I settle on **relleno negro**, a regional speciality made with **chilli anchos**, green pepper, and **achiote** (a dark spice) served over shredded turkey and a hard boiled egg. It is an unqualified failure, tasting of what I can only describe as 'burnt.' I have one spoonful and spend the rest of my lunch trying to expunge the taste with bites of tortillas and bottles of Pepsi Cola. The Matador is not pleased, insulted that I have left the house speciality virtually untouched.

Before leaving, I look around at my fellow diners, hoping for some sort of support. They say nothing, continuing to eat. And then I notice something that might have been better noticed 10 minutes before: not one of them has ordered the relleno negro.

REGIONAL VARIATIONS

### Antojitos

**Papadzules** (also called **tortillas yucatecas**) are fresh corn tortillas wrapped around a filling of chopped hard-boiled eggs and then covered with sauce made from **semilla de calabaza** (pumpkin seed) and **epazote** (a herb similar to coriander).

**Panuchos**, botanas, are bean-stuffed tortillas, fried crisp then topped with a tower of shredded turkey or chicken, tomato, lettuce and onions. **Salbutes** are the same as panuchos minus the bean stuffing. **Sopaches**, popular in neighbourhood restaurants, are fried tacos served with very spicy salsa.

### DON'T MISS

- the **habanero**, the hottest chilli known to humanity
- **cochinita al pibil**, pork covered with **recado** (a seasoning paste), wrapped in platano leaves and slow-cooked in a pit
- **papadzules**, or tortilla yucatecas – tortillas dipped in a pumpkin seed sauce and filled with chopped hard-boiled eggs
- the refreshing drink of **Horchata**
- the easy-going markets of the peninsula

### Tamales

Tamales from the Yucatán merit special mention for their Mayan touch. There is a variety called **to'owloche**, a Mayan word which means 'wrapped in corn leaves' which are served on festival days, made by home chefs and sold to people in the street. The **vaporcito** is flat, stuffed with meat and wrapped in plátano leaves. A similar tamal, the **chacbi-wah**, is round and stuffed with **carne de puerco** (pork).

### Drinks

**Horchata** is a refreshing drink, sometimes called **agua de arroz** (rice water). It is made in great quantities in the Yucatán wherever there are lots of people. The rice is boiled, preferably in spring water, and soaked for 12 hours. It is drained and blended with almonds, cinnamon, sugar and more spring water and served over ice in clay mugs.

# Mexico City

Defining the cuisine of Mexico City presents certain problems. As the world's most populous city, it is anything but homogenous in terms of ethnic and cultural make-up. This has been the case for centuries now: since before centralization policies of successive federal governments flooded the city with migrants from every corner of the republic; since before Maximilian and Carlotta's brief reign launched the afrancesimiento, a period where the elite embraced everything French including, of course, food; and even since before Cortés and his men rode in the Valley of Mexico on their horses when the city was known as Tenochtitlán. As seat of the most powerful and extensive empire in meso-america, Tenochtitlán kitchens benefited from agricultural goods produced in other parts of the country under Aztec rule. Their city teemed with visitors (some invited, some not) who brought with them typical products and dishes from other parts of the empire. It was only by import from the more temperate south and coastal regions, that chocolate made its way to the great city and into the diets of its most noble citizens.

*Peanut vendors, Mexico City*

Mexico City was the obvious choice to build the capital of New Spain. In this capacity, it received visitors and delegations from all other parts of the Spanish crown's lands. More recently, Mexico City has been the destination for groups of immigrants from Spain, the Middle East, Asia and other parts of South America. International communities mingle with large representations from other parts of Mexico all of which contributes to the cosmopolitan nature of the city. Subsequently, there is a strong demand for a varied cuisine and Mexico City offers it all. A restaurant specialising in Yucatecan food, for example, sits side by side with a place offering the best of Cuban cuisine.

**REGIONAL VARIATIONS**

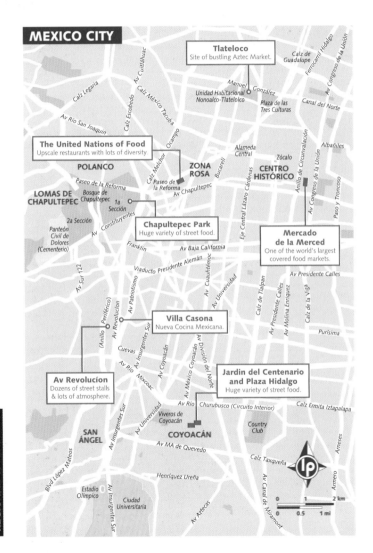

# MEXICO CITY

**Tlateloco**
Site of bustling Aztec Market.

Unidad Habitacional
Nonoalco-Tlatelolco

Plaza de las
Tres Culturas

**The United Nations of Food**
Upscale restaurants with lots of diversity.

**POLANCO**

**ZONA ROSA**

**CENTRO HISTÓRICO**

Alameda Central

Zócalo

Albañiles

**LOMAS DE CHAPULTEPEC**

Bosque de Chapultepec

1a Sección

Paseo de la Reforma

Av Chapultepec

2a Sección

Av Constituyentes

Panteón Civil de Dolores (Cementerio)

**Chapultepec Park**
Huge variety of street food.

**Mercado de la Merced**
One of the world's largest covered food markets.

Franklin

Av Baja California

Viaducto Presidente Alemán

Av Presidente Calles

**Villa Casona**
Nueva Cocina Mexicana.

Purísima

**Av Revolución**
Dozens of street stalls & lots of atmosphere.

Cuevas

Av Río Mixcoac

**Jardin del Centenario and Plaza Hidalgo**
Huge variety of street food.

Av Río Churubusco (Circuito Interior)

Calz Ermita Iztapalapa

Viveros de Coyoacán

**COYOACÁN**

Country Club

**SAN ÁNGEL**

Av MA de Quevedo

Henríquez Ureña

Estadio Olímpico

Ciudad Universitaria

Av Aztecas

Calz Taxqueña

0        1        2 km
0      0.5      1 mi

*Street names on map:*
Calz Legaria · Av Cuitláhuac · Calz México Tacuba · Calz Escobedo · Av Río San Joaquin · Ocampo · Calz Melchor · Manuel González · Calz de Guadalupe · Ferrocarril Hidalgo · Av Congreso de la Unión · Canal del Norte · Bucareli · Anillo de Circunvalación · Av Congreso de la Unión · Paso y Troncoso · Eje Central Lázaro Cárdenas · Av Cuauhtémoc · Av Universidad · Calz de Tlalpan · Av Presidente Calles · Av Molina Enríquez · Calz de la Vigª · Av Sur 122 · Av Patriotismo · (Anillo Periférico) · Av Revolución · Av Insurgentes Sur · Av Coyoacán · Av México Coyoacán · Av División del Norte · Av Universidad · Blvd López Mateos · Av Insurgentes Sur · Armeros · Armero · Av Canal de Miramont

## DON'T MISS

- the astonishing range of **antojitos** not found anywhere else in the Republic
- a visit to **Mercado de la Merced**, one of the world's largest covered food markets
- the neighbourhood restaurants and streetside dining
- sampling **nueva cocina mexicana** (new Mexican cuisine) in some of the city's finest restaurants
- dinner in the exclusive suburb of Zona Rosa, another opportunity to blow your budget at the city's UN of food

As the commercial centre of the country, Mexico City boasts the economic base to support several top-tier restaurants including those featuring **nueva cocina mexicana** (new Mexican cuisine, see the special section Nueva Cocina Mexicana in the Where to Eat & Drink chapter) a movement among some chefs to combine traditional indigenous ingredients with contemporary preparations and presentations. Two particularly popular ingredients are the **flor de calabaza** (squash flower), served in salads or as a filling for **empanadas** (stuffed pastry), and **huitlacoche**, a black fungus that grows on young corn during the rainy season and can be converted into an earthy sauce for meat or fish, or as a filling for **crepas** (crepes).

Mexico City is the capital of the antojito, and you will find a greater variety of tacos, sopes, huaraches, quesadillas, flautas etc than in any other part of the country. Every neighbourhood has a restaurant – perhaps nothing more than a comal, deep fryer and a collection of metal chairs and tables – that prepares antojitos as a quick snack at any time of day. Street vendors crowd on the busiest corners and public plazas, and the best stay open into the evening.

*Flor de Calabasa (squash flower), Tepoztlan market*

### Mercado de La Merced

To get an idea of just how big Mexico City is, take a couple of hours to wander through the Mercado de La Merced, to the south-west of the zócalo. When approaching from that direction, the first building you reach is one that is entirely devoted to packaged candy. These include chocolates, coloured sugar pellets, chains of lollies and enormous bags of **frituras**, flavourless puffed wheat snacks named for their shapes – **lagrimitas** (little tears), **donitas** (little doughnuts) and **ruedas** (wheels). The area devoted to the sale of junk food at La Merced is bigger than entire main markets in other cities.

The next building is devoted to fruit and vegetables. It is bright and airy, in contrast to smaller markets where low-hanging canopies and stays threaten decapitation. The variety is virtually limitless, with nationally grown onions, tomatoes and an infinite variety of chiles seen beside imported beans and anjou pears, each wrapped individually to prevent bruising on their way from California.

And then there is the meat pavilion where hogs' heads hang from hooks, great cylinders of spicy chorizo is stacked on counters and tripe and other entrails are piled high. The Mercado de La Merced is seemingly endless (see the Mercado de La Merced in the Shopping chapter for more details).

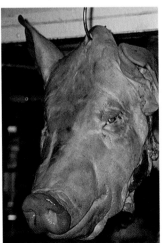

*Mercado de La Merced, Mexico City*                    *Hog's Head*

REGIONAL VARIATIONS

# Gulf Coast
## (including Veracruz, Tobasco)

The Gulf Coast of Mexico is rich in culinary traditions. It was the first region in Mexico to feel the impact of the Spanish as Hernán Cortés began his conquest by founding the city of Veracruz (about half and hour north of the current city) in 1517. Geographically, it is separated from the rest of the country by the Sierra Madre Oriental, which reaches its highest points here. Culturally, there is a definite Caribbean air, with close links to Cuban culture dating from colonial times when Havana served as the capital of Spain's holdings in the area and the port of Veracruz was the stepping stone to the rest of Mexico. The city of Veracruz is home to one of Mexico's best-known **carnavals**, when the seaside malecon is turned into a parade route and the city welcomes its inland cousins for several days of weakened inhibition and raucous celebration (see the boxed text Carnaval! in the Celebrating with Food chapter).

The Aztecs conquered the peaceful Totonaca about 50 years before the arrival of the Spanish and introduced their priests to sacrificial offerings involving human flesh instead of food. The Totonacs were an agricultural society and also great hunters and fishers – so good that the ruler, Chicomacatl, was reportedly enormous, requiring the shoulders of up to eight men to carry him on his litter.

As the principal gateway to the rest of the world, Veracruz has seen many different nationalities pass through its port – welcome or not. The Spanish, French and Americans all invaded at one time or another, usually defeating the Mexican defences, but never staying very long. Slaves from the West Indies arrived in the 19th century, bringing with them Afro-Caribbean traditions. The flow of immigrants of different ethnic backgrounds has given Veracruz a reputation for tolerance in Mexico, and has certainly not harmed its culinary scene. One anthropologist reckons there are 11 different cuisines to be found in Veracruz alone.

The relationship with the sea has shaped the diet of Veracruzanos. One of the most distinctive dishes, the **Huachinango a la Veracruzana**, is fresh red snapper, broiled and bathed in a lightly spiced sauce of tomato and onion. Seafood dominates the menus in the city of Veracruz and also plays a prominent role on those inland. You can get **Cocteles de camaron**, **ostión** or **pulpo** (shrimp, oyster or octopus cocktails) on the cheap at small counter-front restaurants all along the coast. To make them into a **coctel**, the chef mixes the **marisco** (seafood) with onion, tomato and a generous amount of lime juice which 'cooks' the meat in citric acid, pouring it all into a tall glass to be eaten with long-stemmed spoons. Seafood-lovers will be tempted by the sight but should be warned that there are potential dangers to eating raw seafood.

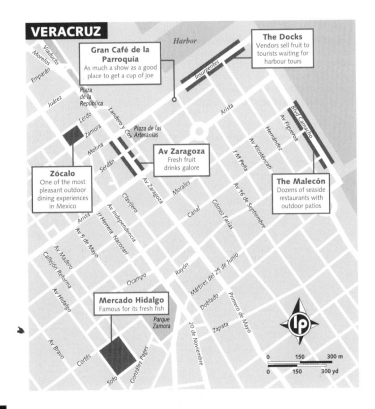

**VERACRUZ**

*Harbor*

**Gran Café de la Parroquía**
As much a show as a good place to get a cup of joe

**The Docks**
Vendors sell fruit to tourists waiting for harbour tours

**Av Zaragoza**
Fresh fruit drinks galore

**Zócalo**
One of the most pleasant outdoor dining experiences in Mexico

**The Malecón**
Dozens of seaside restaurants with outdoor patios

**Mercado Hidalgo**
Famous for its fresh fish

0   150   300 m
0   150   300 yd

## Regional Specialities
### Drinks

The Gulf Coast is perfectly suited to growing **caña de azúcar** (sugarcane). Fields of the tall, succulent plant dominate the landscape on any drive through the state of Veracruz. Sometimes these fields are a bright green, other times burnt black from fires. Sugarcane, in turn, is perfectly suited for making **aguardiente**. The word literally means 'fire water', but one taste of this very strong and unrefined alcohol and you will need no translation. It is very cheap and although more popular on the coast than in other parts of the country, is still not the drink of choice for most people.

REGIONAL VARIATIONS

## Postres

The presence of **cacao**, **vainilla** (vanilla) and caña de azúcar make the Gulf Coast an ideal spot for **repostería** (dessert making). Chocolate and vanilla come from beans grown at a certain altitude on the sides of mountains. Both are processed before becoming useful to the baker and real vanilla extract (simply called 'vainilla' on the label), is widely available and very cheap. You may want to pick up a few bottles to shore up your supplies at home.

*Local pastries, La Parroquia, Veracruz*

## Fish & Seafood

In addition to huachinango a la veracruzana, the cooks of the Gulf Coast have developed a number of fantastic platters showcasing the fruits of their sea. Dishes using **camarones** (shrimps) range from a green soup called **huatape**, made thick with corn masa and coloured by **hojas de chile** (chile leaves) to **camarón para pelar**, whole shrimp boiled in a very weak broth, chilled then served with lime. You peel the skin from the shrimp to get to the tender meat inside. This is a great dish to have on the patio as marimba bands play. **Jaiba** (crab) is served as a botana before meals or in the middle of the afternoon when you've decided to extend the lunch hour just a little longer. Fillets of fish, usually huachinango or **róbalo** are generally prepared on a grill and then topped with different kinds of sauces

### DON'T MISS

• a sip of **aguardiente** (fire water)
• the impressive array of **postres** (desserts) unique to the region
• **huachinango a la Veracruzana** (red snapper)
• **ceviche de marisco** (seafood cocktail) and the wonderful platters showcasing the fruits of the Gulf of Mexico

**REGIONAL VARIATIONS**

# El Bajío
**(including the states of Querétaro, Guanajuato, Michoacán, San Luis Potosí, Aguascalientes, and Zacatecas)**

El Bajío lies in the middle of a triangle formed by the bustling financial and industrial centres of Monterrey, Guadalajara and Mexico City. With plenty of fertile land set on gently sloping mountains and with a temperate climate, the region is known for its agriculture. But it was the discovery of rich silver veins running through its gentle slopes that brought the most settlers.

The cities in the region became very wealthy during the days of the colony. They built baroque churches, public plazas with statues and fountains and beautiful mansions. Most of the silver is gone now, but the attachment to the glory years of the colony remains. Most cities are very protective of this colonial heritage, ensuring the preservation of colonial architecture in their downtown areas. Lunching at a restaurant in a plaza your view of the surrounding hills is rarely blocked. Indeed, it's the setting which provides much of the pleasure when eating your way through the Bajío. In Guanajuato during the September Cervantino Festival – a tribute to the work of 16th century Spanish writer Miguel de Cervantes, author of Don Quixote – you can spend an evening in a plaza-side cafe, enjoying a few plates of botanas while **trobadores** (troubadours), dressed in period costumes, play period instruments and sing in the streets.

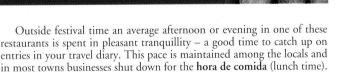

**DON'T MISS**

- **enchiladas queretanas** of Querétaro
- whiling an evening away at a plaza-side café
- tacos with eggs in black chile pasilla sauce
- **papitas del monte** (wild potatoes) from San Luis de Potosí

Outside festival time an average afternoon or evening in one of these restaurants is spent in pleasant tranquillity – a good time to catch up on entries in your travel diary. This pace is maintained among the locals and in most towns businesses shut down for the **hora de comida** (lunch time).

While the colonial influence is strong, the dominant culture is still mestizo. The region represented the northernmost point of Aztec influence as they were prevented from further expansion by the nomadic Chichimec Indians, who also briefly frustrated Spanish efforts to colonize the region in the 1520s. The settlers who stayed inherited a variety of fruit and vegetables including **tuna** (prickly pears) and **nopales** (a variety of cactus). They were also known to drink **pulque**, the maguey plant distillate that is today used in regional recipes for sauces and **estofados** (stews).

There are no extremes in Bajío cuisine, no Sonora-style meat-worshipping or alarming spice as with some Yucatecan dishes. There is a nice, tempered balance of elements which are found throughout the republic. As a result, it is difficult to define a dish typical to the region as birria is to Guadalajara or quesillo is to Oaxaca. Municipalities will have their own specialities – **enchiladas queretanas**, Queretaro-style enchiladas, topped with shredded **lechuga** (lettuce) for example – but nothing of national prominence.

*Boy with watermelons*

## Central Mexico
### (including Puebla, Tlaxcala, Hidalgo and Morelos)

The city of Puebla stands above all other Mexican culinary centres. Two dishes in particular, **mole poblano** and **chiles en nogada**, both products of Puebla kitchens, are testament to its superiority.

The case is convincing. The dish, whether served with **pavo** (turkey) or **pollo** (chicken) is an indescribable wonder, a complex mixture of up to 100 ingredients including several kinds of chile, spices, sesame seed, broth and chocolate, the final item being what characterizes the mole poblano. Despite the work that must go into every batch, mole is widely available in local restaurants. During fiestas and celebrations, mole is a must and your status and the success of your party rests on the quality of your mole (see Mole in the Staples & Specialities chapter).

*Fonda*
*"QueChula*
*esPuebla'*
6 NORTE, Nº 5
Como ud. me vio en la T.V.
*Su Amiga* IRMA TINOCO

Los Invita a Pasar ha Deleitarse con:
Lo Mejor de la "Autentica Cocina Poblana"
Porque Recuerde que Venir a Puebla y
NoComer Mole Poblano es Venir en Vano.

( NO TENEMOS SUCURSALES )

*'To come to Puebla without sampling Mole Poblano is to come in vain'*

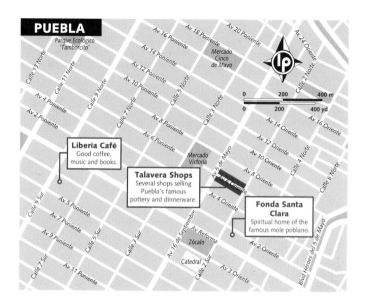

Mole is but one dish that came out of the kitchens of the many convents in the area, where the daughters of the Creole elite were sent to be formally educated and serve the church. Together with their indigenous servants, they created a great many dishes which incorporated old world traditions with Indian ingredients. The region as a whole is characterised by its strong ties to its Spanish heritage. Many of the towns were built where no Indian settlement existed and even after independence, immigration from Spain remained steady.

Other popular moles to feature here include **mole de olla**, a soupy beef-based dish served in bowls, and **pipián verde**, another convent creation, made with ground spices and seeds, green tomatoes, peanuts, and served over pork.

Chiles en nogada, Puebla's other notable dish, is a source of not only culinary pride, but also evokes patriotic sentiments among Mexicans. The origins of the dish go back to 1821 and the signing of the Treaty of Córdoba, which formalised Mexico's independence from Spain. Soon after, one of the leaders of the new republic, Agustin de Iturbide was passing through Puebla. Municipal leaders decided to celebrate the occasion with a

## DON'T MISS

- spoiling yourself in Puebla, Mexico's culinary capital
- Puebla's **mole poblano** and **chiles en nogada**, two of its most famous dishes
- **gusanos de maguey con salsa borracha** (maguey worms with drunken sauce) in Tlaxcala and Hidalgo
- the vegetarian-friendly **sopa de nopales** (soup with cactus leaves)

lavish banquet, inviting the most prominent members of society to dine on the best food the city had to offer. Despite the lavish spread, Iturbide did not eat. The man who would eventually name himself emperor of Mexico, had many enemies and he feared that one would somehow manage to poison his food. So as the platters of roasted meats, seafood cocktails, fresh fruit and pastries passed him, he took nothing. It wasn't until he was presented with a plate of chiles en nogada, the sumptuous green chile poblana stuffed with a stew of beef and fruits, topped with nogada, a white almond-chestnut cream sauce and adorned with red **semillas de granada** (pomegranate seeds), that the general's resistance broke down.

But it is not only the food that has made the word Puebla synonymous with fine dining, but also the dinnerware on which it is served. **Talavera** (the general name for Pueblan pottery) is a Spanish tradition that arrived in Puebla in the early days of the colony. You will notice when you visit that many buildings are adorned with (mostly blue) painted tiles. The same method is used to make full dinner sets or decorative platters.

Puebla certainly dominates the gastronomic scene in central Mexico, but nearby Tlaxcala and Hidalgo have also gained notoriety for **gusanos de maguey con salsa borracha** (maguey worms with drunken sauce). It is a very simple dish consisting of worms that are extracted from the maguey plant and fried in oil, and a sauce made from roasted pasilla chiles, garlic, onion, cheese and pulque (where the drunken bit comes into play).

**Nopale**, the flat, paddle-like leaf of the prickly pear cactus is also popular. They can be eaten raw, cut julienne-style and tossed with a salad or steamed and included in a casserole or stew. **Sopa de nopales** (soup with cactus leaves) is a mainstay in the region's vegetarian restaurants.

# shopping

## & markets

The greatest market in Aztec Mexico was at Tlatelolco, which today forms part of Mexico City. The daily ritual of shopping has changed little since then. Visit any municipal market on any given morning and you will encounter dozens of cooks carefully choosing fruits, vegetables and meats, packing them into a bag made of coloured straw and then heading home to turn their purchases into that day's comida.

You can still visit the area of Tlatelolco where canoes once brought goods from the surrounding areas to sell to the urban elite. Fresh fish, hunted animals, fruits and vegetables (both cultivated and gathered) weighed down these narrow boats as they paddled through the network of lakes and canals that flow through the Valley of Mexico. Some headed for the main **plaza mayor**, the centre of town, where giant warehouses stored offerings while the merchants went on to Tlatelolco. (This place went on to gain notoriety in 1968 as the site where government troops opened fire on a student protest and killed almost 400 demonstrators.)

The produce was inspected by customs agents who doubled as tax collectors, taking the government's share. When the goods arrived at their appropriate stalls housewives and servants rushed to pick their favourite items. And they had a lot of choice. Fruit and vegetable vendors offered plump tomatoes, sweet potatoes, **jícama** roots (sweet turnip), **nopales** (the leaves of the prickly pear cactus) a variety of squash, a greater variety of chiles, mushrooms, edible flowers, onions, oregano, purslane and sorrel.

*Fruit & vegetable seller, Mercado Juarez, Oaxaca City*

Meat and fish sellers displayed rabbits, dogs, gophers, armadillos, iguanas, lizards and venison. A particular speciality meat was the **axolotl**, the larvae of the salamander immortalised by Julio Cortázar's short story of the same name. Fish came from local lakes and were imported in dry form from the Gulf Coast. Shrimps, crabs, clams, snails and oysters all figured prominently. There was trout, herring and whitefish. For the wealthy, speciality shops sold lobster, frog, turtle, snake, eel, octopus, fish caviar and insect eggs.

Today's markets have just as much variety although the likes of dog, eel and snake are no longer widely available.

## Markets

City markets have always been important in Mexican society, not only for commerce but also as a place where friends and acquaintances meet and discuss everything from local gossip to federal politics. In larger cities, markets are losing their social function, but in small towns this aspect is very much alive. (See the Regional Variations chapter for more information on the specific markets mentioned in this section.)

*Mercado de La Merced, Mexico City*

Markets are reflections of the regions and cities they serve. Oaxaca's Mercado de Abastos is a vast, labyrinthine collection of buildings and make-shift stalls, with low-hanging tent-flies that cut tall tourists down to size. There is no apparent order to these mazes: a fruit stand, displaying bright **naranjas** (oranges), **manzanas** (apples), **bananas** (bananas) and **fresas** (strawberries) can stand between stalls of dried, carmine-coloured **chile anchos**, and piles of **almendras** (almonds), roasted **cacahuete** (peanuts) and **cacao** beans. The sales process is aggressive. Vendors call out to every potential customer (which means everyone who passes) "Qué lleva, jóven?" (What will it be, young man?). **El Rogateo** (bargaining) is a part of the game. You win if you convince them to give you a better price, they win if they convince you to buy more. Failing that, the mobile sale might get you, where an accomplice (usually a daughter or son) walks through the aisles with pre-bagged bunches of radishes or bananas, offering them to anyone they pass.

In contrast, there is the Mercado Lucas de Galves in Merida on the Yucatan peninsula. Here, the atmosphere is much more relaxed. Booth tenders sit behind counters or chat with their neighbours, and it is up to you to get their attention. Bargaining is also used as a means of determining the final price, but again, with less rigour.

*Mercado de La Merced, Mexico City*

Bargaining is not always acceptable. In many places, notably the Mercado de la Merced in Mexico City, prices are fairly rigidly controlled and displayed on small placards on sticks that are propped up in their respective products.

The Mercado de la Merced is the largest market in Mexico and one of the largest covered markets in the world. Its wide aisles and high, permanent ceiling enables backpack-clad visitors to walk through the market without fear of knocking down a stack of chiles.

*Woman watching television, Libertat market, Guadalajara, Jalisco*

Despite appearances, markets in Mexico are fairly comprehensive. As well as being places for local farmers to sell the fruits of their labour, most markets sell imported items from North and South America.

From the massive to the minute, visit Tequisquiapan, a beautiful colonial town in the state of Querétaro, about three hours north of Mexico City. Tequis, as it is called by locals, is known for its healing waters. On weekends the small hotels scattered around Tequisquiapan are occupied to capacity by **chilangos** (Mexico City residents) hoping to relax and wash the big-city strain from their bodies.

The market in Tequisquiapan occupies a small space near the main plaza. On a weekday morning, there is not much happening in the way of commerce. Many of the stalls are not even tended, sitting empty until the next market day brings a new shipment of produce for sale. Nevertheless, the market is crowded with people enjoying their breakfast tamal, served from a cart that billows steam into the cool morning air. There is a lot of noise, from animated conversations and a vendor of cassettes who wants to make sure everybody knows what he's selling.

*Mercado Libertad, Guadalajara*

Each small town market has a day or two in the week that are designated as **día del mercado** (Market day) when fresh produce is trucked in. On those days, shoppers come early, eager to get to the best stuff before it is sold out. For the rest of the week a sort of languor prevails. Stalls that might have been jammed packed on market day sit with a few sad-looking onions or tomatoes. Even those stalls that sell non-perishables don't do much business and many don't even bother opening (see Market Day later in this chapter.)

## Meat

You'll know without prompting when you've entered the meat section. The smell of raw flesh is accompanied by the sound of chopping cleavers and electric slicers preparing fillets for sale. Mexicans are frugal about meat, using every part of the slaughtered animal. As a result there are stacks of tripe, buckets of intestines and skinned pigs heads, hanging from hooks that look like props from a production of William Golding's *The Lord of the Flies*. There are chains of **salchichas** (frankfurters), giant blocks of **chorizo** (sausage), and sheets of dried beef called **machaca**. A warning about buying meat: most market stalls do not have refrigeration so it is best to arrive early to get the freshest produce. If you are still uncertain, buy your meat at a supermarket.

## Groceries

There are stalls which sell all types of grocery items from honey to bottled salsas, spices to packed sweets and dried tea blends which can alleviate anything from indigestion to poor performance in bed. Others devote their shelf-space to local drinks like mezcal, tequila and brandy.

## Comedores

Hot food is served in dirt-cheap restaurants known as **comedores**. Unfortunately, you often get what you pay for but these are good places to find out the regional preferences: for example, a Guadalajaran comedor is bound to serve **birria** (stew), in Oaxaca you'll be served chocolate and in Mexico City **atoles** (a corn masa drink, sometimes translated as gruel) will be easy to find.

## Día del Mercado (Market Day)

Big city markets will be well-stocked seven days a week. Small town markets, on the other hand, have specific days where produce arrives. Locals eager to get first pick and take home the freshest foods possible arrive in their droves on market day. In a particular region, the día del mercado will rotate so that nearby markets do not compete directly with each other on a particular day. To find out which is the market day in the place you happen to be staying, ask anyone who looks like they shop: a hotel employee, a store clerk, otherwise ask at the local tourism office.

It's worth getting to know your local shopkeepers and market-sellers if you're staying in one spot for a while, as you're more likely to get a fair price without much hassle and the best quality products may be reserved for you.

*Mercado de La Merced, Mexico City*

## Supermarkets

The **supermercado** is now a universal phenomenon but here range has grown beyond food and into clothing, household items, books, magazines, hardware, virtually anything that can be tossed into a shopping cart and wheeled to a check-out counter.

While there are some advantages to supermarket-shopping, price isn't one of them. Meat is refrigerated and wrapped tightly as opposed to sitting in the open air of a market. Fish is also kept on ice behind a protective glass window. The selection of dry goods, items like ketchup, mayonnaise, cereals, cookies, spices, condiments, and canned goods is greater. Frozen foods, from ice creams to breakfast waffles are also widely available. Larger stores will have a deli section with a selection of cheeses and meats for tortas. Other dairy products like milk, yoghurt and butter, do better in the refrigerated shelves of the supermarket.

Because of their sometimes prohibitive pricing, supermarkets are not to be found just anywhere and tend to be concentrated in the middle and upper class residential neighbourhoods. As a result, they are not often easy to find. Markets, on the other hand, tend to be built (or rather, organised) in the centre of town, where all the action is.

## Speciality Shops
### Panaderías (Bakeries)

There are relatively few genuine bakers here although the ones that do bake on the premises are immensely popular. You may see long queues in bakeries, either early in the morning or early evening, as the batches of fresh bread become available. Bread made from wheat flour is widely used in both restaurants and in the home and it is possible to by commercial brands at any supermarket or corner store. Some cafes will also sell bread, although there is no guarantee that it is as fresh as it ought to be. (For further information, see Breads & Baked Goods in the Staples & Specialities chapter.)

*Hat shop, Tequila, Jalisco*

*Panadería, Puebla*

## Pastelerías (Cake Shops)

**Pastel** means cake but when you see a window display with a 1m-high white frosted wedding cake, you'll know where you are. In addition to wedding cakes, a pastelería may offer **pastel de tres leches**, a very heavy cake made with, as the name indicates, three kinds of milk: evaporated, condensed and evaporated cream. Try one of the small cookie-like nibbles called **pastel margaritas** which may be made with almond marzipan or various fruits. Some even venture into fruit turnovers and eclairs, covered with chocolate and chopped almonds, which are extremely filling and not at all good for you.

*Sweets, Mercado de La Merced, Mexico City*

## Dulcerías (Sweets Shops)

Most basic candy can be bought at the street-corner kiosks found in virtually every city. Drug stores and the check-out aisles at supermarkets are also well-stocked but there are some specialist places that sell their own, homemade sweets. A favourite item is the pastel-coloured salt-water toffee flavoured with fruit and somehow lightly sweet. Chocolate treats are also available in dozens of varieties that use nuts, fruit or other fillings.

## Carnicerías (Butcher Shops)

If you've got a hankering for a good old-fashioned prime rib, or a thick T-bone, or a crown pork roast, be nice to your local butcher. Meat is available wherever food is sold, but the selection of cuts is suited to Mexican cooking methods which essentially involve stove top grilling or frying. But there are Argentine and American restaurants serving inch-thick fillets and top sirloins so custom orders are certainly possible.

## Convenience Stores

In most larger cities, especially those near the US border, you will find convenience stores. American chains and their Mexican hybrids like Circle K, 7-Eleven and Oxxo have become part of the landscape in places like Monterrey, Guadalajara and Chihuahua. They feature walls of refrigerators stacked with beers, soft drinks, milk and water, along with overpriced quick foods such as sliced meat, cheese, bread and eggs. They carry a variety of microwave sandwiches, burgers and tortas, pre-packaged in brightly labeled cellophane. There are even miniature pizzas including a variety known as 'La Mexicana' which is topped with chorizo and chiles. Only eat these out of desperation or pure stupidity as there are few things in these fridges which have not passed though some complicated industrial process. There is also, of course the junk food aisle; a treasure chest of chocolate, cakes, chips and other fried and fat-filled goodies to satisfy any craving under the sun.

## What to Take Home

Depending upon where home is, it may be difficult to find many of the items you've come to know and love during your stay here. Most large centres in Canada and the US have Mexican communities and a small store somewhere that will supply you with some of the basics: a favourite brand of salsa, *Maseca* (a brand of corn flour for tortillas and tamales), **chiles en adobo** (pickled chiles), canned **frijoles refritos** (refried beans) etc. Even some mainstream supermarkets carry these items and with free trade and continued immigration, it is safe to assume that more and more products will become available.

If you have **mole** once, you will want it again. Making it outside of Mexico is very difficult because of the number of ingredients required. There are different brands of mole paste that are concentrated forms of the real thing. You simply add water or stock to bring to the right consistency then pour it over chicken. It may not be as good as the mole you fell in love with, but it will cure your fix.

For those who live in places where the winds of trade have yet to carry them the wonders of Mexican food, a trip to a grocery store before leaving is urged. No packaged product is a proper substitution for the real thing however, and with the exception of chiles and tortillas, there are few Mexican dishes that cannot be duplicated outside of Mexico. Chiles can be purchased in cans in pickled form. **Chipotle chiles** is a wonderful choice. They come in small cans and have a very strong flavour so need not be over-used in your recipes. Use them sparingly and store them for future meals.

Be sure also to pick up some bottled **salsa picante** (hot sauce) before you go. This is a worthy substitute for fresh salsa. Salsa picante need not be limited to Mexican food. It goes fantastically well with things like chips (French Fries), grilled chicken, omelettes or pizza. Buy the small bottles to sneak into restaurants so that lingering flavour of Mexico stays with you, no matter where you eat.

Bakers will want to stock up on genuine vanilla extract. The plant grows abundantly in Mexico and bottles of this dark liquid with the distinctive aroma are very cheap. One purchase can free you forever from the drudgery of imitation extracts.

What you are unlikely to find outside of Mexico is the same kind of fresh tortilla. There are versions of it, of course, in packages or in Mexican restaurants, but there is no substitution for the kind you get in a Mexican home or restaurant, freshly ground and fresh off the comal.

Finally, take home tequila. It is widely available in the blanco variety. But the real quality tequilas, the reposadas and the añejos, have yet to find their way out of Mexico so you should make a purchase at a liquor store (Jalisco has the most variety) or in the airport on your way out. Mexico City airport's duty free area has a particularly good selection. There is a great deal of satisfaction in taking a bottle of fine tequila home and sharing it with friends who usually think of tequila as something to drink only when there is nothing else left.

# where to
# eat & drink

Wherever you go in Mexico, the huge range of places to eat will tempt and satisfy every whim and any purse. Whether you're gorging yourself on the regional speciality at a market comedor, slumming it with the pavement chefs, or treating yourself to nueva cocina mexicana (new Mexican cuisine) in upmarket city restaurants, dining in Mexico is an irresistible opportunity to savour the company of family, friends, lovers or business associates.

Before the onslaught of urbanisation, most Mexicans went home around 2pm to lunch with family, followed by one of the best of all Mexican traditions, the siesta. In the 19th century, the workday didn't resume until maybe 7pm. While some provincial cities and towns still maintain this tradition – with businesses closing between 2-5pm – congestion in the major cities has changed the custom and now most office workers take comida at nearby restaurants which strive to reproduce home cooking. There is a striking number of restaurants, from the kerb-side puestos run by a single cook with a comal, to the 5-star dining rooms with dozens of crisply-dressed waiters catering to your every whim.

Where you eat depends on where you are, who you're with, how much time and money you have and, of course, what you fancy eating.

*Tlacolula, Oaxaca State*

# Budget Eateries

Mexico abounds in budget eateries, many serving up terrific food and unbeatable value. There are no frills, waiters don't run around filling your water, napkins come in dispensers and are not folded into the shape of a swan, and you'll have to go elsewhere for your after-dinner mints. Even so, when you are looking to have a simple and satisfying meal, these are the places to seek out first. Following are some of the options.

### Rotisería

The smell of roasting chickens will hit you from several doors away before you arrive at a rotisería. This is an effective marketing ploy that is coupled with the visual temptation of row upon row of golden chickens turning slowly on long spits. Chicken is all these places serve, and your choice is limited to quarter, half or whole. Whatever the size, you are likely to get a portion of seasoned rice and a stack of tortillas. Beer and soft drinks are available, and make perfect accompaniments for cutting the delectable greasiness of the poultry.

### Tortería

A place specialising in tortas (large sandwiches on crusty rolls), consumed as a quick desayuno or almuerzo. In general, these places also serve tacos and other antojitos, beer and soft drink. Torterías are popular with young people, with many conveniently located near high schools and universities.

While less distinct than tacos, tortas are no less an important part of a busy Mexican's diet. Cheap and filling, these overflowing sandwiches are available in small, non-descript restaurants with hand-written menus posted on the wall. The cooking area is near the front, the better for displaying the cooked meat and releasing the aromas into the street.

A torta can come with virtually anything stuffed inside the crusty white-bread roll. **Pierna** (leg of pork) is one popular filling. The meat is slow cooked then sliced on a large round bisection of a tree (appropriately called a **tronco**) which, after considerable wear, becomes bowl-shaped.

### Lonchería

From the English 'lunch', these places are like torterías, serving sandwiches and other antojitos as small, quick meals.

### Pizzería

Pizza is a truly international food with the only requirement being a flat dough, topped with whatever is available. In Mexico, there are a few large US chains set up which make pizza not terribly distinct from what they make in any of their branches worldwide.

There are also several locally-owned pizzerías that use cheese from Oaxaca, chorizo, **chiles dulces** (sweet chiles) or jalapeño chiles, beans and other uniquely Mexican toppings to give their pizza flavour. Other places dangerously tread the fine line that divides the truly novel from the truly repulsive, with gimmicks such as the Hot Dog Pizza, topped with frankfurter, onion, mustard and pickle. This is hardly authentic national cuisine, though very likely unique to Mexico. Pizza sizes begin with **personal** (about 5 inches) and increase to **pequeña**, **mediana**, and the largest, **familiar** (20-24 inches).

*Ice cream shop, Tepoztlan*

### Paletaría & Nevería

**Paletas** (popsicles) are mostly available commercially in neighbourhood shops big enough to hold a freezer. However, there are also places known as **Neverías** that make their own ice cream (called **helado**) using available fresh fruit. Some shops invite you to stay, and enjoy your helado at the bar stools lining the counter but, in general, this is take away food.

**Taquería**

Tacos are available in all kinds of restaurants but it is only the **taquería** that claims it as their speciality. In general, they are small, without any pretensions of formality. Decorations are sparse, usually limited to whatever promotional posters the Coca-Cola or Corona rep decides to drop off. Sometimes there will be a photo of the local soccer team or a print of the Virgin de Guadalupe.

A taquería will offer tacos with a variety of fillings, from the common al pastor (meat cut from a rotating vertical spit) and choriqueso (spicy sausage and cheese), to the more exotic cabeza (head) and seso (brain). Prices are low, and you should walk out with a full stomach for less than US$2.

### THE TAQUERÍA

A crowded taquería is always an indication of quality. In Querétaro, on Avenida Corregidora, the *El Toro* taquería is always packed. There are only a dozen or so tables, all with four stools supported by wire legs, none of which are the same length. The menu is painted on two walls near an advertisement encouraging you to drink Pepsi Cola, and a warning to take care of your health.

Nothing costs more than US$1.20 including tacos stuffed in a number of ways: al pastor, with cow's head, **longaniza** (sausage) or **sesos** (brain). Each of these run at about US30c but most people ask for four. The ordering process is simple: the waiter takes your order, turns and yells it to the cook.

The kitchens (for there are two at El Toro) are located at the entrance and amount to nothing more than counters with large cutting blocks and a flat grill. The meat is finely chopped, fried and stuffed into small, hot, tortillas. These are then placed in neat rows onto plastic plates lined with a single sheet of paper.

Moments after ordering, the food is on your table along with complementary green and red salsas and a bowl of onions and jalapeño chiles. Each taco takes no more than two or three bites but only the most skilled can eat without spillage.

The waiter will never come back to see how you are doing or to offer dessert or coffee (neither of which they have). It is common to get a second round, however, but it is up to you to get the waiter's attention. In 10 minutes it's all over. Your table is a mess with plastic plates, scrunched up napkins full of grease and little bits of onion and meat. But you've had your fill and all for less than US$2.

## Comedor

This is the name given to those small restaurants that do not exist as stand-alone operations. The most common example are the numerous eateries in markets, all concentrated in one section. Each will have a limited menu, generally specialising in one dish: **mariscos** (shellfish), **pescado** (fish), tacos, stews or soups.

## The Juice Bar

With an abundance of fresh fruit readily available, it is no surprise that there are numerous places devoted to serving fresh juice and little else. These tend to be a perfect stop between meals during a busy day of wandering. Topping the drink list is always **jugo de naranja** (orange juice) which, when made fresh, is a treat for those used to juices made from concentrate and shipped thousands of kilometres. Further down the drink list, the options are wide open: strawberry, carrot, papaya, mango, kiwi, apple, grapefruit and any combination thereof. Some juice stands also serve small snacks, crepes and pastries.

WHERE TO EAT & DRINK

*Zocalo cafe, Oaxaca City*

## Pastelerías & Panadería

**Pastelerías** (cake shops) and **panaderías** (bakeries) are not for sit-down meals, but they're perfect for breakfast on the go, selling fresh croissants, pastries and even a regular old **dona** (doughnut) with chocolate sprinkles.

*Tostadas, a dish made with fried corn dough, which has many regional variations*

## Mid-Range

Restaurants can be categorised as mid-range by their prices, from US$2.50 to US$6, but beyond that the quality and service can range from the exquisite to the horrendous. Most will fall somewhere in between but you should ask around if possible to avoid disappointment.

In Mexico there is a breed of mid-range places specialising in more or less the same fare: appetisers like **quesadillas** (tortilla with cheese) or **queso fundido** (cheese fondue), main dishes like **carne a la tampiqueña** (meat, guacamole, enchilada, beans and lettuce), **filete a la mexicana** (grilled white fish with a tomato-based sauce) or **filet mignon** (a thin portion of fried meat with a piece of bacon). Each city has its own standard fare which varies little between restaurants. In coastal cities, for example, you will see a standard filet a la mexicana, while eateries in Merida, Yucatán will always offer their interpretation of **poc chuc** (grilled pork) and **pollo al pibil** (barbecued chicken).

The best of these 'standard fare' places are found in Puebla, Oaxaca, Guadalajara, Veracruz and Merida. The reputations are well-deserved, but not so much for the outstanding quality of the food, but because the regular dishes are just better in these cities than others. As such, when in Mexico City, you can get wonderful poblano or oaxaqueno cooking without leaving town.

Mexico City also has the advantage of an abundance of ethnic restaurants. Nearly all of the world's cuisines are represented here (see boxed text The UN of Food in the Culture of Mexican Cuisine chapter). If you crave some westernised Chinese food, you will find it here along with Italian restaurants that tend to overcook pasta. Food quality aside, service is generally as attentive and friendly as many in the upper range.

## Sanborn's

There is a whole sub-genre of restaurants – with spacious, clean, dining rooms, sharply dressed waiting staff and consistent quality – catering for middle- and upper-class families. The most famous among them is the national institution of *Sanborn's Casa de Azulejos*. In *The Death of Artemio Cruz*, novelist Carlos Fuentes sets a short scene at *Sanborn's*, situated in the historic centre of Mexico City. The author reveals a microcosm of duality in modern Mexico where the waitresses wear uniforms based on traditional native clothing while the upper-class customers eat waffles and sip on Canada Dry.

Other chains have copied *Sanborn's* model with some success, if the number of *Vips*, *Wings* and *El Portón's* scattered throughout the larger cities is any indication.

The food at these places is competent, if unimaginative, and often borders on bland. Prices, inversely, tend to be high. In *El Portón*, for example, the **carne a la Tampiqueña** goes for US$6. For the same price in independent restaurants, you can get a much better version of the same dish, and some atmosphere. The one feature these Sanborn clones do offer is convenience. They are open from early in the morning to late at night. Generally hygiene isn't a concern as table turnover is high. Furthermore, these are among the few restaurants that offer children's menus and, on weekends, clowns often entertain the kids. From the travellers' perspective, for better or worse, you know that the quesadillas you order at the restaurant in Baja California will taste exactly – and we mean exactly – the same as the one you ordered in Mexico City.

---

### HIDDEN COSTS

For the most part, the final bill will be no more than the sum of the items you ordered from the menu. The IVA (Value Added Tax) should be included. However, there are places (notably in Mexico City's Zona Rosa) that will tack on a cover charge without letting you know. Some restaurants also charge for the bread and butter you are given as soon as you sit down, so while rip-offs are rare, keep an eye on your bill just in case.

---

*Diners at the Latino Americano Tower*

## Upmarket

There are two classes of Mexican restaurants in this category. The first, only found in the largest and wealthiest cities, are the restaurants located in the most prestigious hotels that rely on a steady flow of business people with fat expense accounts. The food is generally top-notch, but menus shy away from typical Mexican dishes and toward what the New York investment banker is used to eating. Thick cuts of beef (certified Angus), salmon, and all the latest trends from the Continent are the ever-changing norm. Naturally, prices are high but one measurable advantage is that they provide an extensive wine list, unlike the majority of restaurants here.

The other restaurants in the splurge category put a fine-dining twist on traditional Mexican dishes and ingredients. You can find **chiles rellenos** (stuffed chiles) virtually anywhere, but at a place like the *Fonda Santa Clara* in Puebla, the ingredients never seem fresher, the bread-coating never lighter nor the sauce spiced to such perfection.

### NUEVA COCINA MEXICANA (New Mexican Cuisine)

In a country where most staples haven't changed in thousands of years, something called **nueva cocina mexicana** is bound to be met with a degree of skepticism. But what is new about new Mexican cuisine is not so new at all and, in fact, the term should probably be *re*newed Mexican cuisine.

Alicia Gironella De'Angeli is the head chef at *El Tajin*, a restaurant with a well-deserved reputation for creating new dishes that somehow remain tightly loyal to the best of Mexican culinary traditions.

She runs the restaurant with her husband, Jorge De'Angeli, an Italian born food writer with a Quixotesque white beard. Jorge is also the Mexican representative of Slow Food, an international organisation of restaurateurs and food lovers. The name, with its polar opposition to the kind of food that evokes images of golden arches and greasy bottomed cardboard boxes, says it all. Slow Food is about enjoying food as more than a way to fill your stomach. It is about sitting down to complete meals with friends and eating foods designed to bring optimum pleasure to the palate. Appropriately enough, the logo for the movement is a snail.

*El Tajin* is also the name of an ancient city in the state of Veracruz and Alicia's menu is heavily influenced by the food of the Gulf Coast. Many other dishes are indigenous to the Yucatán, however the ingredients used can be found in dishes right across Mexico, and have been part of the culinary landscape for centuries. The two tenets of El Tajin's cooking are presentation and less animal fat.

Mexicans of means have begun to embrace traditional cooking with vigour recently. **Nueva cocina mexicana** (new Mexican cuisine) combines traditional ingredients and preparations with contemporary influences and presentations. An good example is the use of **huitlacoche**, a black fungus that grows on corn during the wet season. Always considered a delicacy by Indians, it has only recently influenced the higher echelons of Mexican society. It now serves as a basis for sauces and filling for crepes at some of the country's finest restaurants.

Imaginative cooks are rediscovering the flavours of ingredients which were previously overlooked by the upper-class: chiles, tortillas and beans are now being prepared in new and wonderful ways and have taken on a new lease of life (see the boxed text).

The difference in price between these two sub-categories of restaurants can be significant. Entrees in hotel restaurants begin at U$10 while they rarely exceed this mark at most other places.

**WHERE TO EAT & DRINK**

---

We began with a botana of **tostadas** (fried tortillas, in this case very small) topped with **Haísikil-píak** (a purée made with roasted pumpkin seeds, chile, roasted tomato, cilantro and capers – ingredients that were widely used by the Mayans). This was followed by a creamy soup made with **queso azul** from the state of Querétaro. Another soup, **Chipachole de Jaiba**, uses crab from the Gulf Coast.

The main courses included **chamorro**, a dish typical of the Yucatán peninsula made by marinating a leg of pork in **adobo** (a mixture of ground chiles and vinegar) and then oven-roasted at such a low heat that the meat nearly slips off the bone. Another main was the Veracruz-inspired **mondongo jarocho**, a sort of rich gumbo with ham, tripe, chick peas, generous amounts of cilantro and, of course, freshly made tortillas.

Another Mexico City restaurant features nueva cocina mexicana of a different sort. *Villa Casona*, on Av San Antonio in Mixoac, combines international influences with Mexican staples. A ravioli dish, for example, comes covered with a sauce made from a base of roasted chile poblano. Sauces are the key element in the main courses at *Villa Casona* and most are chile-based, although **huitlacoche** and **tamarindo** also make for wonderful accompaniments to beef, chicken or fish. The restaurant is set in the rooms of an old house and is decorated with artwork from various eras. Among the wall hangings is a wooden plate, signed by Guatemalan Nobel Peace Prize winner Rigoberta Menchÿ.

Restaurants like these are simultaneously advancing *and* preserving traditional Mexican food by keeping the country's culinary heritage alive. History, after all, is a living entity, and culinary history is no exception.

# Vegetarians & Vegans

While there is no real tradition of vegetarianism in Mexico, meat has long been a luxury among many Mexicans so there are many wonderful meatless dishes. As a consequence vegetarians won't be disappointed with their culinary tour.

One caveat though is that **manteca de cerdo** (pork lard) is commonly used as a cooking agent which, in itself, soundly defeats just about every tenet of vegetarianism. Many cooks feel that manteca is a key element in the flavour of traditional cooking and stubbornly insist on using it, even if in smaller quantities. However, in homes and restaurants there is a slow shift towards using vegetable oils.

Vegetarians can play it safe by opting for dishes like **chiles rellenos con queso** (stuffed chiles with cheese), quesadillas, **queso fundido** (fondue), stuffed avocado, tortas and many other antojitos that use cheese or beans as their main ingredient. You may find rice dishes such as **arroz a la poblana** (a pilaf with chiles, corn and cheese) or **arroz verde** (green rice) that includes peas in the recipe. Be warned however, many rice dishes are made with **caldo de pollo** (chicken broth) so you should ask (see Useful Phrases at the end of this chapter). Another vegetarian favourite is **elote asado** (roasted young corn) which is sold by street vendors. Whole corns are cooked in their husks over burning coals, then peeled and slathered in a butter and chile mix. The corn is still steaming when it's returned briefly to the grill until the kernels begin to brown.

Most cities have a few vegetarian restaurants and their menus reflect a desire to remain within the context of traditional Mexican cooking while reducing the amount of meat in the diet. As a result, meat substitutes such as soy or gluten are very popular. Juan de Dios, who has owned and operated three popular vegetarian restaurants in Puebla for 15 years, explains that Mexicans are now prepared to embrace a healthier diet, but not psychologically ready to give up the foods which they grew up on and consider as part of their identity. And so, you can order eggs with sausage and receive a version with faux chorizo made from gluten or soya. Veggie burgers, also made with soy or gluten, are very popular as full meals or as spontaneous antojitos.

Dishes at Juan's restaurants are always served with the requisite Mexican condiments: green and red chile sauce, **salsa bandera** (flag sauce), beans, rice and avocado. As a result, the difference between meat and non-meat dishes is minimal (although Mexicans from the north, where meat is king, would disagree). Greens such as broccoli, cauliflower and salads are always on the menu, along with light soups, stews and even tacos, prepared with imaginative fillings such as carrot, potato, parsley.

Another approach is to take traditional ingredients and place them into a vegetarian context. The result may be a soufflé of **elote** (the young corn used in pozoles) or grilled nopales 'a la mexicana'.

Non-vegetarian restaurants, particularly in the proudly carnivorous north, may only be able to prepare meatless versions of certain dishes, but you should not count on either their willingness to accommodate you, or their ability to produce something you'll enjoy. If you don't eat fish, be certain to tell them, as shrimps and other seafood often make their way into casseroles that would otherwise be meatless.

Even though the culture of vegetarianism is increasing, organic vegetables are virtually non-existent. While fertilisers are not overly used (note how much smaller certain vegetables are), pesticides are commonly used on crops across the country.

Vegans will have more trouble and may have to fend for themselves. When asked about vegan options, Juan de Diego looked puzzled. Restaurants offer very few non-salad options for the vegan. If you have the option of cooking for yourself, there will be no problem with an abundance of tortillas, beans, rice and fresh vegetables and fruits available at markets and grocery stores.

**WHERE TO EAT & DRINK**

## Tips for Eating Out
### Pace
Controlling the pace of a meal in a Mexican restaurant is the diner's responsibility. If you are interested in a long, lingering lunch with several drinks and conversation, it is best to set the menu aside for a space of time before ordering. Once a meal is ordered, it is generally delivered promptly, with courses following one after the other in quick succession. If you want to sit back and enjoy a six-inch cigar and sample a few tequilas after your meal, feel free as waiters won't bring the cheque until it's requested.

### IVA
The **Impuesto de Valor Agregado** (IVA, Value Added Tax) is included in the price of bill. Some places don't include the tax and offer discounts for paying cash instead of using a credit card.

### Hours
In the larger cities most places keep long hours, opening for breakfast no later than 7am and closing by 11am. Others specialise in one meal and may close as early as 2pm. On weekends, some places will stay open till the wee hours of the morning, waiting for the after-disco crowd to file in.

## CANTINA EXCURSION

I left my knapsack in my hotel room, took off my khakis and changed into a pair of old jeans and a T-shirt emblazoned with 'University of King's College', then thought better of it and put on another shirt, plain blue, no logo, no words. It was time to check out a cantina.

Near the bus station in Monterrey there are dozens of such bars, their fronts shut to the street in blatant opposition to most popular restaurants, which are completely open. Around the corner from my hotel, there was a cluster of cantinas, tucked away on a side street where prostitutes patrolled the corners. Some played very loud music, mostly **ranchera**, a Mexican version of country featuring accordions and a repetitive, almost torturous base line. I settled on a place called *El Conde* (The Count). A hand-written sign on the door listed the rules: No Minors, No Salesmen, No Buskers, No Charlatans and No Women without proper identification.

My plan was simple, have a drink, observe, and get out intact. I wanted no part of this cantina culture, where every night someone is shot or stabbed, where virtuous women are turned bad by badder men who steal their innocence before callously discarding them on some metaphorical trash heap. I expected to walk into a room where you couldn't see your hand in front of your face for the smoke from the harshest cigarettes known to humanity. I expected nothing less than what old Hollywood films had promised me.

Turns out Hollywood exaggerated. The *El Conde* cantina was no different than my local in Toronto, except the pictures of hockey heroes were replaced with Mexican football stars and the drinks were

### Children

Outside the national chains (Sanborn's, Vips etc) very few restaurants will make special arrangements for children with specific menus, high chairs or treats. This is not to say that children are not welcome, they certainly are, especially on weekends when families go out to dine.

In some ways, Mexican food is perfect for children. Eating with your hands is encouraged, and a tortilla can occupy the gums of an infant for a good hour, allowing you to enjoy your meal in peace.

On the downside, the spiciness of certain dishes might bother some young stomachs. You can always ask the waiter if it is **muy picoso** (very spicy), or stay away from the chile sauces entirely. When it comes to drinking, you may find that there are not many options beyond soft drink, and as such, the amount of sugar intake will rise during your trip.

considerably cheaper. There was an air of machismo. A few guys at the bar took their mezcal in shots and nobody had shaved in the last few days. The only woman in the place was a bored waitress who sat watching television. Not wanting to disturb her, I ordered my drink right from the bartender, sat down and looked around, now *hoping* for a little action: a fight with chairs, bottles smashed over heads, etc. I got none of it, not even an argument, not even a raised voice. Surely I was missing something?

In rural areas cantinas are meeting places where, as a regular, you'll know half the patrons. It's probably here that Hollywood got its idea of cantina culture. In the lawless Mexican countryside of the 19th and early 20th centuries, it was only natural for men to carry guns. And when guns and excessive drinking mix, there are bound to be a few shots fired. Perhaps the owners of these establishments, subscribing to the music-calms-the-savage-beast philosophy, brought in small bands to entertain patrons. Live bands are not unusual today, but the majority of the music is played over loud stereo systems with big bass woofers. In the old days, women were strictly prohibited from entering a cantina. While today the rules have been relaxed, it is still rare to see a woman in a cantina, especially in the country.

In Mexico City, both men and women can visit cantinas that are part museum, part drinking hole and designed for tourists. I have read reports that describe the cantina as a place for only the hardest drinkers, where you are likely to become embroiled in a shot-for-shot contest with a local, where music is played at ear-popping levels and where the action doesn't stop until the darkness lifts. Make your own discoveries.

## Service

An advertising campaign sponsored by the Office of the Presidency brags that, at 3%, Mexico's is the lowest unemployment rate in the Americas. The restaurant industry must have a lot to do with this as there are usually far more waiters than are needed. Most waiting staff in Mexico consists of full-time careerists rather than starving actors or university students paying off loans. Interestingly, the profession is dominated by men, with the main exception being the fabled cantinas, where **meseras** (waitresses) hold court.

There are a few places where you order at the counter, pay, then carry their food back to a table, but this routine is usually the exclusive domain of American fast food joints. Even the most humble taquería will have one or two servers scurrying between tables, taking orders, clearing dirty plates and presenting bills.

## PULQUERÍAS – The Original Mexican Watering Hole

Before the discotheque, before the leather seats of a hotel lounge, before even the venerated cantina, Mexico had pulquerías. Named for the drink they served, these shady, seedy hovels were the working class's favourite drinking spot for the better part of 400 years before better quality liquors and refrigeration forced them into the obscurity in which they languish today.

When the Aztecs ruled Mexico, pulque, made from the maguey plant, was used only in rituals and by the elite. Its production was strictly controlled and drunkenness was severely punished.

When the Spaniards arrived, pulque hit the streets, almost literally. The milky, low-alcohol drink was sold from make-shift stands that were open on all sides and covered with a shingled roof.

The method of service was just as primitive, purveyors would ladle the drink from large basins or open barrels into an awaiting patron's earthenware cup. As the day wore on, and the mood of the patrons got rowdier, these cups would be smashed against the ground once the contents were drained.

Pulquerías defined street life in the popular neighbourhoods for much of the 17th and 18th centuries. They were the meeting spots where people would go to unwind after a hard day at work (although for many, the day consisted of nothing but hard drinking). The heavy boozing led to spontaneous eruptions of music and dancing. Food stands were set up to feed the drinkers when they so desired. Fights were common, as were public displays of affection between lovers.

This behaviour alarmed authorities and, almost from the outset (the first recorded liquor laws were written in 1529), efforts were made to curtail the debauchery. One inspector general reported that pulquerías were "the real centre and originating point of all the crimes and public sins which overwhelms this numerous population". One measure called for the pulquerías to be enclosed in four walls, which brought protests from those who feared that once hidden behind walls, the behaviour would only worsen.

Another law prohibited members of the opposite sex from imbibing with one and other. There were also attempts to limit the kinds of pulque sold, under the belief that certain blends of roots and herbs had more damaging effects on the consumer. None of these measures proved to have any lasting effect. There were too many men who became very wealthy from pulque production, and this ensured a healthy flow of bribes to corrupt officials whenever tighter regulations compelled such action.

But the failure of authorities to quash Mexican's love of pulque was most hampered by one simple fact, the royal treasury was raking in money from the taxes charged on the sale of pulque, especially toward the end of the 18th century when revenues from silver and gold were diminishing. During this time, taxes on pulque rose steadily, doubling in the 20-year period ending in 1784.

The excessive taxes did accomplish the stated goal of reduced consumption – at least legally. But bootleggers, selling illegal and untaxed pulque, did very well indeed during this period.

More worrying for the last of the Spanish colonial administrators, were that pulquerías would become the seat of rebellion, where dangerous ideas of independence could circulate among the common people. A new law was passed in 1811 (about a year after the rebellion against the Spanish Crown began) that would prohibit the consumption of pulque in the pulquerías. As a result, drinking went underground and clandestine pulquerías thrived.

In truth patrons were not so concerned with making revolution as they were with getting drunk, gambling, dancing and making out in back corners. Besides that, the ability of the colonial viceroy to enforce any measures was undermined by the fact that he was losing the war to the rebelling Mexican forces. As a result, by 1821, when the Spanish finally gave up, pulquerías were more numerous than ever.

Following Mexican independence, pulque consumption on a per capita basis rose, and by 1864 there was one pulquería for every 410 residents! Significantly, the government restricted their locations to neighbourhoods outside the city centre, a factor which may have contributed to pulque's eventual demise.

In the meantime, other drinks such as beer brought by German immigrants and the more potent mezcal and tequila began to gain greater popularity and supplant pulque as the intoxicant of choice. True pulque is homemade, not bottled and therefore not very viable for large-scale commercial production. While still available today in certain parts of Central Mexico, it is clear that these are not the glory days of pulque.

In a way, the demise of the pulquería is a loss for Mexico. As you sit in a bar, listening to pre-recorded music instead of a group of local musicians, drinking the beer that tastes the same wherever you order it, from a glass that will be washed and used again instead of smashed against the floor, you can't help but feel a certain misty sense of nostalgia for the days when pulquerías ruled the social scene in Mexico.

**WHERE TO EAT & DRINK**

## Delivery

If you see **servicio a domicilio** advertised, the restaurant delivers. In the street you'll see boys riding mopeds with large thermally insulated boxes attached to the rear fender and painted in restaurant colours, buzzing perilously in and out of traffic delivering food.

The US pizza chains have an armada of mopeds, parked in formation in front of the respective outlet.

You may also see people, usually women, lugging enormous baskets around cities, delivering fresh tortillas, **guiso** (stew), chiles rellenos or other meals to office-bound customers. The food is kept warm in the baskets by several layers of cotton towels carefully wrapped around containers and lain over the edges of the basket.

## La Cuenta (The Bill/Check)

As dining is as much a social event as a means of nourishment, customers are welcome to linger, enjoying a second or third cup of coffee. The waiter won't bring the bill unless specifically asked. When you do wish to leave, it is perfectly acceptable to raise your arm and call out to a waiter, usually with '**Joven**!' (young man!). However, most places are over-stocked with waiting staff, and it's rarely a problem catching someone's eye.

## Tipping

Tips are usually paid separately and the amount depends on the type of restaurant. For mid-range and up, the general expectation is that tips should amount to 10% to 15% of the bill. In smaller fast food places and at lower end comedores tips are not expected.

*Young girl eating coctel de camarón (prawn cocktail), Veracruz*

# Street Food

Step off any intercity bus and you will be struck by the smell of meat, onions and garlic, drifting from a cluster of **puestos** (semi-permanent street stalls) vying for the attention of hungry travellers. But puestos aren't only for transients, as the culture of eating in the street is firmly entrenched in the Mexican gastronomic psyche. Some puestos become neighbourhood institutions, outlasting permanent restaurants by attracting and maintaining a loyal clientele.

The most common puestos are no more than 2m high by 2m wide, made of thin sheets of metal with shutters serving as sun-screens by day and security by night. Depending on the speciality a puesto may have a counter, a chopping block, a deep frying pot, a large comal, and refreshments nestling among large blocks of ice.

Eating from street vendors can be a questionable proposition in any country, no less so in Mexico. Foreigners are generally warned off them but, while many are unhygienic, there are exceptions that are not hard to find. Ask around and look for places with big crowds, especially in parks and plazas where groups of puestos often sell the same thing. In Mexico City, for example, there is a park at the corner of Revolucion and San Antonio (Metro: San Antonio) with about 20 puestos all selling tacos and tortas, with some offering a **comida completa** (a multi-course meal) including soup.

You can immediately identify the best puesto in this park as it has a constant crowd. While other puestos remain empty, this one (marked with a green and yellow awning advertising Coca Cola) teems with customers, their arms outstretched waiting for their order or a second helping. There are three cooks in the tiny, makeshift kitchen, rushing to construct the house speciality, **guarachos** (tortilla shells piled high with chorizo, carne, potato, cilantro and chile salsa). Other places sell tacos of every variety, quesadillas, golden flautas, hamburguesas, stubby hot dogs wrapped in bacon, overflowing tortas, **gorditas** stuffed with ground seasoned meat or melted cheese, **sopes** (tortillas shaped like beaver tails and topped with beans and vegetables), steaming tamales and even corn on the cob.

Another popular item at many puestos is the **chicharrón**, a rich snack made from pork skin that is deep-fried twice to make it rise. This oily delight is then liberally topped with lime juice and bottled **salsa picante** (hot sauce). There's very little to them and they are not much more than textured vehicles for yet another way to take lime and salsa.

You'll find puestos in most neighbourhoods, especially those in working and middle-class areas. Bus stations and big subway stops also attract these sidewalk chefs. At night, they are meeting places, illuminated with a strange brightness by strings of naked light bulbs. You may find yourself there after a movie or to cap off an evening of dancing.

On the coast, you will find puestos selling ice desserts called **nieves** (snow). Easily recognised by the colourful jars of fruit syrup displayed across the top counter, you take your chances with these places because nieve is just ice scraped from blocks probably not made from purified water.

**Jugos** (juices) are also popular, often supplied from a pushcart equipped with a citrus squeezer and a basket of oranges to the side. More complicated juice puestos advertise themselves by lining the entire stand with the myriad of fruits on offer. In addition to a citrus squeezer, these places may have a pulveriser for juicing carrots, beets and other vegetables.

## Mobile Food

Many visitors are woken by the sound of a loud-speakered voice invading their dreams, then growing louder, until it fills the room from the street below. The loud-speakers are attached to a cart or a bicycle (or a hybrid of the two) and are used to enthusiastically announce that the rider is in possession of fine pistachios, tamales, roasted peanuts or some other product you didn't need to be woken for.

You will also encounter strolling vending machines, children with boxes of cigarettes and candy strapped around their necks who roam from plaza to plaza, from restaurant patio to park bench. Although some of these children may be working for exploitive adults, many are just trying to earn a crust so it's worth supporting them.

## Junk Food

Candy kiosks are everywhere, whether stand-alone operations on a side street or as part of a conglomerate of micro-enterprises, or amidst other kiosks selling pirated cassettes, replacement watchbands and umbrellas. They are all very small, barely big enough to hold their owner, yet manage to stuff in enough chocolates, candy, potato chips and sundry junk food to satisfy even the worst case of the munchies. Some just lay their wares out on a towel, then sit on a box and wait for customers to take the bite. There are a number of international brands (Mars, Snickers, Lays, Ruffles etc) complementing the few indigenous Mexican names.

Kiosks often sell soft drinks from ice-packed coolers. Because the deposit on bottles is high you will notice hordes of school children sipping from clear plastic bags filled with orange, red or brown fizzy liquid. Rather than try to compete with the soft drink empires of Coca-Cola or Pepsi, Mexican manufacturers have turned to unique flavours such as apple, mango, peach or guava. Some are more successful than others but none are substitutes for the fresh juice you can get in restaurants and juice bars.

Rodalo
Negrillo
Peto
Sierra

camaron Cri...
"  " de Rio
"  " de Mar
camaron P/filar Mac...
"  ...  P/filar Ri...
pulpo
caracol
Mano de Cangreji
...  blanc...
Filete

# understanding
# the menu

Think of **la carta** (the menu) as a non-edible appetiser, a means
of getting to know the tone and range of a restaurant before getting
into the actual business of eating. The menu is a great way of
learning how Mexicans eat and their attitudes toward food. For
starters, you'll notice that few menus have explanations for
the dishes – it is assumed that the customer will know each of
them well.

On the upside, this is a chance to practise your Spanish. Don't be shy about asking for explanations and recommendations. Most waiters have at least a rudimentary knowledge of English and can give you a basic idea of what's in a particular dish. Staff in better restaurants are generally quite familiar with the best qualities of each dish, in English.

The menu shows that Mexicans have a strong attachment to national dishes (for example, antojitos such as tacos and quesadillas) as well as regional specialities. They also show a commitment to the complete meal – soup, salad, main dish, and dessert (although you are not expected to order them all).

This chapter deconstructs Mexican menus, a guide to the guides if you like. While there are a few dishes outlined for illustration, this isn't meant as a menu-reader – you can find a comprehensive list of dishes in the Spanish-English dictionary towards the back of this book.

*Nuns in coffee shop, Puebla*

## Types of Menus

The menu comes to you as soon as you sit down. That is, provided you are in a restaurant that uses a menu. Many have no need of anything printed, choosing instead to paint your choices on the wall, or write them on neon-coloured bristle board in black marker with the specialities circled. Some may have a verbal menu and if your Spanish isn't up to scratch, you might have to take a gamble.

Other restaurants, perhaps in an effort to reduce errors of communication, opt for a piece of paper that lists all the different dishes available, organised by type of food and then sub-organised by variation. For example, a heading will read Antojitos, followed by a sub-head reading Tacos, followed by a list of different tacos and combinations; **bistec** (beefsteak), **chuleta** (cutlets), **pollo** (chicken), **bisteck con queso** (with cheese), chuleta con queso. Beside each is the price and the customer is to check off the quantity (including beverages), add up the total cost and pass the paper back to the server. Its a bit like using a mail order catalogue, only with less packaging and faster delivery.

---

### THE 'EN' PREFIX

On a menu, or in the supermarket, you will notice the frequent use of the letters '**en**' at the beginning of certain words. Meaning 'in' when combined with a noun, the new word becomes an adjective describing the preparation of a particular dish. Therefore, **entomatado** means 'in tomato' as in **huevos entomatados** (eggs in a tomato sauce), **enpanizado** means 'in bread' or 'breaded' as in **pescado enpanizado** (crumbed fish), and **endulzado** means 'in sweet' or sweetened as in **mayonesa endulzada** (sweet mayonnaise).

---

### Comida Corrida (Set Menu)

The set menu is common, especially at restaurants catering to office workers. The day's specials are listed on signs near the doorway under the heading 'Menu' or 'Comida Corrida'. Prices range from exceptionally cheap to moderate and usually offer great value. The comida generally includes a soup such as **sopa de tortilla**, a chicken broth-based soup featuring strips of yesterday's corn tortillas, or a **crema** which combines a puréed vegetable with rich cream. The next item is a pasta, usually a spaghetti in a light bolognese sauce, followed by the **plato fuerte** (main dish). There is usually a choice of two or three plato fuertes which may be a piece of grilled fish or meat, served with a portion of steamed greens, beans or rice.

**THE MENU**

### Desayuno (Breakfast)

Some restaurants specialise in breakfast, opening from dawn to comida. Those that offer complete service may have a separate breakfast menu. In both cases, breakfasts tend to come as set packages. They generally include a cup of café americano (as opposed to a cappuccino or espresso), a fruit cocktail or a glass of freshly squeezed juice (orange, grapefruit, mango or papaya are common choices), and a main course. Despite being a coffee producer, Mexicans drink a tremendous amount of instant coffee. The **desayuno continental** (continental breakfast) is a universal phenomenon consisting of bread of some sort — from Wonder Bread toast to flaky croissants – served with chilled butter and **mermelada** (fruit jam). Peanut butter, called **mantequilla de cacahuete**, is rare even in shops. As you read down the menu, the breakfasts get heartier, including a few slices of toast, and main dishes like **huevos rancheros** (eggs with chile sauce) or scrambled eggs with potatoes, onions, bacon, ham, cheese, chorizo, chiles or any number of other additions. Hotcakes, called **hotcakes** in Spanish, are also popular.

### Almuerzo (Lunch)

To the extent that Mexicans eat almuerzo, it is usually in an eatery serving tortas or tacos called a **tortería** or a **taquería** for a quick sandwich or plate of **tacos al pastor** (tacos with meat). Menus seem optional here as most customers live, work or study in the neighbourhood and know their favourites. Indeed, the word Tortería written across the front of the awning is enough to let you know that there is a set list of sandwich fillers. A taquería with a huge chunk of meat rotating on a horizontal spit in front of a hot element needs no menu to let a passer-by know that they serve tacos al pastor.

### Comida & Cena (Afternoon & Evening Meals)

The early afternoon meal, the main one in Mexico, was traditionally taken in the home but is now almost the exclusive domain of restaurants. A restaurant's busiest hours are between 2pm and 4pm when the tables are filled with individuals and large groups.

The whole menu is open for the comida. Most are organised as follows:

**Entradas** (appetisers) can include items such as **cóctel de camarones** (shrimp cocktail), **queso fundido** (fondue) and **champiñones** (fried mushrooms).

*A typical Oaxacan breakfast – scrambled eggs with chopped tomato, onion, chile, garnished with chapulines (grasshoppers), chocolate oaxaqueno (chocolate milk), pan de yema (yolk bread), and tacos con queso (with cheese)*

**Ensaladas** (salads) include everything from the simple **de verduras** (mixed greens), to Caesar salad, to fruit salad, to a wonderful spinachy green called **berros** (cress) which, when served with fresh tomato, smoky bacon bits, and a light lime and oil vinaigrette is a wonderful entrée.

**Sopas** (soups) are divided between traditional broth-based soups, cremas and **sopas secas**, which is any dish cooked in water or broth until the liquid has reduced. Sopa secas can include rice, tortilla strips or **fideos** (noodles). But a Spaghetti Bolognese is not a sopa seca, it is a pasta and is listed on the menu as such.

*Corn soup with huitacoche (black corn mould)*

**Platos Fuertes** (main dishes) may be listed under this single heading or, when the selection is greater, listed by main ingredient: **pollos** (chicken), **carnes** (meat, including beef and pork), **pescados** (fish, almost exclusively white fish fillet) and **mariscos** (other seafood such as shrimp, calamari and crab).

**Especialidades** (daily specials) often feature on a small sheet of paper attached to la carta. The specials may never change, daily or otherwise, but they are a refreshing departure from the main menu, which will not vary much from place to place. Especialidades are what makes a restaurant unique and can create a loyal following.

**Postres** (desserts) are a result of European influence and not a traditional part of the Mexican diet. Nevertheless, Mexicans have embraced the idea and most mid and upper-range restaurants will offer a few selections. The most common choices are **flan**, that heavy sweet white custard covered in one of several syrupy toppings, or **helados** (ice cream) made from fresh local fruit. At the end of a large, protein-rich meal, the urge for something sweet may have you heading for the nearest kiosk or small store to get candies, chocolates, or packaged pastries.

*Mexican desserts*

THE MENU

## Drinks

It always seems odd that the first thing you're asked in a restaurant is '**Algo para tomar?**' (Something to drink?), yet drinks tend to be listed in a small section toward the end of the menu. The most basic list will consist of nothing more than beer, soft drink, coffee and bottled water. Other places will have a more complete **lista de vinos**, which literally means 'wine list' but will include all the alcoholic drinks available which, in some cases, won't include wine. For the most part the brand names for the hard stuff will be recognisable, such as Bacardi and Smirnoff. Those unfamiliar with Mexico generally won't recognise tequila and brandy brands, but they are listed under headings and prices will give you some idea of the quality. Experiment!

Wine is not common in Mexican restaurants and when you see wine available, they are usually catering for tourists. In some cases, your choice will be between **tinto y blanco** (red and white) with no choice in either category. Others will let you know if what you are drinking is **nacional** (domestic) or international.

To get your favourite brand of beer, you may have to ask what brands are available as the menu is likely to just have the word **cerveza** (beer) Selection is occasionally limited to the two main breweries, Cuauhtemóc Monteczuma (Dos XX, Bohemia and Carta Blanca) and Modelo (Corona, Negra Modelo and Montejo). These breweries compete for exclusive deals with bars and restaurants.

# a mexican
# banquet

"Homesickness begins with food," said Che Guevara. But you don't have to be from Latin America to be nostalgic for its food, drink or the atmosphere of a sidewalk cafe with a view of the **zócalo** (city square). After a taste of a rich **pozole** (Mexican soup) or **enchilada** (a meat-based tortilla) you will always remember, and thus have a permanent connection to, the food and drink of Mexico.

Fortunately, the Mexican feast is a moveable one and you should be able to throw your own **fiesta mexicana** whether to celebrate a national holiday or simply as an excuse to get back to the foods and drinks you've grown to love.

Food is a major part of any fiesta, second only to the people. **Botanas** (snacks) are the absolute minimum: serve **totopos** (fried tortillas) and **salsa**, **cacahuetes** (peanuts) in their various forms – with lime and chile, roasted or **japonesa** (Japanese-style) covered with a crunchy coating. Sprinkle lime over a bowl of plain potato chips, gently mix and serve with bottled salsa.

More ambitious hosts will move onto **antojitos** (appetisers). Remember that the definition of antojito is broad and the only mandatory element is a large supply of fresh tortillas. After that, your choices for filling is wide open: cheese for **quesadillas**, meat or chicken for **taquitos**, or **frijoles refritos** (refried beans). Antojitos can be heated by frying in oil or by grilling on a large, flat pan, preferably a **comal**.

## Pipian Sauce

This is a great sauce for meat, especially poultry, whether grilled, roasted or from the barbeque. It also keeps well. You don't have to use chicken broth, any vegetable broth will do. I sometimes add a little red wine or beer for fun. The following is a more traditional recipe.

### Ingredients

| | | | |
|---|---|---|---|
| 2 | chile anchos | ½ | teaspoon (2ml) dried thyme |
| 3 | tablespoons cooking oil | ⅓ | cup (75ml) peanuts |
| 1 | small onion, chopped | 1 | chipotle chile, chopped |
| 1 | clove garlic | 1 | teaspoon sugar |
| 4 | cloves | | salt and pepper to taste |
| ½ | teaspoon allspice | 4–5 | cups (1 litre) chicken broth |
| | hot water | ⅓ | (75 ml) cup untoasted |
| ½ | teaspoon (2ml) ground cinnamon | | pumpkin seeds |

Chop the chile anchos and heat the oil. Quickly fry the chiles, just enough to toast them, and transfer to a bowl. Cover with hot water to soak for 20 minutes. In the same pan, sauté the onion and garlic until soft (add more oil if necessary). In a separate pan, toast the pumpkin seed, ensuring that they do not burn (5–7 minutes). Combine onions, garlic, seeds and the rest of the spices in a bowl along with the peanuts, chipotle and ½ cup of the broth. Purée in an electric blender in small batches until smooth, then return to the pan. Slowly add the rest of the broth until the desired consistency is achieved (should be thick, like melted ice cream). Now it is ready to be served with your meat.

If you fancy a sit-down meal, give it a Mexican feel by creating your own chile salsa. Begin with a variety of your favourite chiles (depending on availability). Once they are roasted and the seeds are removed, you can flex your creative muscle. The basic secondary ingredients are onions, garlic, cilantro, olive oil and peeled tomatoes. The portion you decide to add will alter the flavour. Experiment. When you are happy with the flavour, let it simmer while you prepare your favourite cut of meat on a grill and pour the sauce generously over the meat (see Salsa Verde recipe in the Staples and Specialities chapter).

At Mexican house parties, botanas and antojitos are served as long as people keep eating them and sometimes even after they've stopped. The festivities can last well into the evening and most guests will arrive late. In fact it's common, even customary, to show up to a party a couple of hours after it was supposed to begin.

Your own guests may be slightly more punctual but they will be no less thirsty. Mexican beer is now sold worldwide and two brands in particular, Corona and Dos XX, have enjoyed considerable success in foreign lands. When you buy the beer, pick up a dozen limes to cut into wedges and plant in the mouth of an open bottle before serving. The lime-in-beer combination is a practice you will rarely see in Mexico (legend has it the reason behind the lime is to repel flies and so to serve them is to admit you have pests), but the light lager taste of most domestic brews is perfectly accented with a gentle squeeze of lime juice.

Your party will also be the ideal time to demonstrate the pleasure of a good tequila. The best tequilas should be served to only your best friends and it is well worth the trouble to whip up a batch of **sangrita** (see the Sangrita recipe in the Drinks chapter) to be served chilled with a **reposado** (a tequila that has been aged two to 12 months), or **añejo** (a dark whisky-coloured tequila).

And then there is music, which emerges from the Mexican fiesta as just another way of making noise, of expressing oneself, whether you're musical or not. Little girls know the lyrics to every song on FM radio and the repertoire of the average busker is impressively broad. At parties, the music comes spontaneously. A guitar appears from nowhere and someone is cajoled into playing, first feigning resistance before breaking into a robust **corrido** (a ballad). The singer is soon joined by other voices making conversation impossible as they draw the whole party into a single, mass chorus.

Mexican music is an eclectic mix of styles and sensibilities. The traditional corrido, with their roots in medieval troubadours, tell stories of love and loss and other public scandals. More contemporary styles include **ranchera,** a sort of country music featuring a heavy bass beat and accordions.

**Rock en español**, a continent-wide movement is full of Mexican groups and musicians. Likewise, singers Luis Miguel and Veronica Castro enjoy international prominence. But perhaps the most festive music comes from the Gulf Coast, where the influence of Caribbean rhythms from Cuba, Puerto Rico and the Dominican Republic mean that musical styles known as **salsa, merengue** and **soca** have worked their way into the Mexican musical fabric.

As the drink flows freely, someone inevitably pushes the dining room table or the sofa to one side and couples begin to dance. Your own inclination may be to stand to the side and watch but it's not likely you'll be allowed; someone will find you and pull you onto the floor. There are dancing styles for each type of music, the easiest among them being merengue, which consists of little less than hip wiggles and turns. The most difficult style is that which comes from the north, a sort of tribute to disequilibrium, where partners clutch each other and swing their entire bodies from side to side as though imitating a wrestling match. Now with all this dancing, people are likely to be hungry and as host, you would be wise to have another round of antojitos ready to go.

Parties will often last to those hours where night and morning become one. By the end of it, guests are either exhausted, drunk or a little of both. Driving while under the influence is all too common, especially in rural areas where there are few taxis. However in the cities, it is easy enough to call a cab to pick you up and take you safely home.

## Fit & Healthy

Our bodies don't always share our enthusiasm for new places and the food and drink we may find there. The result may be as benign as a slight discomfort marked by an extra trip or two to the toilet. Fortunately, the more serious maladies are rare and the less serious ones can be avoided (for the most part) by taking some basic precautions.

The first line of defence is common sense – if a particular eating establishment doesn't seem hygienic, it possibly isn't so avoid it. Even if you do not get sick, it may not be worth the few hours of worrying that will follow your meal there.

Mexicans are very aware of the problems food and water-borne bacteria and other contaminants can cause. Popular education campaigns implore people to boil drinking water and wash vegetables in treated water. Concern for internal well-being extends to eating out, and a good rule of thumb when choosing a place to eat, especially market comedores and puestos on the street, is to go where the locals go. A reputation for quality food will also attract more customers, meaning the meat and vegetables will have less time to gather anything nasty.

This general guide will help you overcome potential problems.

## Water

The rule is simple: don't drink untreated tap water. This applies to Mexicans and visitors alike. Tap water can be contaminated with any number of bacteria that can cause quite serious illnesses. Pollution in urban water sources is an additional danger.

Fortunately, bottled water is available everywhere. Even the cheapest motel will have a jug for common use in the hall and most will put a complementary bottle in your room upon arrival. Use this for everything where there is a chance you will ingest water, such as brushing your teeth and washing fruit and vegetables.

Bottled water will be marked **agua purificada** (purified water). **Agua de manantial** (spring water) which may cost more but tastes better.

You can also boil water to kill any contaminants or add a consumer product called **Microdyn.** Vegetables soaked in a solution of microdyn and regular tap water will kill any bacteria on the surface of the vegetable and in the water. It can also be used to purify tap water for drinking or making ice, although whenever possible, you should stick to boiled or bottled water for these purposes.

Watch out for ice when ordering drinks in bars or restaurants. Ask the waiter if it has been made with agua purificada and if in doubt, ask for your drink **sin hielo** (without ice).

## Diarrhoea

It is so common for foreigners to experience diarrhoea when visiting Mexico that doctors in the country have taken to calling the condition **la turista**. You might know it as 'Mocteczuma's revenge'. Diarrhoea is often caused by your body adjusting to a different climate or diet and may be only temporary, but it also can be a symptom of a more serious condition.

Diarrhoea is best prevented by avoiding untreated water. In restaurants, eating raw vegetables and salads may lead to diarrhoea later on. Ask the waiter if the food was washed using agua purificada. As an extra measure, sprinkle lime juice on the salad or eat raw garlic. You may also wish to take a dose of a commercial anti-diarrheal like Pepto-Bismol to coat the inner lining of your stomach.

When you do find yourself spending more time in the bathroom than seems normal, you may find relief from Lomotil or Immodium, available at most Mexican pharmacies. Both will plug you up effectively but do not cure the problem and should only be taken when absolutely necessary. You should also be sure to replace the fluids you are losing by drinking plenty of bottled water, black tea with a little sugar or soft-drinks that have gone flat.

While recovering, you may want to give your stomach a break by avoiding spicy foods like chiles or chorizo. When in doubt, ask your waiter '**Es muy picante?**' or '**Pica mucho?**' (Is it very spicy?). You should also avoid raw vegetables or fruit that does not require peeling as these can exacerbate the problem.

Rehydration is important following any spell of diarrhoea. The World Health Organization recommends the following solution to help you maintain fluid levels and electrolyte balance. Mix one litre of water with $3/4$ teaspoon of salt, 1 teaspoon of baking soda, 1 cup of orange juice and 4 tablespoons of sugar. (As a precaution, you may wish to pack the dry ingredients before you go).

If your diarrhoea includes blood or mucus, is accompanied by fever or lethargy, or persists for more than five days, it may be an indication that you have picked up something that requires attention. Don't take Immodium or Lomotil in these cases and consult a doctor as soon as possible.

## Heat

Most of Mexico isn't that hot, but low-lying and coastal areas are subject to high temperatures, especially in summer. Drinking lots of fluids (especially purified water and fruit juices) is the best way to prevent problems associated with heat. Stay out of the sun during the hottest hours of the day (between noon and 3pm). Have lunch on a shaded patio and then find yourself a hammock under a tree for a short, refreshing siesta.

## Children

Children may find that some Mexican foods can cause stomach upsets. While Mexican children are more accustomed to chiles than their foreign counterparts, they are still not ready for adult doses. Mexican restaurants are conscious of this and it shouldn't be necessary to make a special order.

## Allergies

Most Mexican dishes are presented in a what-you-see-is-what-you-get manner and so avoiding foods that provoke an allergic reaction is mostly a question of perusing the plate. The exception to this rule are sauces, including mole. Most mole recipes call for peanuts including the most famous mole poblano and mole negro. Those allergic to shellfish should be wary of certain casseroles that will include shrimp or crab as secondary ingredients to meat or fish. Raw shellfish of any kind should be avoided by allergics and non-allergics.

Cooking with alcohol is not common in Mexico. There are some dishes however, many of which add the word **borracho** (drunken) to their name that do include some sort of alcoholic seasoning, usually beer.

## Diabetics

The only real concern for diabetics may be the high-calorie content of many Mexican foods, a result of the tendency to use plenty of oil as a cooking agent for meat, vegetables and tortillas. The only other potential concern could be that Mexicans tend to eat heavier meals in mid-afternoon. Otherwise, Mexican foods do not generally present any hidden sugars that may unbalance your insulin levels. Nevertheless, those with severe diabetes should certainly consult their physician before travelling.

## Fat & Cholesterol

Mexican cuisine is traditionally high in fat and cholesterol, given its reliance on **manteca** (lard) as a cooking agent. There is a trend toward lighter eating and lard is sometimes replaced with olive oil. Dishes with the adjective **dorado** (golden) will definitely be rich in oil.

## Hangovers

**Cruda**, the Spanish word for hangover, looks as bad as the English one feels. Bad tequila or mezcal can lead to especially bad morning-afters. Everyone has their own cure: aspirin, fizzy tablets, greasy meat or complicated juice concoctions. In Jalisco, **birria** (a goat meat, chile and tomato stew with a subtle combination of spices served with raw onion and lime juice) is said to be a sure-fire way to get you back in shape.

READING

## Recommended Reading

Pilcher, Jefferey M. *Que vivan los tomales: Food and the Making of the Mexican Identity.* Albuequerque: U of New Mexico Press, 1998
Developed from the author's doctoral dissertation, this is a highly readable and fascinating guide to the history of Mexican cuisine. It delves deeply into the different issues that have affected the Mexican diet over the past 500 years and looks at the part food has played in shaping the contemporary Mexican identity and, in particular, the role of the woman (as it relates to food) throughout the history of Mexican society.

Esquivel, Laura *Like Water for Chocolate*
In this single volume, Laura Esquivel has brought food, identity and history together. It was a best seller in Mexico when it was published in 1990, inspired the most successful Mexican film of all time and has been translated into several languages.

Esquivel, Laura *Suculentas Íntimacias...*
This collection of essays, published in 1998, gathers essays, speeches, articles, reviews and other writings from the previous eight years. In these, Esquivel digs more deeply into the philosophical elements of cooking and eating, its importance to her own sense of Mexicanidad and for Mexican women in general.

Rulfo, Juan *The Burning Plain*
This collection of short stories, published in the 1950s by one of Mexico's best loved authors, does not deal directly with food, but tells the stories of poor Mexicans and their new relationship with the land they worked following the revolution. Rulfo was born in Jalisco, and many of the stories are set in the region.

Anything by Diana Kennedy
This British-American author has been decorated by the Mexican government for her work in bringing Mexican cuisine to the English-speaking world. She is a pioneer in the field and has travelled extensively to every part of the republic, collecting recipes and stories which have been published in several volumes. Her most significant work is *The Cuisines of Mexico*. Although having been published in the early 1970s, it may be difficult to find. More recently she has come out with *My Mexico: A Culinary Odyssey with More Than 300 Recipes* which, in addition to recipes, includes anecdotes from her many travels in the country.

## Local Cookbooks

These follow in the tradition of Josefina Velázquez de León, the daughter of an upper-class family tracing its roots back to the conquistadores, who devoted her career to travelling throughout the Republic to learn about all the different ways of cooking that the country had to offer. She published her findings in over 150 cookbooks. For another good general cookbook with representations from all the major regions, pick up Patricia Quintana's *El Sabor de Mexico*. This glossy volume, highlighted by beautiful photography is also available in English as *The Taste of Mexico*, published by Stewart, Tabori and Chang of New York. Ms Quintana has also included extensive explanations of the history, culture and social significance of food in Mexico.

# eat your words
## language guide

# Pronunciation

As transliterations give only an approximate guide to pronunciation, we've included this guide for those who want to try their hand at pronouncing Mexican Spanish more like a native speaker.

## Vowels

a      as the 'u' in 'nut'
e      as the 'e' in 'met'
i      similar to the 'i' in 'machine', but shorter
o      similar to the 'o' in 'hot'
u      as the 'oo' in 'fool'

## Consonants

b      as the 'b' in 'book' at the start of a word or after **m**, **n** or **ng**;
       elsewhere, somewhere between English 'b' and 'v'
c      as the 'c' in 'cat' before **a**, **o** or **u**;
       as the 's' in 'sin' before **e** or **i**
ch     as the 'ch' in 'cheese'
d      as the 'd' in 'dog' at the start of word; elsewhere as the 'th' in 'this'
g      as the 'g' in 'gone' if followed by **a**, **o** or **u**; like the 'h' in 'hello' before **e** or **i**
h      always silent
j      as the 'h' in 'hill' or as the 'ch' in German 'Bach'
ll     between the 'ly' sound in 'million' and the 'y' in 'yes'
ñ      like the 'ny' in 'canyon'
q      as the 'k' in 'king'. The letter 'q' is always followed by a silent 'u'.
r      a rolled sound. Stronger when at the start of a word or in a word
       with a double 'r'.
s      as the 's' in 'sin'. Sometimes silent when in the middle of a word.
t      as the 't' in 'top' or as the 'th' in 'this'
v      as the 'v' in 'velvet' or somewhere between English 'b' and 'v'
x      as the 'x' in 'taxi' when between two vowels;
       as the 's' in 'sin' when before a consonant;
       sometimes also pronounced as the 'sh' in 'shoe' or as the 'h' in 'hot'
y      as the 'ee' in 'free' at the end of a word or when it stands alone;
       as the 'y' in 'yellow' elsewhere
z      as the 's' in 'sin'

## Combined Letters

gue/gui    in these combinations, the 'u' is silent unless it has diaeresis (ü).

## Stress

When a word ends in **n**, **s** or a vowel, stress falls on the second-last syllable. When a word ends in a consonant other than **n** or **s**, the final syllable is stressed. Any deviation from these rules is indicated by an accent, as in **atún**.

## Eating Out

(cheap) restaurant
**ehl res-tor-ahn-te (bahr-ah-toh)**     *el restaurante (barato)*

please
**por fah-vor**     *por favor*

Do you speak English?
**a-blah oos-tehd een-gles?**     *¿Habla usted Inglés?*

Table for (one/two/three/four).
**oon-ah me-sa pah-rah (oo-noh/ dos/tres/kwah-troh)**     *Una mesa para (uno/dos/tres/ cuatro)*

Can I see the menu?
**pweh-doh ver ehl men-oo/lah kahr-tah?**     *¿Puedo ver el menú/la carta?*

Do you have a menu in English?
**tee-en-en oon-ah kahr-tah en een-gles?**     *¿Tienen una carta en Inglés?*

What's the speciality of this region?
**kwahl es lah es-pes-ee-ah-lee-dahd de lah re-hee-on?**     *¿Cuál es la especialidad de esta región?*

What are today's specials?
**kwahl-es son lahs es-pes-ee-ah-lee-dahd-es pah-rah oy?**     *¿Cuáles son las especialidades para hoy?*

What's that?
**keh es es-oh?**     *¿Qué es eso?*

I'd like the set lunch.
**kee-see-ehr-ah ehl men-oo del dee-ah**     *Quisiera el menú del día.*

What does it include?
**keh een-kloo-yeh?**     *¿Qué incluye?*

Does it come with salad?
**vee-en-eh kon en-sah-lah-dah?**     *¿Viene con ensalada?*

What's the soup of the day?
**kwahl es lah so-pah del dee-ah?**     *¿Cuál es la sopa del día?*

What do you recommend?
**keh meh re-ko-mee-en-dah?**     *¿Qué me recomienda?*

What are they eating?
**keh es-tahn ko-mee-en-doh eh-yos?** ¿Qué están comiendo ellos?

I'll try what she's having.
**voy ah peh-deer loh keh**
**eh-yah pee-dee-oh** Voy a pedir lo que ella pidió.

What's in this dish?
**keh trah-eh es-teh plat-ee-yoh?** ¿Qué trae este platillo?

Do you have sauce?
**tee-en-eh oos-tehd sal-sah?** ¿Tiene usted salsa?

Is that dish spicy?
**es-eh plat-ee-yoh es-tah moo-ee** ¿Ese platillo está muy
**kon-dee-men-tah-doh/pee-koh-soh?** condimentado/picoso?

Not too spicy.
**no moo-ee kon-dee-men-tah-doh/** No muy condimentado/picoso.
**pee-koh-soh**

It's not hot.
**no es-tah kal-ee-en-te** No está caliente.

I didn't order this.
**no or-deh-neh es-toh** No ordené esto.

Can I have a (beer)?
**meh dah oon-ah (ser-veh-sah)?** Me da una (cerveza)?

Do you have a highchair for the baby?
**tee-en-eh oon-ah see-yee-tah** ¿Tiene una sillita para el bebé?
**pah-rah ehl beb-eh?**

| This food is … | **es-tah koh-mee-dah** | Esta comida está … |
| | **es-tah …** | |
| burnt | **keh-mah-dah** | quemada |
| cold | **free-ah** | fría |
| delicious | **eks-kee-sit-a** | exquisita |
| stale | **pa-sa-dah** | pasada |
| undercooked | **seen koh-sehr** | sin cocer |
| spoiled | **eh-chah-dah ah pehr-dehr** | echada a perder |

Waiter, there's a fly in my soup.
**mes-eh-rah/roh, ah-eeh oon-ah** Mesero/a, hay una mosca
**mos-kah en mee so-pah** en mi sopa.

Can you please bring me …?
**meh pweh-de trah-ehr por** ¿Me puede traer por favor …?
**fah-vor …?**

Thank you, that was delicious.
**grah-see-ahs, es-too-voh**
**del-ee-see-oh-soh**
*Gracias, estuvo delicioso.*

Please pass on our compliments to the chef.
**por fah-vor fehl-ee-see-teh-nos**
**ahl chef**
*Por favor felicítenos al cocinero.*

The bill, please.
**lah kwen-tah, por fah-vor**
*La cuenta, por favor.*

Is service included in the bill?
**ehl ser-vi-see-oh es-tah**
**een-kloo-ee-doh en lah kwen-tah?**
*¿El servicio está incluido en la cuenta?*

| | | |
|---|---|---|
| more | **mas** | *más* |
| ashtray | **oon se-ni-she-roh** | *un cenicer* |
| bread | **pahn** | *(mas) pan* |
| cup | **oon-ah ta-sah** | *una taza* |
| fork | **oon ten-e-dor** | *un tenedor* |
| glass | **oon bah-soh** | *un vaso* |
| knife | **oon koo-chil-yoh** | *un cuchillo* |
| napkin | **oon-ah ser-vil-yet-ah** | *una servilleta* |
| pepper | **pi-mee-en-tah** | *(mas) pimienta* |
| plate | **oon plat-oh** | *un plato* |
| salt | **sal** | *(mas) sal* |
| spoon | **oon-ah koo-chah-rah** | *una cuchara* |
| teaspoon | **koo-chah-ree-tah** | *una chucharita* |
| toothpick | **oonpal-il-yoh** | *un palillo* |
| (bottled) water | **ag-wah** | *(mas) agua purificado* |
| wine | **vee-noh** | *(mas) vino* |

## Vegetarian & Special Meals

I'm a vegetarian.
**soy ve-het-ar-ee-ah-noh/nah**
*Soy vegetariano/a*

I'm a vegan, I don't eat meat or dairy products.
**soy ve-het-ar-ee-ah-noh/nah,**
**no ko-moh kar-ne oh lak-tay-os**
*Soy vegetariano/a, no como carne o lácteos.*

Do you have any vegetarian dishes?
**tee-en-eh al-goon plat-ee-yoh**
**ve-het-ar-ee-ah-noh?**
*¿Tiene algún platillo vegetariano?*

Is there meat in this dish?
**es-teh plat-ee-yoh kon-tee-en-eh**
**kar-ne?**
*¿Este platillo contiene carne?*

Can I get this without the meat?
  **meh pweh-de dahr es-teh**
  **plat-ee-yoh seen kar-ne?**
¿Me puede dar este platillo
 sin carne?

Does this dish have gelatin?
  **es-teh plat-ee-yoh tee-en-eh**
  **hel-ah-tee-nah?**
¿Este platillo tiene gelatina?

Can you recommend a vegetarian dish?
  **meh pweh-de re-ko-men-dahr oon**
  **plat-ee-yoh ve-het-ar-ee-ah-noh?**
¿Me puede recomendar un
 platillo vegetariano, por favor?

| I don't eat ... | **no ko-moh ...** | No como ... |
|---|---|---|
| meat | **kar-ne** | carne |
| chicken | **pol-yoh** | pollo |
| poultry | **av-es** | aves |
| fish | **pes-kah-do** | pescado |
| seafood | **mar-is-kos** | mariscos |
| pork | **pwer-koh** | puerco |
| cured/processed meats | **kar-nes pro-seh-sah-dahs** | carnes procesadas |

| Is it ...? | **Es ...?** | ¿Es ...? |
|---|---|---|
| gluten-free | **seen gloo-ten** | sin gluten |
| lactose-free | **seen lak-tay-os** | sin lácteos |
| wheat-free | **seen tree-go** | sin trigo |
| salt-free | **seen sal** | sin sal |
| sugar-free | **seen as-oo-kahr** | sin azúcar |
| yeast-free | **seen lev-ah-doo-rah** | sin levadura |

I'm allergic to ...
  **soy ahl-er-hee-koh ah ...**
Soy alérgico a ...

Does it contain eggs/dairy products?
  **kon-tee-en-eh hway-vos/lak-tay-os?**
  **(ka-kah-wah-tehs)**
¿Contiene huevos/lácteos?

Is it cooked with pork lard/chicken stock?
  **es-tah ko-see-doh kon man-teh-kah/**
  **kal-doh deh pol-yoh?**
¿Está cocido con manteca/
 caldo de pollo?

I'd like a kosher meal.
  **me gus-tah-ree-ah oon plat-ee-yoh**
  **hoo-dee-oh**
Me gustaría un platillo judío.

Is this kosher?
  **es-toh es hoo-dee-oh?**
¿Esto es judio?

Is this organic?
  **es-toh es nah-too-rahl?**
¿Esto es natural?

## Family Meals

You're a great cook!
**oos-tehd es oon/ah gran
koh-see-neh-roh/rah!**
*¡Usted es un/a gran cocinero/a!*

This is brilliant!
**es-toh es eks-kee-see-toh!**
*¡Esto es exquisito!*

Do you have the recipe for this?
**tee-en-eh lah re-set-ah de es-toh?**
*¿Tiene la receta de esto?*

Is this a family recipe?
**es-tah es oon-ah re-set-ah de
fam-ee-lee-ah?**
*¿Esta es una receta de familia?*

Are the ingredients local?
**los in-gred-ee-en-tes son de
lah re-hee-on?**
*¿Los ingredientes son de
la región?*

I've never had a meal like this before.
**noon-kah ah-bee-ah ko-mee-doh
oon-plat-ee-yoh ko-moh es-te**
*Nunca había comido un platillo
como este.*

Could you pass the (salt) please?
**meh po-dree-ah pas-ahr (lah sal)
por fah-vor?**
*¿Me podría pasar (la sal)
por favor?*

Thanks very much for the meal.
**moo-chahs grah-see-ahs por lah
ko-mee-dah**
*Muchas gracias por la comida.*

I really appreciate it.
**de ver-dahd loh dees-froo-te**
*De verdad lo disfruté.*

If you ever come to (Australia), I'll cook you a local dish.
**see al-goo-nah ves vah ah
(ah-oos-trah-lee-ah), leh
koh-see-nahr-eh oon plat-ee-yoh
de lah loh-kahl-ee-dahd**
*Si alguna vez va a (Australia),
le cocinaré un platillo
de la localidad.*

## Buying Stuff

Where's the nearest (market)?
**don-de es-tah (ehl mer-kah-doh)
mas ser-kan-oh?**
*¿Dónde está (el mercado)
más cercano?*

How much?
**kwon-toh?**
*¿Cuánto?*

| Where can I find ...? | don-de pweh-doh en-kon-trahr ...? | ¿Dónde puedo encontrar ...? |
|---|---|---|
| biscuits | bis-ket | bísquet |
| bread | pan | pan |
| honey | mee-el | miel |
| fruit and vegetables | froo-tah eeh ver-doo-ras | frutas y verduras |
| frozen foods | a-lee-men-tos kon-hel-ah-dos | alimentos congelados |

| Can I have a ...? | meh pweh-de dahr ...? | ¿Me puede dar ...? |
|---|---|---|
| bottle | oon-ah bo-tel-yah | una botella |
| box | oon-ah ka-khah | una caja |
| can | oon-ah lat-ah | una lata |
| packet | oon pah-ket-e | un paquete |
| sachet/bag | oon-ah bol-see-tah | una bolsita |
| tin of ... | oon-ah lat-ah de ... | una lata de ... |

Can I taste it?
**pweh-doh pro-bahr-loh/lah?**     ¿Puedo probarlo/a?

Will this keep in the fridge?
**es de re-free-he-rah-see-on?**     ¿Es de refrigeración?

How much is (a kilogram of cheese)?
**kwon-toh kwes-tah ehl**     ¿Cuánto cuesta el (kilo de queso)?
**(ki-loh de ke-soh)?**

Do you have anything cheaper?
**tee-en-eh al-goh mas bahr-ah-toh?**     ¿Tiene algo más barato?

Is this the best you have?
**es-teh es ehl mekh-hor keh**     ¿Este es el mejor que tiene?
**tee-en-eh?**

What's the local speciality?
**kwahl es lah es-pes-ee-ah-lee-dahd**     ¿Cuál es la especialidad de la
**de lah re-hee-on/loh-kahl-ee-dahd?**     región/localidad?

Give me (half) a kilogram, please.
**meh dah (me-dee-oh) ki-loh,**     Me da (medio) kilo, por favor.
**por fah-vor**

I'd like (six slices of ham).
**kee-see-ehr-ah (seh-ees**     Quisiera (seis rebanadas
**re-ban-ah-dahs de ha-mon)**     de jamón).

## Making Your Own Meals

Where can I find the (sugar)?

**don-de pweh-doh en-kon-trahr**     *¿Dónde puedo encontrar*
**(ehl as-oo-kahr)?**     *(el azúcar)?*

| I'd like some ... | **kee-see-ehr-ah al-goh de ...** | *Quisiera algo de ...* |
|---|---|---|
| bread | **pahn** | *pan* |
| butter | **mahn-tek-il-yah** | *mantequilla* |
| cheese | **keh-soh** | *queso* |
| chocolate | **chok-oh-lah-te** | *chocolate* |
| eggs | **hway-vos** | *huevos* |
| flour | **ah-ree-nah** | *harina* |
| ham | **ha-mon** | *jamón* |
| honey | **mee-el** | *miel* |
| jam | **mer-mel-ah-dah** | *mermelada* |
| margarine | **mahr-gah-ree-nah** | *margarina* |
| marmalade | **mer-mel-ah-dah** | *mermelada* |
| milk | **le-che** | *leche* |
| olives | **a-say-too-nah** | *aceitunas* |
|   black | **neg-rah** | *negras* |
|   green | **ver-de** | *verdes* |
|   stuffed | **rel-ye-nas** | *rellenas* |
| olive/sunflower oil | **a-say-te de ol-ee-vah/ de hi-ra-sohl** | *aceite de oliva/ de girasol* |
| pepper | **pi-mee-en-tah** | *pimienta* |
| salt | **sal** | *sal* |
| sugar | **as-oo-kahr** | *azúcar* |
| yoghurt | **yog-ür** | *yogur* |

## At The Bar

Shall we go for a drink?

**keh tal see vah-mos a toh-mahr**     *¿Qué tal si vamos a tomar una*
**oon-ah ko-pah/oon trah-goh?**     *copa/un trago?*

Thanks, but I don't feel like it.

**grah-see-ahs, pe-roh no ten-goh**     *Gracias, pero no tengo ganas.*
**gah-nahs**

I'll buy you a drink.

**teh in-vee-toh oon-ah ko-pah/**     *Te invito una copa/un trago.*
**oon trah-goh**

What would you like?

**keh te gus-tah-ree-ah toh-mahr?**     *¿Qué te gustaría tomar?*

You can get the next one.
**too in-vee-tahs lah proks-ee-mah**          *Tú invitas la próxima.*

I'll have (a vodka and lemonade).
**ah mee meh trah-eh oon vod-kah**          *A mí me trae (un vodka y*
**ee lim-on-ah-dah**                                   *limonada).*

| I'll have/a ... | yoh kee-ehr-oh ... | Yo quiero ... |
|---|---|---|
| beer | oon-ah ser-veh-sah | *una cerveza* |
| brandy | oon bran-dee | *un brandy* |
| champagne | oon-ah sham-pan-yah | *una champaña* |
| cider | oon-ah see-drah | *una cidra* |
| cocktail | oon kok-tel | *un coctel* |
| liqueur | oon lee-kor | *un licor* |
| rum | oon ron | *un ron* |
| whisky | oon gwis-kee | *un wisky* |
| bottle of wine | oon-ah bo-tel-yah de vee-no | *una botella de vino* |
| glass of wine | oon-ah koh-pah de vee-no | *una copa de vino* |
| (two) glasses | (dos) ko-pahs | *(dos) copas* |

I'm next.
**yoh see-goh**                                        *Yo sigo.*

Excuse me.
**dees-kool-pe-meh**                                *Discúlpeme.*

I was here before this lady/gentleman.
**ye-geh ahn-tehs keh lah da-mah/**          *Llegué antes que la dama/*
**ehl kah-bal-yeh-roh**                             *el caballero.*

No ice.
**seen ee-el-oh**                                      *Sin hielo.*

Can I have ice?
**meh pweh-de trah-ehr ee-el-oh,**            *Me puede traer hielo.*

Where's the toilet?
**don-de es-tahn lohs bahn-yos?**             *¿Dónde están los baños?*

Is food available here?
**ai al-goh de koh-mehr ah-kee?**               *¿Hay algo de comer aquí?*

I don't drink (alcohol).
**no beb-oh (al-kol)**                               *No bebo (alcohol).*

Cheers.
**sal-ood**                                               *Salud.*

This is hitting the spot.
**es-toh meh es-tah kah-yehn-doh mahl**   *Esto me está cayendo mal.*

So, do you come here often?
**vee-en-e oos-tehd seh-gwee-doh
ah-kee?**

*Viene usted seguido aquí?*

One more and I'll be under the table.
**oon-ah mas ee tehr-mee-nahr-eh
de-bah-khoh de lah mes-ah**

*Una más y terminaré debajo de
la mesa.*

Same again.
**loh mees-moh**

*Lo mismo.*

I really, really love you.
**de vehr-dahd te ah-moh**

*De verdad, de verdad te amo.*

I'm a bit tired, I'd better get home.
**es-toy oon po-koh kahn-sah-doh/
dah, mekh-hor meh voy ah ka-sah**

*Estoy un poco cansado/a,
mejor me voy a casa.*

I'm feeling drunk.
**meh see-en-toh bohr-rah-choh/
chah**

*Me siento borracho/a.*

I think I've had one too many.
**kreh-oh keh yah tuv-eh
bas-tahn-tes**

*Creo que ya tuve bastantes.*

I'm pissed.
**es-toy as-tah ehl gor-roh**

*Estoy hasta el gorro.*

I feel ill.
**meh see-en-toh mahl**

*Me siento mal.*

I want to throw up.
**kee-ehr-oh voh-mee-tahr**

*Quiero vomitar.*

He/she's passed out.
**ehl/eh-yah es-tah pehr-dee-doh/
dah**

*Ella ya está perdido/a.*

I'm hung over.
**es-toy kroo-doh/dah**

*Estoy crudo/a.*

What did I do last night?
**keh ee-she a-noh-che?**

*¿Qué hice anoche?*

I'm never, ever drinking again.
**noon-kah ha-mahs vol-ve-reh
ah to-mar oo-nah go-ta mas**

Nunca, jamás, volveré a tomar
unagota más

The definite article (**la** or **el**, corresponding to 'the' in English) or indefinite article (**una** or **un**, corresponding to 'a' or 'one' in English) is included with each noun. Either the definite or indefinite article has been chosen according to the way the word is most likely to be used. Just remember, **el** becomes **un**, while **la** becomes **una**.

## A

| | | | |
|---|---|---|---|
| abattoir | *ehl mat-ah-deh-roh* | el | matadero |
| agriculture | *lah ag-ree-kool-too-rah* | la | agricultura |
| alcoholic sodas | *lahs beb-ee-das al-kol-lee-kas* | las | bebidas alcohólicas |
| ale | *lah ser-veh-sah* | la | cerveza |
| allspice | *lah pi-mee-en-tah ing-leh-sah* | la | pimienta inglesa |
| almond | *lahs al-men-dras* | las | almendras |
| amaretto | *ehl ah-mar-eht-toh* | el | amareto |
| anchovy | *lah ahn-cho-ah* | la | anchoa |
| angelica | *lah ee-ehr-bah ahn-gel-ee-kah* | la | hierba angélica |
| animals | *lohs ah-nee-mah-lehs* | los | animales |
| anise | *ehl ah-nees* | el | anís |
| aperitif | *ehl a-per-ee-tee-voh* | el | aperitivo |
| appetiser | *lohs bo-tan-ah; el en-tre-mes* | los | antojitos; el entremes |
| apples | *lahs man-tha-nas* | las | manzanas |
| apricot | *ehl chah-bac-ah-no* | el | chavacano |
| artichoke | *lah al-ka-cho-fa* | la | alcachofa |
| ashtray | *ehl se-ni-seh-roh* | el | cenicero |
| asparagus | *ehl es-parr-ah-go* | el | espárrago |
| aubergine | *lah be-ren-ken-ah* | la | berenjena |
| avocado | *ehl ag-wah-ka-te* | el | aguacate |
| awful | *or-reeb-leh* | | horrible |

## B

| | | | |
|---|---|---|---|
| bar | *un bahr* | un | bar |
| baby corn | *ehl eh-lot-eh* | el | elote |
| baby food | *lah kom-eed-ah deh beh-beh* | la | comida de bebé |
| bacon | *ehl toh-see-noh* | el | tocino |
| bacon (from the back) | *ehl toh-see-noh deh loh-moh* | el | tocino de lomo |
| bake | *orr-neh-arr* | | hornear |
| baked | *ahl orr-noh/orr-neh-ah-doh* | al | horno/horneado |
| baker | *ehl pahn-ah-der-oh* | el | panadero |
| bakery | *lah pahn-ah-der-ee-ah* | la | panadería |

| baking soda | *ehl bi-karh-bon-ah-toh de so-dee-oh* | el | bicarbonato de sodio |
| bamboo shoot | *lohs brot-ehs de bam-boo* | los | brotes de bambú |
| banana | *ehl plah-tahn-oh* | el | plátano |
| barbecue | *lah bahr-bah-koh-ah* | la | barbacoa |
| barbecue grill | *un a-sahd-or* | un | asador |
| barley | *lah se-ba-dah* | la | cebada |
| bass | *ehl rob-ah-loh* | el | robalo |
| batter | *lah mah-sah* | la | masa |
| bay | *ehl lah-oo-rel* | el | laurel |
| bean sprout | *ehl ger-meen-ah-doh de soh-yah* | el | germinado de soya |
| beef | *lah kar-ne de res* | la | carne de res |
| beef jerky | *lah mah-chah-kah* | la | machaca |
| beer | *lah ser-veh-sah* | la | cerveza |
| bees | *lahs abeh-khas* | las | abejas |
| beetroot | *ehl bet-ah-bel* | el | betabel |
| best | *ehl/lah me-khor* | el/la | mejor |
| betel | *lah ar-eh-kah* | la | areca |
| bill | *lah koo-ehn-tah* | la | cuenta |
| bird | *ehl pah-khah-roh* | el | pájaro |
| birthday | *lohs cum-ple-ahn-yohs* | los | cumpleaños |
| birthday cake | *ehl pahs-tel de cum-ple-ahn-yohs* | el | pastel de cumpleaños |
| bitter lemon | *ehl li-mon ahg-ree-oh* | el | limón agrio |
| bitters | *lah ser-ve-sah ah-mahr-gah* | la | cerveza amarga |
| black bean | *ehl free-gohl neg-roh* | el | frijol negro |
| black olive | *lah ah-say-too-nah neg-rah* | la | aceituna negra |
| black pudding | *lah mor-see-yah* | la | morcilla |
| black truffle | *lah troo-fah* | la | trufa |
| blackberry | *lah zahr-zah-mor-ah* | la | zarzamora |
| blender | *lah lee-koo-ah-dor-ah* | la | licuadora |
| blueberry | *ehl ah-rahn-dah-no* | el | arándano |
| boil | *her-bir* | | hervir |
| boiled | *her-bee-doh/ko-see-doh* | | hervido/cocido |
| bone | *ehl hway-soh* | el | hueso |
| borage | *lah bohr-rah-kah* | la | borraja |
| bottle opener | *ehl des-tah-pah-dor* | el | destapador |
| bourbon | *ehl gwis-kee dee sen-ten-oh* | el | whisky de centeno |
| bowl | *ehl plaht-on* | el | platón |
| braise | *koh-ser ah few-goh len-toh* | | cocer a fuego lento |
| bran | *ehl sahl-vah-doh* | el | salvado |
| brandy | *ehl bran-dee* | el | brandy |
| brazil nut | *lah noo-es del brah-sil* | la | nuez del Brasil |

| English | Pronunciation | Spanish |
|---------|---------------|---------|
| bread | *ehl pahn* | el pan |
| breakfast | *ehl des-ai-yoo-oh* | el desayuno |
| breast | *lah pech-oo-gah* | la pechuga |
| brill | *ehl ro-dab-ah-yoh* | el rodaballo |
| brilliant | *bree-yan-te/exs-eh-len-teh* | brillante/excelente |
| brisket | *kar-ney par-ah ah-sahr* | carne para asar |
| broad bean | *lah ahb-ah* | la haba |
| broccoli | *ehl brok-o-lee* | el brócoli |
| broth | *ehl kahl-doh* | el caldo |
| brown lentil | *lahs len-tek-as* | las lentejas |
| brown rice | *ehl ah-rros in-teg-ral* | el arroz integral |
| brussels sprouts | *lahs kol-es de broo-sel-as* | las coles de Bruselas |
| bubble | *lah bur-boo-kah* | la burbuja |
| buckwheat | *ehl al-fohr-fon* | el alforfón |
| bull | *ehl to-roh* | el toro |
| butcher | *ehl kahr-nee-she-roh* | el carnicero |
| butter | *lah man-tek-il-yah* | la mantequilla |
| butter bean | *lah hoo-dee-ah blan-kah* | la judía blanca |
| buttermilk | *ehl swe-roh de lah le-chay* | el suero de leche |
| butterscotch | *ehl dul-say de as-oo-kahr kon man-tek-il-yah* | el dulce de azúcar con mantequilla |
| to buy | *komp-rahr* | comprar |

## C

| English | Pronunciation | Spanish |
|---------|---------------|---------|
| cabbage | *lah kol; ehl re-pol-yoh* | la col; el repollo |
| café | *kaf-eh* | café |
| cake | *ehl pas-tel* | el pastel |
| cake shop | *lah pas-tel-er-ee-ah* | la pastelería |
| can (aluminium) | *lah lat-ah* | la lata |
| can opener | *ehl ah-bray-lah-tas* | el abrelatas |
| candy | *ehl dul-say* | el dulce |
| cantaloupe | *ehl me-lon* | el melón |
| capers | *lah al-kah-pah-rrah* | la alcaparra |
| caramel | *ehl kara-me-loh* | caramelo |
| caraway seed | *lohs karh-vees* | los carvis |
| cardamom | *ehl kahr-dah-moh-moh* | el cardomomo |
| cardoon | *ehl kahr-doh* | el cardo |
| carrot | *lah zan-a-or-ee-ah* | la zanahoria |
| cashew | *ehl ah-nah-karh-doh* | el anacardo |
| cauliflower | *lah kol-i-flor* | la coliflor |
| caviare | *kav-ee-ahr* | el caviar |

| English | Pronunciation | Gender | Spanish |
|---|---|---|---|
| cayenne | *ehl chee-lay kay-en-ah* | el | chile cayena |
| celeriac | *ehl a-pee-oh/nab-oh* | el | apio/nabo |
| celery seed | *sem-ee-yah de a-pee-oh* | | semilla de apio |
| cereal | *ehl ser-ee-al* | el | cereal |
| chair | *lah see-yah* | la | silla |
| champagne | *ehl cab-ah; lah sham-pan-yah* | el | cava; la champaña |
| chanterelle | *ehl mees-kah-loh* | el | mízcalo |
| chargrilled | *ahl karb-ohn* | al | carbón |
| chayote | *ehl cha-yoh-te* | el | chayote |
| cheese | *ehl ke-soh* | el | queso |
| blue | *a-sul* | | azul |
| cottage | *ehl rek-wes-on* | | requesón |
| cream | *krem-ah* | | crema |
| goat's | *de ka-bra* | | de cabra |
| hard | *doo-roh* | | duro |
| semi-firm | *may-dee-oh doo-roh* | | medio duro |
| soft | *blan-doh* | | blando |
| chef | *ehl chef* | el | chef (m) |
| cherry | *lah se-ray-sah* | la | cereza |
| cherry tomatoes | *mi-nee hi-to-mah-tes dul-ses* | las | mini jitomates dulces |
| chervil | *ehl per-i-fol-yoh* | el | perifollo |
| chestnut | *lah kas-tan-yha* | la | castaña |
| chewing gum | *ehl chic-leh* | el | chicle |
| chick pea | *ehl gar-ban-soh* | el | garbanzo |
| chicken | *ehl pohl-yoh* | el | pollo |
| chicory | *lah a-chi-ko-ria* | la | achicoria |
| chilli | *ehl chi-leh* | el | chile |
| chilli sauce | *lah sal-sah pee-kahn-te; ehl a-khi* | la | salsa picante; el ají |
| Chinese cabbage | *lah kol chi-nah* | la | col china |
| chips | *pa-pas ah lah fran-se-sah* | | papas a la francesa |
| chive | *lohs se-bol-yeen-ehs* | los | cebollinos |
| chocolate | *ehl chok-oh-lah-tay* | el | chocolate |
| chopping board | *lah tab-lah – ehl tron-koh* | la | tabla; el tronco |
| chops | *lahs choo-let-tah de kar-ne* | las | chuletas de carne |
| porkchops | *lahs choo-let-tah de ser-doh* | las | chuletas de cerdo |
| chopsticks | *lohs pal-il-yos chee-nos* | los | palitos chinos |
| chorizo | *ehl choh-ree-soh* | el | chorizo |
| chowder | *lah so-pah/kre-mah* | la | sopa/crema |
| Christmas Day | *lah nahv-ee-dahd* | la | Navidad |
| Christmas Eve | *lah no-cheh-bwehn-ah* | la | Nochebuena |
| chump | *lah kar-ne de ka-deh-rah* | la | carne de cadera |
| cider | *lah si-drah* | la | cidra |

| English | Pronunciation | | Spanish |
|---|---|---|---|
| cilantro | *ehl sil-ahn-troh* | el | cilantro |
| cinnamon | *lah kan-el-ah* | la | canela |
| citrus | *ehl si-tree-koh* | el | cítrico |
| clam | *lah al-meh-kah* | la | almeja |
| clove | *ehl kla-voh* | el | clavo |
| cockerel | *ehl gal-yee-toh* | el | gallito |
| cockle | *ehl ber-ber-ech-oh* | el | berberecho |
| cocktail | *ehl kok-tel* | el | cóctel |
| cocoa | *lah koh-koh-ah* | la | cocoa |
| coconut | *ehl koh-koh* | el | coco |
| cod | *ehl bak-al-ow* | el | bacalao |
| coffee | *ehl ka-fay* | el | café |
| coffee grinder | *ehl mohl-ee-noh de ka-fay* | el | molino de café |
| coffee machine | *lah ma-kee-nah de ka-fay* | la | maquina de café |
| coke | *koh-kah* | | coca-cola (coca) |
| cold (adj) | *free-oh/ahh* | | frío/a |
| cold water | *ehl ag-wah free-ah* | el | agua fría |
| condiments (incl. spices) | *lohs kon-dee-men-tohs* | | condimentos |
| conserves | *lohs kon-ser-va-dohr-es* | los | conservadores |
| consomme | *ehl kon-som-e* | el | consomé |
| cookies | *lahs gal-yet-ahs* | las | galletas |
| coriander | *ehl sil-ahn-troh* | el | cilantro |
| cork | *un kor-choh* | un | corcho |
| corn | *ehl may-iz* | el | maíz |
| corn flakes | *lahs oh-kwel-ahs de may-iz* | las | hojuelas de maíz |
| cornmeal | *lah ah-ree-nah de may-iz* | la | harina de maíz |
| courgette | *ehl ka-lab-ah-síhn* | el | calabacín |
| couscous | *ehl kus-kus* | el | cuscús |
| crab | *ehl kan-gre-koh* | el | congrejo |
| cracked wheat | *ehl tree-goh res-kwe-brah-doh* | el | trigo resquebrado |
| cranberry | *ehl ah-rahn-dah-noh* | el | arándano |
| cranberry sauce | *lah sal-sah de ah-rah-dah-noh* | la | salsa de arándano |
| crayfish | *lah ha-ee-ba de ree-oh* | la | jaiba de rio |
| cream | *lah kre-mah/nat-ah* | la | crema/nata |
| clotted cream | *lah kre-mah es-pes-ah* | la | crema espesa |
| sour cream | *lah kre-mah a-si-dah* | la | crema ácida |
| whipping cream | *lah kre-mah bat-ee-dah* | la | crema batida |
| crème caramel | *flan* | | flan |
| cress | | | berro |
| croissant | *ehl ber-roh* | el | cuerno |
| croquette | *ehl kwer-noh* | la | croqueta |
| | *elah krok-et-ah* | | |

| English | Pronunciation | Spanish |
|---|---|---|
| cucumber | *ehl pep-ee-noh* | el pepino |
| cumin | *ehl kohm-ee-noh* | el comino |
| cup | *lah ta-sah* | la taza |
| cure | *lah ku-rah* | la cura |
| currant | *lah grow-sel-yah* | la grosella |
| curry | *ehl kur-ree* | el curry |
| curry powder | *ehl pohl-voh de kur-ree* | el polvo de curry |
| cutlery | *lohs koo-bee-her-tos* | los cubiertos |
| cutlet | *oon-ah choo-let-ah* | una chuleta |
| to celebrate | *fes-teh-har* | festejar |
| to celebrate (an event) | *se-leh-brar* | celebrar |

## D

| English | Pronunciation | Spanish |
|---|---|---|
| a dozen | *oo-nah do-se-nah* | una docena |
| a drink | *oo-nah koh-pah* | una copa |
| dab | *un poh-kee-toh* | un poquito |
| (to go on) a date | *(ten-er) oo-nah see-tah* | (tener) una cita |
| dates | *daht-il-es* | los dátiles |
| deep-fry | *fray-ir* | freir |
| deer | *ehl see-er-voh/ven-ad-oh* | el ciervo/venado |
| delicatessen | *lah sal-chee-choh-neh-ree-ah fee-nah* | la salchichonería fina |
| dental floss | *ehl eeh-loh dent-al* | el hilo dental |
| dessert | *ehl pos-tray* | el postre |
| dessert spoon | *lah koo-cha-ree-tah de pos-tray* | la cucharadita de postre |
| dewberry | *lah zar-zam-or-ah* | la zarzamora |
| diabetic | *dee-ah-be-tee-koh/kah* | diabético/a |
| diarrhoea | *lah dee-ahr-reh-ah* | la diarrea |
| dill | *ehl e-nel-doh* | el eneldo |
| dining car | *ehl va-gon* | el vagón restaurante |
| dinner | *lah se-nah* | la cena |
| set dinner | *lah koh-mee-dah* | comida |
| dirty | *soo-see-oh/ah* | sucio/a |
| donkey | *ehl bur-roh* | el burro |
| dried fruit | *lahs froo-tahs se-kahs* | las frutas secas |
| drinks | *lahs beb-ee-das* | las bebidas |
| duck | *ehl pa-toh* | el pato |
| dummy (baby's) | *un choo-pon* | un chupón |
| dumplings | *ehl boo-din* | el budín |
| to drink | *beb-er/toh-mar* | beber/tomar |

## E

| each | *ka-dah* | | cada |
| earth | *lah tee-ehr-rah* | la | tierra |
| Easter | *lah pas-koo-ah;* | | Pascua; |
| | *se-ma-nahsan-tah* | | Semana Santa |
| eel | *lah ahn-gwee-lah* | la | anguila |
| egg custard | *flan* | | flan |
| eggplant | *lah be-ren-ken-ah* | la | berenjena |
| eggs | *lohs blan-kee-yos/hwe-vos* | los | blanquillos/huevos |
| endive | *lah en-dib-ee-ah* | la | endibia |
| enough | *bahs-tan-te/soo-fee-see-en-teh* | | bastante/suficiente |
| environment | *ehl med-ee-oh am-bee-ehn-teh* | el | medio ambiente |
| excellent | *eks-eh-len-te/* | | excelente/ |
| | *fan-tas-tee-koh/kah* | | fantástico/a |
| eye | *ehl o-koh* | el | ojo |
| to eat | *kom-er* | | comer |

## F

| farm | *lah gran-ha* | la | granja |
| farmer | *ehl ag-ree-kool-tohr;* | el | agricultor; |
| | *lah ag-ree-kool-toh-rah* | la | agricultora |
| fat | *gor-doh/dah* | | gordo/a |
| fennel | *ehl in-ok-oh* | el | hinojo |
| fennel seed | *lah sem-ee-yah de in-ok-oh* | la | semilla de hinojo |
| fenugreek | *al-or-ah/fe-neh-greh-koh* | | alhora/fenegreco |
| fig | *ehl ee-goh* | el | higo |
| fillet | *ehl fil-et-ay* | el | filete |
| first course | *lah en-trah-dah* | la | entrada |
| fish (alive) | *ehl pes* | el | pez |
| fish (as food) | *ehl pes-kah-doh* | el | pescado |
| fish shop | *lah pes-kah-der-ee-yah* | la | pescadería |
| flank | *ehl ee-har* | el | ijar |
| flavour | *ehl sa-bor* | el | sabor |
| flounder | *lah plah-tee-ha* | la | platija |
| flour | *lah ah-ree-nah* | la | harina |
| flower | *lah flor* | la | flor |
| food processor | *lah mes-klah-dor-ah* | la | mezcladora |
| food | *lah ko-mee-dah* | la | comida |
| fork | *ehl ten-e-dor* | el | tenedor |
| frankfurter | *lah sal-chee-chah* | la | salchicha |

| English | Pronunciation | | Spanish |
|---|---|---|---|
| free-range | de gran-ha | de | granja |
| fresh | fres-kah - koh | | fresca/o |
| fresh garden pea | lah a-rah-veh-ha | la | araveja |
| fresh juice | ehl hoo-goh fres-koh | el | jugo fresco |
| fried | free-toh | | frito |
| frog | lah rah-nah | la | rana |
| fruit cake | ehl pas-tel de froo-tahs | el | pastel de frutas |
| fruit juice | ehl hoo-goh de froo-tahs | el | jugo de fruta |
| fruit punch | ehl pon-chay de froo-tahs | el | ponche de frutas |
| fry | fray-ir | | freir |
| frying pan | ehl sahr-ten | el | sartén |

## G

| English | Pronunciation | | Spanish |
|---|---|---|---|
| game | ka-sah | | caza |
| garlic | ah-khoh | el | ajo |
| garlic press | ehl ex-prim-i-dor de ah-khoh | el | exprimidor de ajo |
| gelatin | lah gel-at-ee-nah | la | gelatina |
| gherkin | ehl pep-in-il-yoh | el | pepinillo |
| giblets | lohs men-oo-dil-yos | los | menudillos |
| gin | lah hin-eb-rah | la | ginebra |
| ginger | ehl hen-ee-bray | el | jengibre |
| glutinous rice | ehl ah-rros gloot-in-oh-soh | el | arroz glutinoso |
| goat | lah ka-bra/chi-vah | la | cabra/chiva |
| good restaurant | un boo-en res-tor-an-tay | un | buen restaurante |
| goose | ehl gan-soh | el | ganso |
| gooseberry | lah grow-sel-yah es-pee-noh-sah | la | grosella espinosa |
| gram | gram-oh | | gramo |
| grapefruit | oon-ah tor-on-ha | una | tonronja |
| grapes | lahs oo-bahs | las | uvas |
| grappa | di-ges-tee-voh it-al-ee-ah-noh | | digestivo Italiano |
| to grate | ral-yahr | | rallar |
| grater | ehl ral-yah-dor | el | rallador |
| gravy | sal-sah | la | salsa |
| grayling | ehl tee-mah-loh | el | tímalo |
| green capsicum | ehl pee-men-ton | el | pimentón |
| green lentil | lah len-tek-ah ver-deh | la | lenteja verde |
| green olive | lah a-say-too-nah ver-day | la | aceituna verde |
| green pepper | ehl pee-men-ton | el | pimentón |
| green split pea | ehl chi-cha-roh se-koh | el | chícharo seco |
| greengrocer | lah ver-dul-her-ee-ah/ froo-the-ree-ah | la | verdulería/frutería |

| greens | *lahs ver-doo-ras* | las | verduras |
| to grill | *ah-sahr* | | asar |
| grilled | *a-sa-doh/ah lah par-ril-yah* | | asado/a la parilla |
| guava | *lah gwa-yah-bah* | la | guayaba |
| guinea pig | *ehl kon-eh-hee-yoh de in-dee-ahs* | el | conejillo de indias |

## H

| haddock | *ehl a-bah-deh-ho* | el | abadejo |
| hake | *mer-loo-sah* | la | merluza |
| half a litre | *un med-ee-oh lee-troh* | un | medio litro |
| half | *med-ee-oh/ah* | | medio/a |
| halibut | *ehl ah-lee-boot* | el | halibut |
| ham | *ehl ha-mon* | el | jamón |
| hamburger | *lah am-bür-gway-sah* | la | hamburguesa |
| handmade | *eh-cho a ma-noh* | | hecho a mano |
| hare | *lah lee-eb-ray* | la | liebre |
| haricot bean | *lah a-loo-bee-ah* | la | alubía |
| hazelnut | *lah av-el-yah-nah* | la | avellana |
| heart | *ehl ko-ra-son* | el | corazón |
| heat | *ehl kal-ohr* | el | calor |
| hen | *lah gal-yee-nah* | la | gallina |
| herbalist | *lah/ehl ee-er-ber-ah/oh* | la/el | hierbera/o |
| herbs | *lahs ee-er-bas* | las | hierbas |
| herring | *ehl a-ren-kay* | el | arenque |
| hominy | *ehl may-iz moh-lee-doh* | el | maíz molido |
| honey | *lah mee-el* | la | miel |
| horseradish | *ehl rab-ah-noh pee-kan-teh* | el | rábano picante |
| hot (temperature) | *kal-ee-en-tay* | | caliente |
| hot (food) | *pi-kahn-te/pi-koh-soh/sah* | | picante/picoso/a |
| hot water | *ehl ag-wah kal-ee-en-tay* | el | agua caliente |
| to be hungry | *ten-er am-breh* | | tener hambre |
| to have | *ten-er* | | tener |

## I

| ice | *ehl ee-el-oh* | el | hielo |
| icecream | *un el-ah-doh* | un | helado |
| icing sugar | *ehl as-oo-kahr glas* | el | azúcar glass |
| ingredient | *in-gred-ee-en-tay* | | ingrediente |

## J

| English | Pronunciation | Spanish |
|---|---|---|
| Jalapeno pepper | *ehl chi-leh hal-ah-pen-yoh* | el chile jalapeño |
| jam | *lah mer-mel-ah-dah* | la mermelada |
| jelly | *lah mer-mel-ah-dah* | la mermelada |
| Jerusalem artichoke | *ehl top-ee-nam-bür* | el topinambur |
| juice | *ehl zu-moh/hoo-goh* | el zumo/jugo |
| juicer | *ehl ex-prim-i-dor de hoo-gohs* | el exprimidor de jugos |
| juniper | *ehl eneb-roh* | el enebro |

## K

| English | Pronunciation | Spanish |
|---|---|---|
| kettle | *lah ol-yah pa-rah er-vear ag-wah* | la olla para hervir agua |
| kidney | *un rin-yon* | un riñón |
| kilogram | *un ki-loh* | un kilo |
| kipper | *ehl a-ren-kay a-oo-mah-doh* | el arenque ahumado |
| kitchen | *lah ko-see-nah* | la cocina |
| kiwi | *ehl ki-wee* | el kiwi |
| knife | *un koo-chee-yoh* | un cuchillo |
| boning | *un koo-chee-yoh pa-rah des-weh-sahr* | un cuchillo para deshuesar |
| bread | *un koo-chee-yoh pa-rah pan* | un cuchillo para pan |
| butter | *un koo-chee-yoh pa-rah man-tek-il-yah* | un cuchillo para mantequilla |
| carving | *un koo-chee-yoh pa-rah trin-chahr* | un cuchillo para trinchar |
| paring | *un koo-chee-yoh pa-rah pel-ahr* | un cuchillo para pelar |
| serrated | *un ku-chee-yoh de see-her-rah* | un cuchillo de sierra |
| knuckle | *ehl noo-dee-yoh* | el nudillo |
| kosher | *per-mi-tee-doh por lah lay hoo-dee-ah* | permitido por la ley judía |
| kumquat | *lah na-ran-kah chin-ah* | la naranja china |
| to kill | *mat-ahr* | matar |

## L

| English | Pronunciation | Spanish |
|---|---|---|
| ladle | *ehl koo-chah-ron* | el cucharón |
| lager | *lah-ger* | lager |
| lamb | *ehl kor-deh-roh* | el cordero |
| land | *lah tee-er-rah* | la tierra |
| lard | *lah man-teh-kah* | la manteca |

| | | | |
|---|---|---|---|
| lavender | *lah lav-an-dah* | la | lavanda |
| leek | *ehl pwer-roh* | el | puerro |
| leg | *lah pee-er-nah* | la | pierna |
| legumes | *lah leg-oom-bray* | la | legumbre |
| lemon | *ehl li-mon* | el | limón |
| lemon balm | *ehl bal-sa-moh de li-mon* | el | bálsamo de limón |
| lemonade | *lah lim-on-ah-dah* | la | limonada |
| lime | *lah li-mah* | la | lima |
| liqueur | *ehl li-kor* | el | licor |
| liquorice | *ehl reg-ah-lis* | el | regaliz |
| liver | *ehl ee-gah-doh* | el | hígado |
| lobster | *lah lan-gos-tah* | la | langosta |
| loin | *ehl loh-moh* | el | lomo |
| lunch | *ehl al-mwer-so/lah koh-mee-dah* | el | almuerzo; la comida |
| set lunch | *ehl koo-bee-her-toh* | | cubierto |
| lunchtime | *oh-rah deh lah ko-mee-dah* | | hora de la comida |
| lychee | *ehl li-che* | el | lichi |

## M

| | | | |
|---|---|---|---|
| macadamia | *lah noo-es de mak-a-day-mee-ah* | la | nuez de macadamia |
| mace | *lah ma-sis* | la | macis |
| mackerel | *lah kah-bal-yah* | la | caballa |
| madeira | *ehl vee-noh de ma-deh-ee-rah* | el | vino de Madeira |
| main course | *ehl plat-oh preen-see-pal* | el | plato principal |
| mandarin | *lah man-da-ree-nah* | la | mandarina |
| mangetout pea | *ehl chi-cha-roh mol-yar* | el | chícharo mollar |
| mango | *un man-goh* | un | mango |
| margarine | *lah mahr-gah-ree-nah* | la | margarina |
| marinades | *lahs mahr-een-ah-das* | las | marinadas |
| to marinate | *mahr-een-ar* | | marinar |
| marjoram | *lah mek-or-ah-nah* | la | mejorana |
| market | *ehl mer-kah-doh* | el | mercado |
| marmalade | *lah mer-mel-ah-dah* | la | mermelada |
| marrow | *ehl too-eh-tah-no* | el | tuétano |
| marzipan | *ehl maz-ah-pan* | el | mazapán |
| mayonnaise | *lah lah may-on-ay-sah* | la | mayonesa |
| meal | *lah koh-mee-dah* | | comida |
| medium (cooked) | *med-ee-oh* | | medio |

| English | Pronunciation | Spanish |
|---|---|---|
| melon | *me-lon* | el melón |
| menu | *un men-oo; lah kahr-tah* | un menú; la carta |
| meringue | *ehl mer-en-gay* | el merengue |
| milk | *lah le-chay* | la leche |
| skimmed milk | *lah le-chay des-krem-ah-dah* | la leche descremada |
| millet | *ehl mee-kho* | el mijo |
| mince | *pee-kahr* | picar |
| mincer | *ehl pee-kah-dor* | el picador |
| mineral water | *ehl ag-wah min-er-al* | el agua mineral |
| mint | *lah men-tah* | la menta |
| mixing bowl | *ehl re-see-pee-en-the pa-rah mes-klahr* | el recipiente para mezclar |
| morel | *kah-gar-ree-ah (on-goh)* | cagarria (hongo) |
| mortar | *ehl molk-ah-keh-te* | el molcajete |
| muesli | *ehl moo-es-lee* | el muesli |
| mulberry | *lah mo-rah; ehl mo-rahl* | la mora; el moral |
| multi-course meal | *kom-eed-ah kom-plet-ah* | comida completa |
| mung bean | *lah se-mee-yah or-ee-en-tal* | la semilla oriental |
| mussel | *ehl mek-il-yon* | el mejillón |
| mustard | *lah mos-ta-sah* | la mostaza |
| mutton | *ehl kor-deh-roh* | el cordero |

## N

| English | Pronunciation | Spanish |
|---|---|---|
| napkin | *lah ser-vil-yet-ah* | la servilleta |
| near | *ser-cah* | cerca |
| nearby restaurant | *un res-tor-an-tay ser-kee-tah* | un restaurante cerquita |
| neck | *ehl kwel-yoh* | el cuello |
| net | *lah re-ehd* | la red |
| noisy | *rwee-doh-sah - ah* | ruidosa/o |
| noodles | *lohs fe-day-os* | los fideos |
| nougat | *ehl too-rron* | el turrón |
| nutcracker | *lahs kas-kah-noo-eh-sehs* | las cascanueces |
| nutmeg | *lah noo-ehs mos-kah-dah* | la nuez moscada |

## O

| English | Pronunciation | Spanish |
|---|---|---|
| oatmeal | *lah av-ay-nah* | la avena |
| octopus | *ehl pul-poh* | el pulpo |
| offal | *lohs des-poh-kohs* | los despojos |

| English | Pronunciation | Spanish |
|---|---|---|
| oil (cooking) | *ehl a-ay-tay* | el aceite |
| olive oil | *ehl a-say-tay de ol-ee-vah* | el aceite de oliva |
| olives | *lah a-say-too-nahs* | las aceitunas |
| omelette | *ehl om-eh-let* | el omelete |
| oregano | *ehl or-eh-gah-no* | el orégano |
| organic | *or-gan-ik-oh – ah* | orgánico/a |
| oven | *ehl orr-no* | el horno |
| ox | *ehl boo-ay* | el buey |
| oxtail | *ehl ra-boh de boo-ay* | el rabo de buey |
| oyster | *lah os-trah* | la ostra |

## P

| English | Pronunciation | Spanish |
|---|---|---|
| pan | *oo-na kah-sway-lah – kah-ceh-roh-lah* | una cazuela; cacerola |
| papaya | *lah pa-pay-ah* | la papaya |
| paprika | *ehl pee-men-ton pah-pree-kah* | el pimentón paprika |
| parma ham | *ehl ha-mon par-meh-sah-no* | el jamón parmesano |
| parsley | *ehl per-ek-il* | el perejil |
| parsnip | *lah chir-iv-ee-ah* | la chirivía |
| passion fruit | *lah gra-nah-dil-yah* | la granadilla |
| pasta | *lah pahs-tah* | la pasta |
| pastrami | *ehl pas-tra-nee* | el pastrami |
| pastry | *ehl pas-tel-ee-toh* | el pastelito |
| patisserie | *oo-nah pas-tel-er-ee-ah* | una pastelería |
| peach | *ehl doo-rahs-noh* | el durazno |
| peanut | *ehl ka-kah-wah-teh* | el cacahuete |
| pears | *lahs peh-rahs* | las peras |
| pecan | *lah noo-es pah-kah-nah* | la nuez pacana |
| peeler | *ehl pel-ah-dohr* | el pelador |
| pepper | *lah pi-mee-en-tah* | la pimienta |
| peppermint | *lah men-tah* | la menta |
| pepperoni | *ehl pep-eh-ron-ee* | el pepperoni |
| perch | *lah pehr-kah* | la perca |
| pestle | *lah ma-noh de mohr-tehr-oh* | la mano de mortero |
| pheasant | *ehl fai-san* | el faisán |
| pickle | *pep-ee-noh* | un pepino |
| pickled | *en ah-doh-boh* | en adobo |
| pickling onion | *lahs se-bol-yahs en vin-a-greh* | las cebollas en vinagre |
| picnic | *un pik-nik* | un picnic |
| pig | *ehl ser-doh* | el cerdo |
| pigeon | *lah pa-lom-ah* | la paloma |

| English | Pronunciation | Spanish |
|---|---|---|
| pike | *ehl loo-see-oh* | el lucio |
| pinenut | *ehl peen-yon* | el piñón |
| pineapple | *lah peen-yah* | la piña |
| pinto bean | *lah hoo-dee-ah peen-tah* | la judía pinta |
| pistachio | *ehl pis-tach-oh* | el pistacho |
| plaice | *lah plat-ee-kah* | la platija |
| plain flour | *ah-ree-nah blan-koh* | harina blanco |
| plant | *oo-na plan-tah* | una planta |
| to plant | *sem-brahr* | sembrar |
| plate | *un plat-oh* | un plato |
| plum | *lah si-roo-el-ah* | la ciruela |
| plum tomatoes | *ehl hee-tom-ah-tay* | el jitomate |
| poach | *es-kal-fahr* | escalfar |
| polenta | *pohl-en-tah* | la polenta |
| pomegranate | *lah gran-ah-dah* | la granada |
| popcorn | *lahs pah-lom-ee-tas (de may-iz)* | las palomitas (de maíz) |
| poppy | *lah ah-mah-pol-ah* | la amapola |
| pork | *lah kar-nay de ser-doh* | la carne de cerdo |
| pork sausages | *ehl choh-ree-soh* | el chorizo |
| port | *ehl o-por-toh* | el oporto |
| pot | *lah ol-yah* | la olla |
| potato masher | *ehl a-plas-tah-dohr de pa-pas* | el aplastador de papas |
| potatoes | *lahs pa-pas* | las papas |
| poultry | *lahs av-es* | las aves |
| prawn | *ehl kam-ah-ron* | el camarón |
| preservative | *ehl kon-ser-vah-dohr* | el conservador |
| pressure cooker | *lah ol-yah de pres-see-on* | la olla de presión |
| prune | *lah si-roo-el-ah pa-sah* | la ciruela pasa |
| puffball | *un pas-tel de krem-ah* | un pastel de crema |
| pulses | *lahs leg-oom-brays* | las legumbres |
| pumpkin | *lah ka-lab-ah-sah* | la calabaza |

## Q

| English | Pronunciation | Spanish |
|---|---|---|
| quail | *lah kod-or-nees* | la codorniz |
| quality | *kah-li-dahd* | la calidad |
| quarter | *un kwahr-toh* | un cuarto |
| quince | *ehl mem-bril-yoh* | el membrillo |

## R

| English | Pronunciation | Spanish |
|---|---|---|
| rabbit | *ehl kon-eh-kho* | el conejo |
| radish | *rab-an-oh* | el rábano |

| English | Pronunciation | Spanish |
|---|---|---|
| raisin | *lahs pas-ahs* | las pasas |
| rare (cooked) | *un kwahr-toh* | un cuarto |
| raspberry | *lah fram-bway-sah* | la frambuesa |
| raw | *kroo-dah - oh* | cruda/o |
| receipt | *ehl re-see-boh* | el recibo |
| red cabbage | *lah kol roh-kah* | la col roja |
| red capsicum (pepper) | *ehl pee-men-ton roh-koh* | el pimentón rojo |
| red kidney bean | *lohs free-kohl-es neh-gros* | los frijoles negros |
| red lentil | *lah len-the-kah roh-kah* | la lenteja roja |
| red onion | *la se-bol-yah* | la cebolla roja |
| red pepper | *ehl pee-men-ton roh-koh* | el pimentón rojo |
| reservation | *lah re-serv-ah-see-on* | la reservación |
| restaurant | *un res-tor-an-tay* | un restaurante |
| rhubarb | *ehl rwee-bar-doh* | el ruíbarbo |
| ribs | *lahs kos-til-yas* | las costillas |
| rice | *ehl ah-rros ...* | el arroz ... |
| brown | *in-teg-ral* | integral |
| glutinous | *gluh-tee-noh-soh* | glutinoso |
| short-grain | *de grah-noh kor-toh* | de grano corto |
| wild | *sal-vak-hat* | salvaje |
| rice pudding | *ah-rros kon lay-che* | arroz con leche |
| ripe | *mah-doo-roh* | maduro |
| roast | *rost-ee-sahr* | rostizar |
| roasted | *rost-ee-sah-doh* | rostizado |
| rocket | *har-ah-mah-goh* | el jaramago |
| rolled oats | *lah av-ay-nah* | la avena |
| rolling pin | *ehl rod-ee-yoh* | el rodillo |
| rosemary | *ehl ro-meh-roh* | el romero |
| rum | *ehl ron* | el ron |
| rump | *ehl loh-moh* | el lomo |
| runner bean | *lah hoo-dee-ah es-kar-lah-tah* | la judía escarlata |
| rye whisky | *ehl gwis-kee kan-ah-dee-en-say* | whiskey canadiense |
| to reserve (a table) | *re-serv-ahr* | reservar |

## S

| English | Pronunciation | Spanish |
|---|---|---|
| a smell | *un oh-lohr* | un olor |
| saffron | *ehl az-ah-fran* | el azafrán |
| sage | *lah sal-vee-ah* | la salvía |
| sago | *ehl sa-goo* | el sagú |

| English | Pronunciation | | Spanish |
|---|---|---|---|
| sake | *ehl sah-keh* | el | sake |
| salad | *lah en-sah-lah-dah* | la | ensalada |
| salad bowl | *lah en-sah-lah-day-rah* | la | ensaladera |
| salami | *ehl sal-ah-mee* | el | salami |
| salmon | *ehl sal-mon* | el | salmón |
| salt | *lah sal* | la | sal |
| salt and pepper mills | *ehl mol-een-eh-roh* | el | molinero |
| salted pork | *lah kar-nay de pwer-koh sah-lah-dah* | la | carne de cerdo salada |
| sandwich | *ehl sand-gwich* | el | sandwich |
| sardine | *lahs sahr-di-as* | las | sardinas |
| sauce | *lah sal-sah* | la | salsa |
| saucepan | *ehl sahr-ten* | el | sartén |
| to sauté | *sal-teer-ahr* | | saltear |
| savoury | *sal-ah-doh - ah* | | salado/a |
| scales | *la pe-sah* | la | pesa |
| scallions | *lah se-bol-yah lahr-gah* | la | cebolla larga |
| scallop | *ehl fes-ton* | el | festón |
| scampi | *lahs gam-bas* | las | gambas |
| scissors | *lahs tik-her-as* | las | tijeras |
| sea vegetables | *lah al-gah* | la | alga |
| seafood | *lohs mar-is-kos* | | mariscos |
| second/main course | *ehl seg-oon-doh plat-oh – ehl plat-oh fwer-teh* | | segundo plato; plato fuerte |
| semolina | *lah sem-ol-ah* | la | sémola |
| service | *`ehl ser-vi-see-oh* | el | servicio |
| sesame seed | *lahs sem-ee-yahs de ses-amo* | las | semillas de sesamé |
| set menu | *lah koh-mee-dah koh-ree-dah* | la | comida corrida |
| shallot onion | *ehl cha-lot-eh* | el | chalote |
| to shallow-fry | *fray-ir* | | freir |
| shandy | *ehl pen-ah-cheh* | el | penaché |
| shank | *ehl tah-yoh* | el | tallo |
| sharpening stone | *ehl ah-fee-lah-dohr* | el | afilador |
| shellfish | *lohs mar-is-kos* | los | mariscos |
| sherry | *he-res* | el | jerez |
| shin | *ha-rreh-teh* | el | jarrete |
| short-grain rice | *ah-rros de gra-noh kohr-toh* | | arroz de grano corto |
| shoulder | *ehl loh-moh* | el | lomo |
| shrimp | *lohs kam-ah-roh-nes* | los | camarones |
| sieve | *ehl kol-a-dor* | el | colador |
| to sift | *ser-neer* | | cernir |

| simmer | *ko-ser a fwe-goh len-toh* | | cocer a fuego lento |
| sirloin | *ehl seer-leeh-on* | el | sirloin |
| size (of anything) | *ehl tam-ah-nyo* | el | tamaño |
| skewer | *lah broh-che-tah* | la | brocheta |
| small | *pay-keh-nya -o* | | pequeña/o |
| smoke | *ehl oo-moh* | el | humo |
| smoked | *a-oo-mah-doh* | | ahumado |
| snacks | *lohs an-toh-hee-tohs* | los | antojitos |
| snap peas | *lohs chi-chah-rohs ver-days* | los | chícharos verdes |
| snapper | *ehl gwa-chin-an-goh* | el | huachinango |
| soda water | *ehl ag-wah min-er-al* | el | agua mineral |
| soft drink | *ehl re-fres-koh* | el | refresco |
| sole | *ehl len-goo-ah-doh* | el | lenguado |
| soup | *lah so-pah* | la | sopa |
| soup spoon | *lah koo-chah-rah pa-rah so-pah* | la | cuchara para sopa |
| soya bean | *lah sem-ee-yah de sol-yah* | la | semilla de soya |
| soya sauce | *lah sal-sah de sol-yah; lah sal-sah chin-ah* | la | salsa de soya; la salsa china |
| spanish onion | *lah se-bol-yah es-pah-nyo-lah* | la | cebolla española |
| spare rib | *lah kos-tee-yah* | la | costilla |
| sparkling wine | *ehl vee-noh es-poo-moh-soh* | el | vino espumoso |
| spicy | *pee-kan-te/ kon-dee-men-tah-doh/ah* | | picante/ condimentado/a |
| spinach | *lah es-pee-na-ka* | la | espinaca |
| spirits | *lohs li-kor-ehs* | los | licores |
| spoon | *lahkoo-chah-rah* | la | cuchara |
| spring onions | *lah se-bol-yah lahr-gah* | la | cebolla larga |
| squash | *lah ka-lab-ah-sah* | la | calabaza |
| squid | *ehl kal-a-mahr* | el | calamar |
| stale | *pa-sah-doh/ran-see-oh* | | pasado/rancio |
| stale (bread) | *pan doo-roh* | | (pan) duro |
| steak | *ehl bis-tek* | el | bistec |
| steam | *ehl vay-pohr* | el | vapor |
| steamer | *lah o-yah de vay-pohr* | la | olla de vapor |
| steep | *se-pahr* | | cepar |
| stew | *ehl gwee-soh* | el | guiso |
| stewed | *ehl gwee-sah-doh* | | guisado |
| still water | *ag-wah min-er-al sin gas* | la | agua mineral sin gas |
| stocks | *lohs kal-dohs* | los | caldos |
| stomach | *ehl es-to-mah-goh* | el | estómago |
| stout | *lah ser-veh-sah neg-rah* | la | cerveza negra |
| straw | *ehl poh-poh-teh* | el | popote |

| strawberry | *lah fre-sah* | la | fresa |
| stuffing | *ehl rel-ye-noh* | el | relleno |
| sturgeon | *ehl es-too-ree-on* | el | esturión |
| sugar | *ehl as-oo-kahr* | el | azúcar |
| sun-dried tomatoes | *lohs heet-oh-mat-tehs-se-kos* | los | jitomates secos |
| sunflower oil | *ehl a-say-tay de hi-ra-sohl* | el | aceite de girasol |
| supermarket | *ehl su-per-mer-kah-doh* | el | supermercado |
| swede | *ehl nab-oh swe-koh* | el | nabo sueco |
| sweet | *dul-say* | | dulce |
| sweet basil | *lah al-ba-aka* | el | albahaca |
| sweet cicely | *per-i-fol-yoh klo-ro-soh* | el | perifollo cloroso |
| sweet potatoes | *ehl ka-moh-teh* | el | camote |
| sweetcorn | *ehl ehl-oh-tay tee-her-noh* | el | elote tierno |
| to smell | *o-lehr* | | oler |

# T

| tablecloth | *ehl man-tel* | el | mantel |
| tail | *ehl rah-boh; lah koh-lah* | el | rabo; la cola |
| tap water | *ag-wah de lah yav-eh* | la | agua del llave |
| tarragon | *ehl es-trah-gon* | el | estragón |
| tartare | *lah sal-sah tahr-tah-rah* | la | salsa tártara |
| tea | *ehl té* | el | té |
| tea spoon | *lah koo-chah-ree-tah* | la | cucharadita |
| tea | *ehl té ...* | el | té ... |
|   chamomile |   *man-sah-nee-yah* | | manzanilla |
|   peppermint |   *de men-tah* | | de menta |
|   rose hip |   *es-kahr-ah-moo-ho* | | escaramujo |
|   lemon |   *lee-mon* | | de limón |
|   with milk |   *kon le-cheh* | | con leche |
|   herbal |   *her-boh-lah-ree-oh* | | herbolario |
|   decaffeinated |   *des-kah-fay-nah-doh* | | sin cafeine |
|   green |   *ver-day* | | verde |
| teaspoon | *lah koo-chah-rah-dee-tah* | la | cucharita |
| tonic water | *ehl ag-wah ton-eek* | el | agua tónic |
| tequila | *ehl tek-ee-lah* | el | tequila |
| terrible | *ter-ree-bleh/de pen-ah* | | terrible/de pena |
| thyme | *ehl to-mil-yoh* | el | tomillo |
| tin (can) | *lah lat-ah* | la | lata |
| tin opener | *ehl a-bray-lat-ahs* | el | abrelatas |
| tip (gratuity) | *oon-ah prop-ee-nah* | una | propina |

| English | Pronunciation | Spanish | |
|---|---|---|---|
| to take (away) | *yev-ahr* | | llevar |
| to take (food) | *tom-ahr* | | tomar |
| toast | *tos-tah-dah/oh* | | tostada/o |
| toaster | *ehl tos-tah-dohr* | el | tostador |
| tofu | *ehl ke-soh de so-kah* | el | queso de soja |
| toilet paper | *ehl pa-pel ee-hee-eh-nee-koh* | el | papel higiénico |
| toilets | *lohs ba-nyos; ehl tok-ah-dohr* | los | baños; el tocador |
| tomatoes | *lohs hee-toh-mah-tehs* | los | jitomates |
| tongs | *lahs ten-ah-sahs* | las | tenazas |
| tongue | *lah len-gwa* | la | lengua |
| too much/many | *dem-ah-see-ah-doh(s)* | | demasiado(s) |
| toothpick | *pal-ee-yoh* | | palillo |
| topping | *lah koo-bee-her-tah* | la | cubierta |
| tripe | *lah tree-pah* | la | tripa |
| trout | *lah troo-chah* | la | trucha |
| tuna | *ehl a-tun* | el | atún |
| turbot | *ehl ro-dab-al-yoh* | el | rodaballo |
| turkey | *ehl pa-voh* | el | pavo |
| turmeric | *lah kur-koo-mah* | la | cúrcuma |
| turnip | *ehl nab-oh* | el | nabo |

## V

| English | Pronunciation | Spanish | |
|---|---|---|---|
| vanilla | *lah vay-nil-yah* | la | vainilla |
| veal | *lah ter-neh-rah* | la | ternera |
| vegetable | *oon-ah leg-oom-bray* | una | legumbre |
| vegetable marrow | *ehl ka-lab-ah-sihn* | el | calabacín |
| vegetable oil | *ehl a-say-tay veg-et-ahl* | el | aceite vegetal |
| vegetarian | *oon-ah/un veg-et-ar-ee-ah-noh/nah* | un/una | vegetariano/a |
| venison | *ehl ven-ad-oh* | el | venado |
| vine | *lah vid* | la | vid |
| vinegar | *ehl vin-ag-reh* | el | vinagre |
| balsamic | *bal-sah-mee-koh* | | bálsamico |
| cider | *see-drah* | | sidra |
| malt | *mal-tah* | | malta |
| rice | *ehl vin-ag-reh de a-rros* | | de arroz |
| wine | *vee-noh* | | vino |
| vineyard | *un vee-nay-doh* | un | viñedo |
| vitamins | *lahs vee-tah-mee-nahs* | las | vitaminas |
| vodka | *ehl vod-kah* | el | vodka |

## W

| English | Pronunciation | Spanish |
|---|---|---|
| waiter | *ehl mes-eh roh; lah mes-eh-rah* | el mesero; la mesera |
| walnut | *lah noo-es de nog-ahl* | la nuez de nogal |
| to want | *kehr-her/des-eh-ahr* | querer/desear |
| water | *ehl ag-wah* | el agua |
| mineral water | *ehl ag-wah min-er-al* | el agua mineral |
| water bottle | *lah kan-teem-ploh-rah* | la cantimplora |
| watercress | *ehl beh-rroh* | el berro |
| watermelon | *lah san-dee-ah* | la sandía |
| wedding cake | *ehl pas-tel de bo-dah* | el pastel de boda |
| well done (cooked) | *bee-en koh-see-doh* | bien cocido |
| wheat | *ehl tree-goh* | el trigo |
| wheat germ | *ehl ger-men de tree-goh* | el germen de trigo |
| whisk | *lah bat-ee-dor-ah* | la batidora |
| whisky | *ehl gwis-kee* | el whisky |
| white cabbage | *lah kol; ehl re-pol-yoh* | la col; el repollo |
| white poppy seed | *lah sem-ee-yah de a-mah-poh-lah* | la semilla blanca de amapola |
| white pudding | *ehl bu-din blan-koh* | el budín blanco |
| whitebait | *lah mohr-rah-yah* | la morralla |
| whiting | *lah pes-kah-dil-yah* | la pescadilla |
| wholewheat | *ehl tree-goh in-teg-ral* | el trigo integral |
| wholewheat flour | *lah ah-ree-nah de tree-goh in-teg-ral* | la harina de trigo integral |
| wild boar | *ehl ha-bah-lee* | el jabalí |
| wild rice | *ehl ah-rros sal-vak-hat* | el arroz salvaje |
| wine | *ehl vee-noh* | el vino |
| dry | *vee-noh sek-oh* | vino seco |
| fruity | *ah froot-as* | a frutas |
| full | *kom-plet-ah-men-the sek-oh* | completamente seco |
| house | *vee-noh de lah ka-sah* | vino de la casa |
| red | *ehl vee-noh teen-toh* | tinto |
| sweet | *ehl vee-noh (mu-ee) dul-se* | (muy) dulce |
| white | *ehl vee-noh blan-koh* | blanco |
| very dry | *ehl vee-noh mu-ee sek-oh* | vino muy seco |
| lightly sweet | *lee-ge-rah-men-the dul-se* | ligeramente dulce |
| semi-dry | *se-mee sek-oh* | semi-seco |
| winery | *lah bo-deh-gah* | la bodega |
| wooden spatula | *lah es-pat-u-lah de mah-der-ah* | la espátula de madera |
| Worcestershire sauce | *lah sal-sah in-glay-sah* | la salsa inglesa |

## Y

| yellow capsicum (pepper) | *ehl pi-mee-en-toh a-ah-ree-yoh* | el | pimiento amarillo |
| yellow split pea | *ehl chee-chah-roh a-mah-ree-yoh ke-brah-doh* | el | chícharo amarillo quebrado |
| yoghurt | *ehl yo-gür* | el | yogur |

## Z

| zucchini | *ehl ka-lab-ah-sí hn* | el | calabacín |

## Mexican Culinary Dictionary

In Spanish, nouns always have a feminine or masculine form. With some exceptions, there are some ways to tell which form a word should take. Generally speaking, feminine forms end in 'a' and are preceded by the definite article **la** (the) or the indefinite article **una** (a). Masculine forms end in 'o' and are preceded by the definite article **le** (the) or the indefinite article **un** (a). Even if they don't end in 'a' or 'o', the gender of most words can be determined. For example, words derived from ancient Greek are often feminine, such as those ending in '-dad' (**la eternidad**) and in '-cion' (**la nacion**).

In this dictionary, either the definite article (**la** or **el**) or the indefinite article (**una** or **un**) has been included with each noun, according to which one is most likely to be used with each word. However, in most cases, the articles are interchangeable. Thus **una copa**, (a drink) may also be **la copa**, (the drink)'. Just remember, **el** becomes **un**, while **la** becomes **una**.

The Spanish alphabet contains three consonants not found in the English alphabet: **ch**, **ll** and **ñ**. Words beginning with **ch** appear between 'c' and 'd' words. Words containing **ch** are listed after the alphabetical listings containing 'c'; for example, under 'a' **achiote** (a kind of spice) is listed after **acocil** (shrimp).

The letter **ñ** is always listed after the letter 'n'. Thus you'll find **año** (year) after all words beginning with 'an'.

In older dictionaries, the letter **ll** is listed as a separate letter, but contemporary Spanish no longer does so. This dictionary follows the contemporary Spanish usage, so the letter **ll** appears under the 'l' listing.

## A

el **abadejo** *ehl a-bah-deh-ho* codfish

el **abarrote** *ehl a-bahr-roh-the* groceries

la **abarrotería** *lah a-bahr-roh-teh-ree-ah* grocery store

la **abeja** *lah a-beh-khah* bee

**abierta** *a-bee-her-tah* open

el **abrebotellas** *ehl a-bray-boh-tel-yas* bottle opener

el **abrelatas** *ehl a-bray-lat-ahs* can opener

**abrir** *a-breer* to open

el **abulón** *ehl a-byoo-lon* abalone

el **aceite** *ehl a-say-tay* oil

–**de girasol** *deh hi-ra-sohl* sunflower oil

–**de oliva** *deh ol-ee-vah* olive oil

–**vegetal** *veh-et-ahl* vegetable oil

la **aceituna** *lah ah-say-too-nah* olive

–**negra** *neg-rah* black olive

–**verde** *ver-day* green olive

las **acelgas** *ah-sel-gas* bok choy

el **aciento** *ehl a-see-en-toh* lard

el **acocil** *ehl a-koh-seel* small red shrimp

la **achicoria** *lah a-chi-ko-ria* chicory

el **achiote** *ehl a-cheeh-oh-the* also called **annatto**, this red, musky-flavoured spice is obtained from seeds of the **annatto** tree. More of a colouring agent than a spice, when finely ground to a paste **achiote** gives a beautiful orange-yellow colour to **mole**, sauces and other foods.

**aderezar** *a-dehr-e-sahr*
to dress, sprinkle

el **aderezo** *ehl a-dehr-e-soh*
dressing (salad)

el **adobo** *ehl ah-doh-boh* paste of garlic, vinegar, herbs and **chiles**, used as a sauce, marinade or pickling agent

**afilado** *ah-fee-lah-doh*
sharp (knife)

el **afilador** *ehl ah-fee-lah-dohr*
sharpening stone

el **agave** *ehl ah-gah-beh* American aloe, also known as 'century plant', source of alcoholic beverages such as **pulque**, **mezcal** and **tequila**

**agregar** *a-greh-gahr* to add

un **agricultor** *oon a-gre-kool-toh*
farmer

la **agricultura** *lah a-gree-kool-tur-ah*
agriculture

el **agua** *ehl ag-wah* water
–**caliente** *kal-ee-en-tay* hot water
–**con gas** *kohn gas* soda water
–**de arroz** *deh ah-rros* rice water (*see* **horchata**)
–**de jamaica** *deh ha-mah-ee-kah* a drink made by steeping the red flower of the Jamaica plant in warm water then serving it chilled
–**de la llave** *deh lah yav-eh* tap water
–**de manantial** *–deh man-ahn-tee-ahl* spring water
–**en botella/enbotellada** *ehn boh-tay-yah/enh-boh-tey-yah-dah* bottled water

(las)–**fresca** *(lahs) fres-ka* fruit-flavoured water
–**fría** *free-ah* cold water
–**mineral** *min-er-al* mineral water
–**mineral sin gas** *min-er-al sin gas* still water
–**purificada** *puh-ree-fee-kah-dah* purified water
–**tónic** *ton-eek* tonic water

el **aguacate** *ag-wah-ka-te* avocado

el **aguamiel** *ehl ag-wah mee-el*
agave juice

el **aguardiente** *ehl ag-wahr-di-ente*
sugar cane alcohol

**ahumado** *a-oo-mah-doh* smoked

el **ajo** *ehl ah-khoh* garlic

la **alacena** *ah-lah-se-nah* a simple cupboard covered with a curtain for keeping non-perishables

las **albahacas** *lahs al-ba-akas*
sweet basil

las **albóndigas** *lahs al-bohn-di-gas*
meatballs

la **alcachofa** *lah al-ka-cho-fa*
artichoke

las **alcaparras** *lahs al-kah-pah-rrahs*
capers

el **alforfón** *ehl al-fohr-fon*
buckwheat

la **alga** *lah al-gah* seaweed, algae

**¿Algo para tomar?**
*al-goh pa-rah toh-mahr*
Would you like something to drink?

la **alhora** *al-or-ah* fenugreek

los **alimentos** *lohs a-lee-men-tos* food

el **almacén** *ehl al-mah-sen*
general store/shop

la **almeja** *lah al-meh-kah* clam

la **almendra** *lah al-men-drah*
almond

el **almuerzo** *ehl al-mwer-so* brunch, also translated as 'lunch', a late-morning snack typically consisting of a quick plate of **tacos** or a sandwich

la **alubía** *lah a-loo-bee-ah* haricot bean

el **amarillo** *a-mah-ree-yoh* yellow (*see* **mole amarillo**)

la **anchoa** *lah ahn-cho-ah* anchovy

la **anguila** *lah ahn-gwee-lah* eel

el **anís** *ehl ah-nees* anise, a plant related to those which produce cumin, dill and fennel – its flowers and leaves are used in salads and as a garnish. The seeds are known as aniseed.

los **antojitos** *lohs an-toh-hee-tohs* 'little whimsies', small portions of classical Mexican dishes, such as **burritos**, **empañada** and **tostada**, served as snack food for street eating or as appetisers.

el **antro** (slang) *ehl an-troh* nightclub

el **añejo** *ehl ahn-yeh-oh* aged, used to describe certain cheeses, meat and **tequila**

el **apio** *ehl ah-pee-oh* celeriac

el **aplastador de papas** *ehl a-plas-tah-dohr deh pa-pas* potato masher

el **arándano** *ehl a-rahn-dah-noh* bilberry
–**agrio** *ah-gri-oh* cranberry

las **aravejas** *lahs a-rah-veh-has* fresh garden peas

la **areca** *lah ar-eh-kah* betelnut

el **arenque** *ehl a-ren-kay* herring/kipper

¡**Arriba ...!** *ahr-ree-bah ...!* Long live ...!

el **arroz** *ehl ah-rros* rice (*see* **sopa seca**)

–**a la Mexicana** *ah lah meh-hee-kah-nah* Mexican rice, may be coloured red with **achiote** or saffron and sprinkled with peas, or cooked in tomato stock with onions, peas and carrots

–**a la poblana** *ah lah po-blah-nah* Puebla-style rice, a pilaf with **chiles**, corn and cheese

–**con leche** *kon lay-che* rice pudding

–**de grano corto** *deh grah-noh kor-toh* short-grain rice

–**glutinoso** *gloot-in-oh-soh* glutinous rice

–**integral** *in-teg-ral* brown rice

–**salvaje** *sal-va-khay* wild rice

–**verde** *ver-day* green rice, made with peas

el **asadero** *ehl a-sa-deh-ro* white cheese used in **quesadillas**

un **asado** *a-sa-doh* roast/barbeque

un **asador** *oon a-sahd-or* barbeque grill

**asar** *ah-sahr* to grill

un **asiento** *oon a-see-en-toh* seat

el **atole** *ehl a-tol-eh* a thin porridge or gruel of maize flour or corn-flour boiled with water, milk, sugar, cinnamon and puréed fresh fruit, usually served hot for breakfast

el **atún** *ehl a-tun* tuna

el **autoservicio** *ehl ah-u-toh-ser-vi-see-oh* self-service

la **avena** *lah av-ay-nah* rolled oats, a breakfast staple usually served with milk

las **aves** *lahs av-ay* poultry

el **azafrán** *ehl ahz-ah-fran* saffron

el **azúcar** *ehl ahs-oo-kahr* sugar

el **azúcar glass** *ehl as-oo-kahr glas* icing sugar

**B**

el **babero** *ehl bab-her-oh* bib (child's)

el **bacalao** *ehl bak-al-ow* cod; dried cod is used in a variety of Mexican dishes

el **balché** *bahl-cheh* Mayan alcoholic drink

**bálsamico** *bal-sah-mee-koh* balsamic

el **bálsamo de limón** *ehl bal-sa-moh deh li-mon* lemon balm

las **banderillas** *lahs bahn-dehr-ee-yahs* long flaky pastries

la **barbacoa** *lah bahr-bah-koh-ah* Mexican-style barbecue; a whole lamb, goat or chicken is teamed with **chiles**, **epazote**, onions, tomatoes, cabbage, carrots and **garbanzo**, then baked in the ground in a bed of roasted **maguey** leaves, or it may be made simply with chile sauce. The Yucatecáan **barbacoa** is **cochinta** or **pollo a la pibil** baked in banana leaves.

**¡Basta!** *bahs-tah!* Enough!

**bastante** *bahs-tahn-the* enough

la **batidora** *lah bat-ee-dor-ah* whisk

**beber** *beb-ehr* to drink

la **bebida** *lah beb-ee-dah* drink
—**alcohólica** *al-kol-lee-ka* alcoholic soda

el **berberecho** *ehl ber-ber-ech-oh* cockle

la **berenjena** *lah be-ren-ken-ah* aubergine/eggplant

el **berro** *ehl beh-rroh* watercress

el **betabel** *ehl bet-ah-bel* beet/beetroot

el **biberón** *ehl bi-ber-ohn* baby's feeding bottle

el **bicarbonato de sodio** *ehl bi-karh-bon-ah-toh deh so-dee-oh* bicarbonate of soda (baking soda)

**bien cocido** *bee-en koh-see-doh* well done (cooked)

el **bif** *beef* beef, also called **carne de res** or **carne de vaca**; a steak is **bifstec** or **bistec**

la **birreria** *la bi-rree-ree-ah* restaurant specialising in **birria**

la **birria** *lah bi-rree-ah* soupy stew made with meat (usually goat). Goat, lamb or veal is marinated and steam-baked in a tomato-based broth. (Jalisco)

**blanco** *blahn-koh* white

**blando** *blan-doh* soft

los **blanquillos** *lohs blan-kee-yos* eggs (also **huevos**)

la **bodega** *lah bo-deh-gah* winery

el **bolilo** *ehl boh-lee-yo* large, French-style roll, served with most meals

**borracho** *boh-rrah-cho* drunk; also the use of wine, beer, tequila or other liquor in cooking. For example, **frijoles borrachos** (drunken beans) which are flavoured with beer.

la **borraja** *lah bohr-rah-kah* borage, a European herb. The flowers and leaves are used in salads, the leaves to flavour teas and vegetables.

el **borrego** *ehl boh-rreh-goh* lamb – other words for lamb include **carnero** and **cordero**

una **bota de vino** *oo-na bo-tah deh vee-noh* leather wine bottle

la **botana** *lah bo-tan-ah* appetiser

la **botella** *lah bo-tel-yah* bottle

un **botellón de agua** *oon boh-tay-yohm deh ag-wah* a large blue bottle of purified drinking water el **brasero** *ehl brah-sehr-oh* a charcoal-burning barbecue for grilling meats and roasting **chiles**

la **brocheta** *lah broh-che-tah* skewer/kebab

el **brócoli** *ehl brok-o-lee* broccoli

los **brotes de bambú** *lohs brot-ehs deh bam-boo* bamboo shoot

el **budín** *ehl boo-din* pudding; trifle; moist cake

**¡Buen provecho!**
*bwen pro-veh-choh!*
Enjoy your meal!

**buena** *boo-en-nah* good

**¡Buena suerte!**
*bwen-ah swer-te!*
Good luck!

**Buenas noches.**
*bwen-ahs no-ches*
Good evening.

**Buenas tardes.**
*bwen-ahs tahr-des*
Good afternoon.

**Buenos días.**
*bwen-ohs dee-ahs*
Good morning.

el **buey** *ehl boo-ay* ox

el **buñuelo** *ehl bun-yoo-el-oh* **tortilla**-sized fritter, fried then sprinkled with sugar and cinnamon

el **burrito** *ehl boor-ree-toh* any combination of beans, cheese, meat, chicken or seafood seasoned with **salsa** or **chile** and wrapped in a wheat-flour **tortilla**

el **burro** *ehl bur-roh* donkey

la **butifarra** *lah boo-tee-fahr-rah* a dried speciality pork sausage (Chiapas)

# C

la **caballa** *lah kah-bal-yah* mackerel

**caballito** *kah-bah-yee-toh* large-sized (glass)

el **caballo** *ehl kah-bal-yoh* horse

la **cabeza** *lah kab-eh-sah* head

la **cabra** *lah ka-bra* goat

el **cabrito** *ehl kab-ree-toh* **milk-fed** kid, rubbed with butter or oil and seasoned with salt, pepper and lime, then roasted whole on a spit

el **cacahuete** *ehl ka-kah-weh-teh* peanut

los **cacahuetes japoneses** *lohs ka-kah-wah-tehs hah-pohn-eh-sehs* Japanese-style peanuts, covered with a crunchy coating

el **cacao** *ehl kah-kah-oh* cocoa/cacao/chocolate

la **cacerola** *lah ka-sehr-oh-lah* casserole dish

el **café** *ehl kaf-eh* café/coffee
–**americano** *ah-me-ri-cah-noh* American
–**con leche** *kon le-cheh* coffee with milk
–**de olla** *deh oh-yah* coffee sweetened with **piloncillo**
–**espresso** *es-preh-soh* espresso coffee

**cagarria (hongo)** *kah-gar-ree-ah (on-goh)* morel, an edible, wild mushroom

el **calabacín** *ehl ka-lab-ah-síhn* courgette/zucchini, vegetable marrow

la **calabaza** *ka-lab-ah-sah* pumpkin/squash (*see* **flor de calabaza**)

el **calamar** *ehl kal-a-mahr* squid

el **caldo** *ehl kal-doh* meat broth/stock

–de pollo *deh pohl-yoh* chicken broth/soup with lots of chicken and large chunks of vegetables, such as carrots, potatoes, corn and **garbanzos**, and sometimes even rice; served with **tortillas**, lime wedges and **salsa**

–de pornil *deh pohr-neel* as for **caldo de pollo**, only with pork

–de res *deh rehs* as for **caldo de pollo**, only with beef

**calentar** *kal-en-tahr* to heat

**calentar previamente** *kal-en-tahr preh-bee-ah-men-teh* to preheat

la **calidad** *lah kah-li-dahd* quality

**caliente** *kal-ee-en-te* hot (temperature)

el **calor** *ehl kal-ohr* heat

el **camarón** *ehl kam-ah-rohn* shrimp/prawn

–para pelar *pa-rah peh-lahr* whole shrimp boiled in a very weak broth, milled then served with lime

**cambiar** *kahm-bee-ahr* to change

el **camote** *ehl ka-moh-teh* sweet potato

(de) **campo** *(deh) kahm-poh* farm fresh; from the countryside

la **canela** *lah kan-el-ah* cinnamon

el **cangrejo** *ehl kan-gre-koh* crab

–moro *moh-roh* stone crab

la **cantimplora** *lah kan-teem-ploh-rah* water bottle

la **cantina** *lah kan-teen-nah* traditional Mexican bar

la **caña de azúcar** *lah kah-nya deh as-oo-kahr* sugar cane

**cañita** *kah-nyee-tah* small-sized (glass)

el **capeado** *ehl kah-pee-yah-doh* fried vegetables with cheese (Chiapas)

la **capirotada** *lah kah-pee-roh-tah-dah* Mexican-style bread pudding

las **capulínes** *lahs kah-poo-lee-nehs* black cherries

el **cardo** *ehl kahr-doh* cardoon (vegetable)

la **carne** *lah kar-ne* meat

–asada *ah-sah-dah* thinly cut, broiled tenderloin or steak, usually served with sliced onion and grilled sweet pepper strips, rice, **frijoles** and **guacamole**

–a la Tampiqueña *ah lah tam-pee-keh-nya* a plate piled with a small piece of meat, **rajas de chile poblano**, a **taco** or enchilida, **frijoles**, **guacamole** and shredded lettuce

–de cerdo *deh ser-doh* pork

–de cerdo salada *deh ser-doh sah-lah-dah* salted pork

–de res *deh res* beef

–de vaca *deh vah-kah* beef

–para asar *par-ah ah-sahr* brisket

–para taquear *par-ah ta-keh-ahr* meat for use in a **taco**

el **carnero** *ehl kah-neh-roh* mutton

el **carnicería** *ehl kahr-nee-seh-ee-ah* butcher shop

el **carnicero** *ehl kahr-nee-she-roh* butcher

una **carta** *oon-ah kahr-tah* menu; also letter

los **carvis** *lohs karh-vees* caraway seed

el **cascanueces** *lahs kas-kah-noo-eh-sehs* nutcracker

la **cáscara** *lah kas-kah-rah* skin (of fruit), rind, shell, husk

**casera** *kah-seh-rah* homemade

la **castaña** *lah kas-tan-ya* chestnut

**caza** *ka-sah* game (animals)

una **cazuela** *oon-ah kas-we-lah* casserole/casserole dish

la **cebada** *lah se-ba-dah* barley

la **cebolla** *lah se-bol-yah* onion
  –**en vinagre** *en vin-a-greh* pickling onion
  –**española** *es-pah-nyo-lah* spanish onion
  –**larga** *lahr-gah* spring onions
  –**roja** *roh-ya* red onion
  **celebrar** *se-leh-brar* to celebrate (an event)

la **cena** *lah se-nah* supper/dinner – the evening meal, usually lighter than **la comida** (lunch)

el **cerdo** *ehl ceer-doh* pig/pork
el **cenicero** *ehl se-ni-seh-roh* ashtray
el **cereal** *se-ree-al* cereal
la **cereza** *lah se-re-sah* cherry
  **cernir** *ser-neer* to sift

la **cerveza** *lah ser-veh-sah* beer/ale
  –**amarga** *ah-mahr-gah* bitter
  –**clara** *kla-rah* blonde/light beer
  –**de barril** *deh bahr-reel* draught beer
  –**negra** *neg-rah* stout
  –**obscura** *os-koo-rah* dark beer

el **ceviche** *ehl she-vee-cheh* a cocktail with shrimp, oysters or crab, mixed with **escabeche**

---

### CH ...

Words beginning with **ch** appear under a separate listing after all 'c' words (see next page).

---

la **cidra** *lah si-drah* cider
el **ciervo** *ehl see-her-voh* deer
el **cilantro** *see-lahn-troh* coriander (Chinese parsley/cilantro)
la **ciruela** *lah si-roo-el-ah* plum
  –**pasa** *pa-sah* prune

(tener) **una cita** *(ten-er) oo-nah see-tah* (to go on) a date
el **cítrico** *ehl si-tree-koh* citrus
las **claras de huevos** *lahs kla-rahs deh hway-vohs* egg whites
el **clavo** *ehl kla-voh* clove
la **clayuda** *lah klah-yoo-dah* a large, crisp tortilla (also spelled **tlayuda**)
  **coca** *koh-kah* head; nut; coca plant
de **coca** *deh koh-kah* free/gratis
**cocer** *koh-sehr* to cook
  –**a fuego lento** *few-goh len-toh* to braise/simmer
  **cocido de carne** *ko-see-doh deh kar-ne* a stew made of beef and vegetables
la **cocina** *lah koh-see-nah* kitchen
  **cocinar** *kok-see-nahr* to cook
el **coco** *ehl koh-koh* coconut
el **cóctel** *ehl kok-tel* cocktail
  –**de camarón** *deh kam-ah-rohn* shrimp cocktail
la **cochinita pibil** *lah koh-chi-nee-tahpee-beel* barbecued pork (Yucatecáan)
la **codorniz** *lah kod-or-nees* quail
la **col** *lah kol* cabbage
  –**china** *chi-nah* Chinese cabbage
  –**roja** *roh-kah* red cabbage
el **colador** *ehl kol-a-dor* sieve
las **coles de Bruselas** *lahs kol-es deh broo-sel-as* brussels sprouts
la **coliflor** *lah kol-i-flor* cauliflower
el **comal** *ehl kom-ahl* a flat, rimless iron pan used to cook **tortillas** and **antojitos**
  **comer** *kom-er* to eat
la **comida** *lah koh-mee-dah* lunch, the biggest meal of the day, taken between 1 and 4pm

–**completa** *kom-plet-ah* multi-course meal

–**corrida** *koh-ree-dah* set menu (also **el cubierto** and **menú del dia**)

–**de bebé** *deh beh-beh* baby food

el **comino** *ehl kohm-ee-noh* cumin

**comprar** *komp-rahr* to buy

las **conchas de vainilla** *lahs kohn-chahs deh vay-nil-yah* a mini loaf topped with vanilla icing

**condensado** *kon-dehn-sah-do* condensed

**condimentado** *kon-dee-men-tah-doh* seasoned/spicy

los **condimentos** *lohs kon-dee-men-tohs* condiments (including spices)

el **conejillo de indias** *ehl kon-eh-khi-yo deh in-dee-ahs* guinea pig

el **conejo** *ehl kon-eh-kho* rabbit

**congelar** *kon-gel-ahr* to freeze

el **congrejo** *ehl kon-greh-hoh* crab (also **la jaiba**)

el **comedore** *lohs koh-meh-dohr-ehs* dining room

los **conservadores** *lohs kon-ser-va-dohr-es* conserves

una **copa** *oo-nah koh-pah* a drink

el **corazón** *ehl ko-ra-son* heart

un **corcho** *onn kor-choh* cork

el **cordero** *ehl kohr-deh-roh* lamb/mutton

la **cordoñiz** *lah kod-or-nis* quail

la **corrida** *lah kohr-ree-dah* run; also the name given to the Veracruz fiesta

–**de toros** *deh toh-rohs* bullfight

el **corrido** *ehl kohr-ree-doh* a Mexican style of music originating from medieval troubadours; also a ballad

el **corzo** *ehl kor-zoh* deer

las **costillas** *lahs kos-tee-yas* ribs

la **crema** *la krem-ah* cream; also a combination of puréed vegetable and cream

–**ácida** *a-si-dah* sour cream

–**batida** *bat-ee-dah* whipping cream

–**espesa** *es-pes-ah* clotted cream

**cremoso** *krem-oh-so* creamy

las **crepas** *lah kreh-pahs* crêpes

la **croqueta** *lah krok-et-ah* croquette

**cruda** *kroo-dah* raw

la **cruda** *lah kroo-dah* hangover

**¿Cuánto cuesta?** *kwon-toh kwes-tah?* How much is it?

una **Cuba libre** *oon-ah koo-bah lee-breh* rum and cola (also simply **cuba**)

la **cubierta** *lah koo-bee-her-tah* topping

el **cubierto** *ehl koo-bee-her-toh* set menu (lunch; *see* **la comida**)

los **cubiertos** *lohs koo-bee-ehr-tos* cutlery

el **cuello** *ehl kwel-yoh* neck

la **cuenta** *lah kwen-tah* bill/check

**La cuenta, por favor.** *lah kwen-tah por fah-vor* The bill, please.

el **cuerno** *ehl kwer-noh* croissant

**Cuesta bastante.** *kwes-tah bas-tahn-te* It's expensive.

el **cuitlacoche** *ehl kwee-tlah-koh-cheh* black corn fungus (also **huitlacoche**)

la **culebra** *lah koo-leh-brah* snake

los **cumpleaños** *lohs cum-ple-ahn-yohs* birthday

la **cura** *lah ku-rah* cure

la **cúrcuma** *lah kur-koo-mah* turmeric

una **cuchara** *oon-ah koo-chah-rah* spoon

–**para sopa** *pa-rah so-pah* soup spoon

una **cucharada** *oon-ah koo-chah-rah-dah* tablespoon (measurement)

una **cucharadita** *oon-ah koo-chah-rah-dee-tah* teaspoon (measurement)

la **cucharita** *lah koo-chah-rah-dee-tah* teaspoon

el **cucharón** *ehl koo-chah-ron* ladle

un **cuchillo** *oon koo-chil-yoh* knife

–**de sierra** *deh see-her-rah* serrated knife

–**para deshuesar** *pa-rah des-weh-sahr* boning knife

–**mantequilla** *man-tek-il-yah* butter knife

# CH

el **chabacano** *ehl chah-vah-kah-noh* apricot

el **chacbi-wah** *ehl chak-bee-wah* round **tamales** stuffed with pork

el **chalote** *ehl cha-lot-eh* shallot onion

las **chalupas** *lahs chah-loo-pahs* small pancake with **chile**, beans and cheese

los **champiñones** *lohs cham-pee-nyo-nehs* fried mushrooms

el **chamorro** *ehl chah-mohr-roh* A Yucatécan dish – a leg of pork marinated in **adobo** then oven-roasted at a very low heat

el **chapulino** *ehl cha-poo-lee-noh* grasshopper

el **charalo** *ehl cha-rah-loh* sardine-like fish

la **chaya** *lah cha-yah* type of spinach (Mayan)

el **chayote** *ehl cha-yoh-the* known in the USA as 'mirliton', this gourd-like fruit was once the main food of the Aztecs and Mayas. About the shape of a very large pear, it can be prepared in much the same ways as the squash, or may be stuffed and baked or used raw in salad.

**chelear** *cheh-leh-ahr* to go drinking in a social atmosphere, from **chela**, meaning 'beer' or 'drink beer'

los **cheques de viajero** *lohs che-kehs deh vee-ah-keh-roh* travellers cheques

los **chetos** *lohs cheh-tohs* **frituras** with a cheese flavouring

el **chícharo** *ehl chi-cha-roh* pea

–**amarillo quebrado** *a-mah-ree-yoh ke-brah-doh* yellow split pea

–**mollar** *mol-yar* mangetout pea

–**seco** *se-koh* green split pea

–**verde** *ver-day* snap pea

la **chicharra** *lah chi-chahr-rah* cricket (insect)

los **chicharrónes** *los chi-chah-ron-ehs* deep-fried pork rinds, usually sold by street vendors with a topping such as mild chile sauce or a sprinkling of chile powder and fresh lime; also a flour-based fried snack

los **chicles** *lohs chic-lehs* chewing gum

los **chilaquiles** *lohs chi-lah-kee-lehs* crisp **tortillas** topped with chicken, onion, cream, fresh cheese and **salsa**, this popular breakfast choice is sometimes made with scrambled eggs and **chorizo**

el **chile** *ehl chi-leh* chile – a huge variety of fresh and dried chiles is available at Mexican markets. Some varieties are pickled and sold in bottles.

–**ancho** *an-choh* 'broad chile', so named for its size and shape, this chile has wrinkled, reddish-brown skin and is the most common form of dried **chile poblano**

–**cayena** *kay-en-ah* cayenne

–**chipotles** *chi-poht-lays* smoke-dried version of **chile jalapeño**

–**dulce** *dul-say*
sweet chile (not spicy)

–**en adobo** *en ah-doh-boh*
pickled chile

–**en nogada** *en noh-gah-dah* a green **chile poblano** stuffed with a stew of beef and fruits, topped with **nogada** and adorned with pomegranate seeds

–**habanero** *ah-bah-neh-roh*
an extremely spicy type of chile

–**jalapeño** *hal-ah-pen-yoh* Jalapeno pepper, often eaten in pickled form

–**mulato** *moo-lah-toh* dried **chile poblano**, its almost-black colour means it can be substituted for **chilhuacle negro** in the dish **mole negro**

–**poblano** *poh-blah-noh* medium-green to purple-black chile, often dried to produce **chile ancho** and **chile mulato**, this mildly hot, arrow-shaped chile is often used for stuffed peppers

–**relleno** *rel-ye-noh* green **chile poblano** stuffed with cheese,

covered in egg batter and fried

–**serrano** *seh-rah-noh* fiery green chile used in **moles** and **salsa**

los **chiles el chimichurri** *lohs chi-lehs ehl chi-mee-chuh-ree* a melange of olive oil, vinegar, chopped parsley, oregano, onion, garlic, seasoned with salt, pepper and cayenne

**chilhuacle negro** *cheel-how-kleh neh-groh* very dark, spicy strain of **chilhuacle**, a chile about the shape and size of a small bell pepper

el **chilpecho** *ehl chil-peh-choh* shrimp soup

la **chimolera** *lah chi-moh-leh-rah* a textured pestle with a round head

**Chipachole de Jaiba** *chi-pah-cho-leh deh ha-ee-bah* a soup made with crab

la **chirivía** *lah chir-iv-ee-ah* parsnip

la **chiva** *lah chi-vah* goat

el **chocolate oaxaqueno** *ehl choh-koh lah-teh oh-ah-shah-keh-noh* chocolate milk

los **chongos zamoranos** *lohs chon-gohs zah-moh-rah-nohs* popular dessert of curdled milk, sugar, cinnamon and egg yolks

el **choriqueso** *ehl choh-ree-keh-soh* **chorizo** and cheese

el **chorizo** *ehl choh-ree-soh* spicy pork sausage, fried with eggs as break-fast, or cooked with potatoes as a filling for **tacos**

una **chuleta** *oon-ah choo-let-ah* cutlet

**chuletas de carne** *choo-let-tah deh kar-ne* chops

–**de cerdo** *deh ser-doh* porkchops

un **churro** *oon choo-roh* long, stuffed doughnut covered with sugar

# D

los **dátiles** *lohs daht-il-ehs* dates

**De acuerdo.**
*deh ah-kwehr-doh*
Okay.

el **dedo** *ehl de-doh* finger

**delgado** *del-gah-doh* thin

**demasiado(s)** *dem-ah-see-ah-doh(s)* too much/many

el **desayuno** *ehl des-ah-yoo-noh* breakfast – Mexicans usually eat meat for breakfast, including one or more of the staples – **tortillas, frijoles** and **chiles**. Many also have **atole.**

los **despojos** *lohs des-poh-kohs* offal

el **destapador** *ehl des-tah-pah-dor* bottle opener

**DF (Distrito Federal)** *ehl de eff-ay* the Federal District, in which central Mexico City lies

**diabético/a** *dee-ah-be-tee-koh/-kah* diabetic

**día del mercado** *dee-ah dehl mehr-kah-doh* market day

la **diarrea** *lah dee-ahr-reh-ah* diarrhoea

el **diente de ajo** *ehl dee-en-te deh ah-khoh* clove of garlic

**digestivo Italiano** *di-ges-tee-voh it-al-ee-ah-noh* grappa

el **dinero** *ehl dee-ner-oh* money

**dividir (entre)** *dee-vih-dihr (en-treh)* to share (with); to divide

**una docena** *oon-ah doh-se-nah* a dozen

**¿Dónde está …?**
*don-de es-tah …?*
Where's …?

**una dona** *oon-ah do-nah* doughnut

las **donitas** *lahs doh-nee-tahs* **frituras** shaped like little doughnuts

**dorado** *dor-ah-doh* deep fried

el **dulce** *ehl dul-say* sweet/candy

**–de azúcar con mantequilla** *deh as-oo-kahr kon man-tek-il-ya* butterscotch

la **dulcería** *duhl-say-ree-ah* sweet/candy shop

el **durazno** *ehl doo-ras-noh* peach

# E

la **edad** *lah eh-dahd* age

el **elote** *ehl el-oh-the* maize/corn; also corn on the cob, sold (roasted) on streets all over Mexico as a fast-food snack, flavoured with **chile** powder and/or mayonnaise

**–tierno** *tee-her-noh* sweetcorn

la **empanada** *lah em-pan-ah-dah* pastry turnover with a savoury meat and vegetable filling, baked or fried. Empanada can also be filled with fruit and served as a dessert. They range in size from the huge **empanada gallega** (family size) to tiny **empanaditas** (ravioli-size).

**encebollado** *en-she-bol-yah-doh* served with onions (see also **higado encebollado**)

los **encurtidos** *lahs ehn-koo-tee-dohs* table condiment consisting of a bowl of **chiles** marinated in vinegar, combined with onions, carrots and other vegetables

las **enchiladas** *lahs en-chih-lah-dahs* meat or cheese wrapped in **tortillas** and smothered in red or green **salsa**, cream and melted cheese

**–adobados** *ah-doh-bah-dohs* beef or chicken **enchiladas** in **adobo** sauce

–**queretanas** *keh-reh-tan-ahs* **enchiladas** topped with shredded lettuce and other raw vegetables

–**rojas** *roh-hahs* meat or cheese **enchiladas** with a red **chile ancho** sauce, the most popular **enchiladas** on menus

–**suizas** *swee-sahs* mild and creamy Swiss-style **enchiladas** filled with chicken or cheese, served with creamy tomato sauce flavoured with nutmeg

–**verdes** *veh-dehs* served with a delicate green **tomatillo** sauce

la **endibia** *lah en-dib-ee-ah* endive

**endulzada** *en-dul-zahd-ah* sweetened

el **enebro** *eneb-roh* juniper

el **eneldo** *ehl e-nel-doh* dill

**enfrijolado** *en-free-khoh-lah-doh* anything cooked in a bean sauce, most commonly corn **tortillas** in a smooth black bean sauce and topped with thinly sliced onions and crumbed cheese. Other toppings include chicken and hard-boiled eggs.

**enlatado** *en-lah-tah-doh* canned

**enmolada** *ehn-moh-lah-dah* anything cooked in a **mole** sauce

**ensalada** *lah ehn-sah-lah-dah* salad

–**César** *seh-sahr* Caesar salad, Italian immigrant César Cardini created this salad in his hotel restaurant in Tijuana in 1925. These days anchovies are often featured in this salad, but the original didn't have have them.

–**de vegetales** *deh beh-hee-tah-lehs* vegetable salad of cooked vegetables, a mix of fresh vegetables, or a combination of the two

–**mixta** *meeks-tah* a delicious mix of lettuce, red tomatoes, cucumber, peas, avocado and fresh onion rings

la **ensaladera** *lah en-sah-lah-day-rah* salad bowl

**en su propio jugo** *ehn soo proh-pee hoo-goh* (cooked) in its own juice

**entender** *en-ten-dehr* to understand

**Ya entiendo.**
*ya en-tee-en-doh*
I understand.

**entomatado** *en-toh-mah-tah-doh* in a tomato sauce

la **entrada** *lah en-trah-dah* appetiser

el **entremes** *ehl en-tre-mes* appetiser

el **epazote** *ehl eh-pas-oh-the* wormseed, a pungent herb similar to **cilantro**, used in sauces, **frijoles** and **quesadillas**

**escabeche** *es-kah-beh-cheh* pickled

**escalfar** *es-kal-fahr* to poach (eggs)

el **escamole** *ehl ehs-kah-moh-leh* ant eggs, a delicacy that looks like rice usually sautéed in butter and wine as an accompaniment to meat or served with **tortillas**, avocado and salad

**escaramujo** *es-kahr-ah-moo-ho* rosehip

la **escocesa** *ehs-koh-seh-sah* vegetable soup

el **espárrago** *ehl es-parr-ah-goh* asparagus

la **espátula de madera** *lah es-pat-u-lah deh mah-der-ah* wooden spatula

las **especialidades** *lahs ehs-peh-see-ah-lee-dah-dehs* daily specials

las **especias** *lahs ehs-peh-see-ahs*
spices

**espeso** *es-pes-oh*
thick (as in cream)

la **espinaca** *lah es-pee-na-ka* spinach

la **espuma** *lah es-poo-mah*
foam (as in beer)

**esquites** *ehs-kee-tehs* fresh corn cooked in butter, **epazote** and onions, served with fresh lime juice, **chile** powder and grated cheese

el **estación** *ehl ehs-tah-see-ohn*
(in) season

el **estofado** *ehl es-toh-fah-doh* stew; also an Oaxacan **mole** served over chicken or pork, its unique flavour derived from tomatoes, almonds, bread, raisins, cloves and ground **guajillo chiles.** May be sweet and spicy or lightly spicy hot.

el **estómago** *ehl es-to-mah-goh*
stomach

–**de cordero relleno** *deh kor-deh-roh rel-ye-noh* haggis

el **estragón** *ehl es-trah-gon* tarragon

la **estufa** *lah es-too-fah* stove/heater

el **esturión** *ehl es-too-ree-on* sturgeon

el **exprimidor de ajo** *ehl ex-prim-i-dor deh ah-khoh* garlic press

–**de jugos** *deh hoo-gohs* juicer

**¿Es muy picante?**
*ehs mwy pee-kan-tay*
Is it very spicy?

# F

el **faisán** *ehl fai-san* pheasant

**familiar** *fah-mee-lee-ahr*
a large pizza (50 to 55 cm)

el **fenegreco** *fe-neh-greh-koh*
fenugreek

**¡Felicidades!**
*fel-ee-see-dah-dehs!*
Congratulations!

**¡Feliz cumpleaños!**
*feh-lees kum-ple-an-yos*
Happy birthday!

**¡Feliz santo!**
*feh-lees san-toh!*
Happy saint's day!

**festejar** *fes-teh-har* to celebrate

el **festón** *ehl fes-ton* scallop

la **fiesta** *lah fee-es-tah*
party/celebration

el **filete a la Mexicana** *ehl fil-et-tay ah lah me-hee-kah nah* grilled white fish with a tomato-based sauce

**fino/a** *fee-noh/-nah* fine

el **flan** *ehl flahn* a caramel egg custard flavoured with vanilla and covered in a syrupy topping

–**napolitan** *nah-poh-lee-tahn* whiter and thicker than the custard-style flan, sometimes flavoured with liqueur

las **flautas** *lahs flaw-tahs* also known as **tacos dorados**, tube-shaped **tacos**, deep fried and served with cream, cheese and green or red sauce

la **flor** *lah flor* flower

–**de calabaza** *deh kah-lah-bah-sah* large squash flowers used in soups and other dishes

la **fonda** *lah fon-dah*
cheap restaurant

la **frambuesa** *lah fram-bway-sah*
raspberry

**freir** *fray-ir* to shallow fry

la **fresa** *lah fre-sah* strawberry; also upper-class kids from Mexico City (slang) fresca *fres-kah* fresh

los **fideos** *lohs fe-day-os* noodles

frío *free-oh* cold

los **frijoles** *lohs free-khoh-lehs* beans, of which nearly 100 are included in the Mexican cuisine

   –**a la charra** *ah lah chah-rah* 'cowgirl's beans', with pork rind, fried tomatoes, onion and cilantro, and served as a soup

   –**borrachos** *bohr-rah-chohs* 'drunken beans', made as cowgirl's beans and flavoured with flat beer

   –**molidos** *moh-lee-dohs* ground beans

   –**negros** *neh-gros* black beans, served mashed and refried, puréed as a soup or whole, usually seasoned with **epazote**

   –**refritos** *re-free-tohs* mashed pinto beans fried in lard

frito *free-toh* fried

las **frituras** *lah free-to-rahs* flavourless puffed wheat snacks

las **frutas** *lahs froo-tahs* fruit

   –**secas** *se-kahs* dried fruit

fuerte *fwer-the* strong

# G

la **galleta** *lah gal-yet-ah* cookie/cracker

la **gallina** *lah gal-yee-nah* hen

el **gallito** *ehl gal-yee-toh* cockerel

las **gambas** *lahs gam-bas* scampi

el **gamo** *ehl ga-moh* deer

el **ganso** *ehl gahn-soh* goose

el **garbanzo** *ehl gar-bahn-soh* chickpea

la **gastronomía** *lah gas-tro-no-mee-ah* gastronomy

el **gastrónomo** *ehl gas-tro-no-moh* gastronome/gourmet

la **gelatina** *lah gel-at-ee-nah* gelatin

el **germen de trigo** *ehl ger-men deh tree-goh* wheatgerm

el **germinado de soya** *ehl ger-meen-ah-doh deh soh-yah* bean sprout

la **ginebra** *lah hin-eb-rah* gin

gordo *gor-doh* fat

las **gorditas** *las gor-dee-tahs* bread or **tortillas** fried then filled with ground pork and **chorizo**, and topped with cheese and lettuce

un **gramo** *oon gram-oh* gram

la **granada** *lah grah-nah-dah* grenadine/pomegranate

la **granadilla** *lah gra-nah-dil-yah* passion fruit

de **granja** *deh gran-ha* free-range

la **granja** *lah grahn-kah* farm

el **granjero** *ehl gran-kheh-roh* farmer

el **grano** *ehl grah-noh* grain

la **grasa** *lah gra-sah* dietary fat

grasoso *gra-soh-soh* greasy

el **gringo** *ehl green-goh* foreign/blonde/fair; also tourist from the US (slang)

la **grosella** *lah grow-sel-yah* currant

   –**espinosa** *es-pee-noh-sah* gooseberry

guacamole *gwa-kah-moh-lay* mashed avocado mixed with lemon or lime juice, **chile** or red pepper. Tomato, onion and coriander are often added.

los **guarachos** *lohs gwar-rach-os* **tortilla** shells piled high with **chorizo**, meat, potato, cilantro/coriander and **chile salsa**

la **guarnición** *lah gwar-nee-see-on* garnish

guisado *gwee-sah-doh* stewed

un guiso *oon gwee-soh* stew

el gusano *ehl goo-sah-noh* worm

los gusanos de maguey *lohs goo-sah-nohs deh mah-hwey* worms that live in **maguey**, usually placed in the bottom of the bottle as a sign that you've bought true **mezcal**, or served fried

–con salsa borracha *con sal-sah bohr-rah-chah* **maguey** worms with drunken sauce. A dish of **maguey** worms fried in oil and accompanied by a sauce of roasted **pasilla chiles**, garlic, onion, cheese and **pulque**.

## H

la haba *lah ahb-ah* broad bean

el habanero *ehl ah-bah-neh-roh* an extremely spicy type of **chile**

haber *ahb-her* to have

Hace calor.
*ah-se kal-or*
It's hot.

Hace frío.
*ah-se free-oh*
It's cold.

hacer *ah-sehr* to make

haísikil-píak *gwas-ee-keel pee-ak* a purée made with roast pumpkin seeds, **chiles**, roast tomato, coriander and capers

el hambre *ehl ahm-bre* hunger

la hamburguesa *lah am-bür-gwe-se* hamburger

la harina *lah ah-ree-nah* flour

–blanco *blan-koh* plain (white) flour

–de maíz *deh may-iz* cornflour

–de trigo *deh tree-goh* wheat flour

–de trigo integral *deh tree-goh in-teg-ral* wholewheat flour

hawaiana *ha-gwa-ee-ah-nah* from Hawaii (includes pineapple)

hecho a mano *eh-cho a ma-noh* handmade

un helado *oon el-ah-doh* icecream

helar *el-ahr* to freeze

hervido *her-bee-doh* boiled

hervir *er-vear* to boil

el hielo *ehl ee-eh-loh* ice

la hierba *lah ee-er-bah* herb

–angélica *ee-ehr-bah ahn-gel-ee-kah* angelica, a tall, parsley-like plant – the stalks and leaf ribs are blanched, peeled and boiled, then candied for use as decoration

hierbera *lah ee-er-ber-ah* herbalist

el hígado *ehl ee-gah-doh* liver

–encebollado *en-she-bol-yah-doh* liver with onions

el higo *ehl ee-goh* fig

el hilo dental *ehl ee-loh den-tal* dental floss

el hinojo *ehl in-ok-oh* fennel

las hojas *lahs oh-khahs* leaves – banana, avocado, corn and **maguey** leaves are used in Mexican cooking for the subtle flavour they impart to certain dishes. Banana leaves, corn stalk leaves and corn husks are used to wrap **tamales** for steaming, avocado leaves add flavour to sauces, and **maguey** and banana leaves, apart from being used as aromatic wrappers for food, are used to line earthen cooking pots or cover the food cooked in them.

–de laurel *deh lah-u-rel* bay leaf

–santa *sahn-tah* large anise-flavoured leaf

las **hojuelas de maíz** *lahs oh-kwel-ahs deh may-iz* cornflakes

**¡Hola!**
*oh-lah!*
Hello.

**hora de la comida** *oh-rah deh lah ko-mee-dah* lunch time

la **horchata** *lah or-chat-ah* rice water made by boiling rice then soaking it for 12 hours, after which it is drained and blended with almonds, cinnamon, sugar and spring water (Oaxaca)

**hornear** *orr-ne-ahr* to bake

al **horneado** *ahl orr-neh-ah-doh* baked

al **horno** *ahl orr-noh* baked

el **horno** *ehl ohr-no* oven
–**de lena** *deh leh-na* wood-fired oven

el **huachinango** *ehl wah-chee-nan-goh* red snapper
–**a la Veracruzana** *ah lah beh-rah-croos-ah-na* specialty of the port city of Veracruz, where fresh red snapper is broiled and bathed in a lightly spiced sauce of tomato and onion

el **huarache** *ehl wah-rah-cheh* dough stuffed with beans and topped with cream, cheese and a variety of sauces a common street food

el **huatape** *ehl gwa-tah-peh* a green soup made thick with corn dough and coloured with **chile** leaves

el **huauzontle** *ehl wahn-son-tleh* green vegetable whose buds are dipped in flour and fried

el **hueso** *ehl weh-soh* bone

los **huevos** *lohs hwe-vos* eggs; also testicles (slang)

–**de chocolate** *deh chok-oh-lah-teh* chocolate Easter eggs
–**de naca** *deh-nah-kah* fish roe
–**entomatados** *en-toh-mah-tah-dohs* eggs in a tomato sauce
–**refritos** *reh-free-tohs* fried eggs
–**revueltos** *reh-boo-ehl-tohs* scrambled eggs
–**rancheros** *rahn-cheh-rohs* eggs on **tortillas**, topped with **chile** sauce
–**tibios** *tee-bee-ohs* softboiled eggs

el **huitlacoche** *ehl gwee-tlah-koh-cheh* a black fungus that grows on young corn during the rainy season, used in crêpes, scrambled eggs and soups

el **humo** *ehl oo-moh* smoke

## I

el **ijar** *ehl ee-har* flank/side

**Impuesto de Valor Agregado (IVA)** *ee veh ah* value-added tax

**ir de compras** *eer deh kom-prahs* to go shopping

los **itacates** *lohs ee-tha-kah-tehs* food/provisions

## J

un **jabalí** *oon ha-bah-lee* boar

el **jabón** *ehl ha-bon* soap

la **jaiba** *lah ha-ee-bah* crab (also **congrejo**)
–**de rio** *deh ree-oh* crayfish

el **jalapeño** *ehl hal-al-pehn-yo* a hot green chile from Jalapa, Veracruz

**jaliscense** *hal-ee-sen-she* from the state of Jalisco

el **jamón** *ehl ha-mon* ham
–**parmesano** *par-meh-sah-no* parma ham

el  **jardín** *ehl har-deen* garden
una **jarra** *oon-ah ha-rrah* jar/pitcher
el  **jarrete** *ehl ha-rreh-teh* shin
el  **jengibre** *ehl hen-ee-bray* ginger
el  **jerez** *ehl he-res* sherry
la  **jícama** *lah hee-kam-ah* crunchy, sweet turnip/potato-like tuber often sold by street vendors, sliced and garnished with red **chile** powder and fresh lime
el  **jimador** *ehl hee-mah-dohr* person responsible for the initial stages of the **tequila** making process
el  **jitomate** *ehl hee-toh-mah-te* red tomato, specifically plum or roma
los **jitomates secos** *lohs heet-oh-mat-tehs-se-kos* sun-dried tomatoes
la  **judía** *lah hoo-dee-ah* bean
    –**blanca** *blan-kah* butter bean
    –**escarlata** *es-kar-lah-tah* runner bean
    –**pinta** *peen-tah* pinto bean
el  **jugo** *ehl hoo-goh* juice
    –**fresco** *fres-koh* fresh juice – juice bars serving freshly prepared fruit juice while you wait, are popular in Mexico
    –**de fruta** *deh froo-tahs* fruit juice

# L

la  **langosta** *lah lan-gos-tah* lobster
la  **lata** *lah lat-ah* can (aluminium)
el  **laurel** *ehl lah-oo-rel* bay leaf
la  **lavanda** *lah lav-an-dah* lavender
la  **leche** *lah le-che* milk
    –**descremada** *des-krem-ah-dah* skimmed milk
la  **legumbre** *lah leg-oom-bray* legumes
la  **leña** *lah lay-nya* wood used for cooking

la  **lengua** *lah len-gwa* tongue
el  **lenguado** *ehl len-goo-ah-doh* sole (fish)
las **lentejas** *lahs len-tek-as* brown lentils
    –**roja** *roh-kah* red lentil
    –**verde** *ver-deh* green lentils
la  **levadura** *lah leh-vah-dew-rah* yeast
los **libros** *lohs lee-brohs* books
el  **licor** *ehl li-kor* liqueur
los **licores** *lohs li-kor-ehs* spirits
el  **lichi** *ehl li-che* lychee
la  **licuadora** *lah li-koo-ah-do-rah* electric blender
la  **liebre** *lah lee-eb-ray* hare
la  **lima** *lah li-mah* lime

---

### LA LIMA

Cut limes are as common on the Mexican table as salt and pepper.

---

el  **limón** *ehl li-mon* lemon
    –**agrio** *ahg-ree-oh* bitter lemon
la  **limonada** *lah lim-on-ah-dah* lemonade
la  **lista de vinos** *lah lees-tah deh vee-nohs* wine list
un  **litro** *ehl lee-tro* litre
    **llevar** *yev-ahr* to take (away)
el  **lomo** *ehl lo-moh* loin/rump/shoulder
el  **lonche** *ehl lohn-cheh* sandwich made with a long bun – in Guadalajara most of the bread is scooped out of the middle to make way for a filling of meat, cheese, avocado and mayonnaise or cream

la **lonchería** *lah lon cher-ee-ah* lunch counter; snack bar

la **losa** *lah lo-sah* crockery

el **lucio** *ehl loo-see-oh* pike (fish)

# M

la **macis** *lah ma-sis* mace

la **machaca** *lah ma-chah-kah* meat grinder; also sheets of dried beef or beef jerky

el **machacado** *ehl ma-cha-kah-doh* dried meat (northern specialty)

**maduro** *mah-doo-roh* ripe

el **maguey** *ehl ma-gay* any of the various American agave plants, used to make alcoholic beverages such as **mezcal** – the fibre is often used in making rope

el **maíz** *ehl may-is* corn/maize
–**molido** *moh-lee-doh* hominy (hulled corn), dehusked, whole dried maize kernels with the germ removed, usually boiled in water with bicarbonate of soda to dehusk and soften it before drying or using in cooking

la **malta** *lah mal-tah* malt

la **malteada** *lah mahl-teah-dah* milkshake

el **mamey** *ehl ma-may* mamey, fruit of the *Mammea americana* tree tasting of raspberries and apricots, has a rough brown to grey outer skin, a thin, bitter yellow inner skin and yellowish flesh surrounded by inedible seeds

el **manantial** *ehl man-ahn-tee-ahl* spring/fountain

a **mano** *ah mah-noh* by hand

la **mano de mortero** *lah ma-noh deh mohr-tehr-oh* pestle

el **mantel** *ehl man-tel* tablecloth

la **manteca** *lah man-teh-kah* lard

la **mantequilla** *lah man-te-kil-yah* butter
–**de cacahuete** *deh ka-kah-wah-the* peanut butter

la **manzana** *lah man-sah-nah* apple

la **maquina de café** *lah ma-kee-nah deh ka-fay* coffee machine

la **margarina** *lah mahr-gah-ree-nah* margarine

**marinar** *mahr-een-ar* to marinate

los **mariscos** *lohs mar-is-kos* seafood/ shellfish

la **masa** *lah mahs-ah* ground, cooked corn made into a dough or batter – dried ground corn mixed with lime slake is formed into **masa** dough used for making **tortillas**. Cooks once spent hours preparing the corn and then grinding it on special stones called **metates**. These days people make their daily **tortillas** from **masa** prepared in local factories. Dry **masa** flour is also available in supermarkets.
–**de harina** *deh hah-ree-nah* corn flour
–**de maíz** *deh may-is* corn dough
–**de trigo** *deh tree-goh* wheat flour

la **maseca** *mah-say-kah* corn flour used in **tortillas** and **tamales**

el **matadero** *ehl mat-ah-deh-roh* abbatoir

la **mayonesa** *lah lah may-on-ay-sah* mayonnaise

el **mazapán** *ehl maz-ah-pan* marzipan

la **mediana** *lah meh-dee-ah-nah* a medium-sized pizza

la **medida** *lah meh-dee-dah* a medium-sized glass

**medio** *med-ee-oh* half/medium cooked

el **medio ambiente** *ehl med-ee-oh am-bee-ehn-teh* environment

la **médula** *lah meh-doo-lah* bone marrow, also called **tuétano**. A dish called **sopa de médula** (bone marrow soup) combines large pieces of soft white bone marrow with a spicy tomato and **chile** broth.

el **mejor** *lah me-khor* best

el **mejillón** *ehl mek-il-yon* mussel

la **mejorana** *lah mek-or-ah-nah* marjoram

el **melón** *ehl me-lon* melon/cantaloupe

el **membrillo** *ehl mem-bril-yoh* quince

**menear** *men-eh-ahr* to stir

la **menta** *lah men-tah* peppermint/mint

el **menudo** *ehl meh-noo-doh* tripe stew, a popular hangover remedy with an acquired taste

los **menudillos** *lohs men-oo-dil-yos* giblets

el **mercado** *ehl mer-kah-doh* market

el **merengue** *ehl mer-en-gay* meringue; Dominican music style

la **merienda** *lah meh-ree-ehn-dah* the equivalent of English afternoon tea

la **merluza** *lah mer-loo-sah* hake

la **mermelada** *lah mehr-meh-lah-dah* fruit jam/jelly/marmalade

la **mesa** *lah mes-ah* table

la **mesera** *lah mes-eh-rah* waitress

el **mestizaje** *ehl mehs-tee-sah-hay* mixture

el **metate** *ehl meh-tah-tay* a heavy grinding stone with a flat surface and three legs

el **método** *ehl met-oh-doh* method

el **mezcal** *ehl mes-kahl* a distilled liquor made from **agave**; a worm is usually placed in the bottle

la **mezcladora** *lah mes-klah-dor-ah* food processor

**mezclar** *mes-klahr* to mix

**Microdyn** *mee-kroh-deen* a consumer product used to kill contaminants in water

el **microondas** *ehl mee-kroh-ohn-dahs* microwave

l **miel** *lah mee-el* honey

las **migajas** *lahs mee-gah-yahs* crumbs

el **mijo** *ehl mee-kho* millet

la **milanesa** *lah mee-lah-neh-sah* breaded steak – inferior cuts of beef are pounded to a thin slab, then fried in an egg and bread batter, served with mayonnaise and fresh limes and accompanied by rice, beans and salad

los **mini jitomates dulces** *lohs mi-nee hi-to-mah-tes dul-ses* cherry tomatoes

los **mixiotes** *lohs mee-shoh-tehs* lamb, chicken or rabbit meat wrapped in parchment paper and steamed in a broth, then served with a mild green sauce, sliced avocado and **tortillas**. To eat, untie the string, dribble the sauce into the bag and cut the meat into bite-sized pieces, then fill a tortilla with a portion of meat and avocado, roll up and enjoy.

el **mízcalo** *ehl mees-kah-loh* chanterelle

el **modongo jarocho** *ehl mon-dohn-goh hah-roh-choh* a rich, stew-like dish with ham, tripe, pork, chickpeas, coriander and **tortillas**

la **mojarra** *lah moh-ha-rah* perch

-a la veracruzana *ah lah ver-ah-kroo-sah-nah* spicy baked perch in a tomato, onion and green olive **salsa**

el molcajete *ehl molk-ah-keh-te* a kind of stew; also a bowl made of thick clay, baked to hardness and enamelled. The surface is heavily textured, allowing **salsa** ingredients to be mashed and mixed with greater ease.

el mole *ehl mol-eh* the quintessential Mexican sauce, this **chile**-based sauce is made using a variety of chiles, herbs, spices and chocolate. **Mole** varies from region to region, from restaurant to restaurant and from house to house. Although the sauce originated in Puebla, Oaxaca boasts as many as seven varieties of **mole**. Testimony to how seriously Mexicans regard the **mole**, is the annual **mole** festival, complete with competing cooks, held in the village of San Pedro Actópan, south of Mexico City.

-coloradito *koh-loh-rah-dee-toh* a Oaxacan **mole** made with **chiles**, sesame seeds, almonds, raisins, bananas and spices, ladled over chicken

-de olla *deh oh-yah* from Morelos, this **mole** is cooked in a pot with pork, lamb or smoked meat, and includes cactus fruit and **epazote**

-de xico *deh see-koh* a slightly sweet **mole** from the Jalapa region

-naolinco *nah-oh-leen-koh* a spicy mole from the Jalapa region

-negro *neh-gro* a dark mole from Oaxaca region

-poblano *po-blah-noh* Pueblan-style **mole** consisting of deseeded and puréed **chiles**, onion, coriander, garlic and unsweetened chocolate

moler *mol-her* to grind

los molineros *lohs mol-een-eh-rohs* salt and pepper mills

el molinillo *ehl moh-lee-nee-yoh* a mixing stick with a textured knob at one end that, when spun between two palms, whips liquid into a froth

el molino de café *ehl mohl-ee-noh deh ka-fay* coffee grinder

las molletes *lahs moh-yeh-tehs* a savoury, filled bread roll that makes a filling breakfast or other meal. A large white roll is spread with refried beans and melted cheese and topped with fresh **salsa**.

el mondongo *ehl mon-dohn-goh* a kind of stew with several regional variations

la mora *lah mo-rah* mulberry

la morcilla *lah mor-see-yah* black pudding

a morralla *lah mohr-rah-yah* whitebait

el mortero *ehl moh-teh-roh* mortar and pestle

la mostaza *lah mos-ta-sah* mustard

# N

el nabo *ehl nab-oh* turnip

-sueco *swe-koh* swede

nacional *nah-see-oh-nal* domestic

la naranja *oon-ah na-ran-khah* orange (fruit)

-agria *ah-gree-yah* sour/bitter orange tasting more like a lemon or lime than an orange – the juice is often substituted for vinegar or a mixture of lime and orange juice as a favourite in marinades and sauces

la **naranja china** *lah na-ran-kah chin-ah* kumquat

la **Navidad** *lah nahv-ee-dahd* Christmas Day

la **nevería** *ne-ver-ee-ah* a store that makes its own icecream (called **helado**) using available fresh fruit

el **nieve** *ehl nee-yeh-beh* shaved ice flavoured with fruit juice, sold by pushcart vendors throughout the country as a refreshing treat

el **nixtamal** *ehl neex-tah-mal* mixture of corn and lime used in making dough (*see* **la masa**)

la **Nochebuena** *lah no-cheh-bwehn-ah* Christmas Eve

la **nogada** *lah noh-gah-dah* walnuts or in a walnut sauce

el **nopal** *ehl no-pal* prickly pear cactus – the cactus pads (leaves) are cut into strips and boiled as a vegetable, or may be added to scrambled eggs

el **nudillo** *ehl noo-dee-yoh* knuckle

la **nueva cocina mexicana** *noo-eh-vah koh-see-nah meh-hee-kah-nah* new Mexican cuisine – a movement among some chefs to combine traditional ingredients with contemporary preparations and presentations

la **nuez** *noo-es* nut

   –**anacardo** *ah-nah-karh-doh* cashew

   –**avellana** *av-el-yah-nah* hazelnut

   –**castaña** *kas-tan-yah* chestnut

   –**del Brasil** *dehl brah-sil* brazil nut

   –**de macadamia** *deh mak-a-day-mee-ah* macadamia

   –**de nogal** *lah noo-es deh nog-ahl* walnut

   –**moscada** *lah noo-ehs mos-kah-dah* nutmeg

   –**pacana** *pah-kah-nah* pecan

# O

el **octli** *ehl ok-tlee* alcoholic drink made from a combination of juices from different **agave** plants

el **ojo** *ehl o-koh* eye

   **oler** *ol-her* to smell

la **olla** *lah ol-yah* pot/pan or something cooked or served in a clay pot

   –**de presión** *deh pres-see-on* pressure cooker

   –**de vapor** *deh vay-pohr* steamer

   –**para hervir agua** *pa-rah er-vear ag-wah* kettle

un **olor** *oon ol-ohr* a smell

el **oporto** *ehl o-por-toh* port

   **orgánico** *or-gan-ik-oh* organic

la **ostra** *lah os-trah* oyster

una **oveja** *oon-ah o-beh-khah* sheep

# P

el **pájaro** *ehl pa-khah-roh* bird

la **paleta** *lah pa-let-ah* lollipop/popsicle

el **palillo** *ehl pal-ee-yoh* toothpick

los **palitos chinos** *lohs pal-il-yos chee-nos* chopsticks

la **paloma** *lah pa-lom-ah* pigeon

las **palomitas de maiz** *lahs pa-lom-ee-tas deh may-is* popcorn

el **pan** *ehl pahn* bread

   –**árabe** *ah-ra-bay* pita bread

–de **muerto** *mwer-toh* a heavy bread used as an offering on the Day of the Dead

–de **yema** *deh yeh-mah* a yellow, rich and heavy bread made with egg yolks

–**dulce** *dul-say* a sweet bread

–**duro** *doo-roh* stale (bread)

la **panadería** *lah pahn-ah-der-ee-ah* bakery

los **panuchos** *lohs pah-noo-chos* a finger food taken as an appetiser, these are bean-stuffed **tortillas**, fried crisp then topped with a tower of shredded turkey or chicken, tomato, lettuce and onions

la **papa** *lah pa-pa* potato

–a la **francesa** *ah lah fran-seh-sah* french fries; chips

los **papadzules** *lohs pah-pahd-swu-lehs* fresh corn **tortillas** wrapped around a filling of chopped hard-boiled eggs then covered with sauce from pumpkin seed and **epazote**

el **papel higiénico** *ehl pa-pel ee-hee-eh-nee-koh* toilet paper

las **papitas del monte** *lahs pa-pee-tahs dehl mon-tay* wild potatoes

la **parillada** *lah pahr-ree-yah-dah* flame-grilled meat platter

la **pasa** *lah pas-ah* raisin

**pasado** *pa-sah-doh* stale

**Pascua** *lah pas-koo-ah* Easter

el **pastel** *ehl pas-tel* pastry/cake

–de **boda** *deh bo-dah* wedding cake

–de **crema** *–deh krem-ah* puffball

–de **cumpleaños** *deh cum-ple-ahn-yohs* birthday cake

–de **tres leches** *deh tres le-chays* a very heavy cake made with evaporated milk, condensed milk and evaporated cream

–**margarita** *mahr-gah-ree-tah* a cake made with almonds or various fruits

la **pastelería** *lah pas-tel-er-ee-ah* cake shop

el **pastelito** *ehl pas-tel-ee-toh* pastry

al **pastor** *ahl pas-tohr* shepherd; also grilled pork with pineapple, served in small **tortillas** (*taquitos al pastor*)

las **patas** *lahs pah-tahs* hooves

el **pato** *ehl pa-toh* duck

el **pavo** *ehl pa-voh* turkey

la **pechuga** *lah pech-oo-gah* breast

–de **pollo** *deh pohl-yoh* chicken breast

un **pedazo** *oon ped-ah-soh* a piece

el **pelador** *ehl pel-ah-dohr* peeler

el **penaché** *ehl pen-ah-cheh* shandy made with beer and lemon-flavoured soft drink

**permitido por la ley judía** *per-mi-tee-doh por lah lay hoo-dee-ah* kosher

el **pepinillo** *ehl pep-in-il-yoh* gherkin

el **pepino** *ehl pep-ee-noh* cucumber

**pequeña** *pay-keh-nya* small; a small pizza

la **pera** *lah peh-rah* pear

el **perejil** *ehl per-ek-il* parsley

el **perifollo** *ehl per-i-fol-yoh* chervil

–**cloroso** *kloh-raw-soh* sweet cicely

el **personal** *ehl per-sohn-al* a pizza size (about 12cm)

las **pesas** *las pe-sahs* scales

la **pescadería** *lah pes-kah-der-ee-yah* fish shop

el **pescado** *ehl pes-kah-doh* fish (prepared as food)

el **pez** *ehl pes* fish

el **pib** *ehl peeb* pit used by Mayans in which to cook meat

**pibil** *pee-beel* 'roast in a hole' method of roasting meat, typical of Yucatáan

el **picadillo** *ehl pee-kah-dee-yoh* ground beef and potato mixture

el **picador** *ehl pee-kah-dor* mincer

¿**Pica mucho?**
*pee-kah moo-choh?*
Is it very spicy?

**picante** *pee-kan-te* spicy

**picar** *pee-kahr* to mince

**picoso** *pi-koh-soh* hot (food)

la **pierna** *lah pee-er-nah* leg

el **piloncillo** *ehl pee-lohn-see-yoh* raw brown sugar

el **pimentón** *ehl pee-men-ton* sweet pepper/capsicum

–**paprika** *pah-pree-kah* paprika

la **pimienta** *lah pi-mee-en-tah* black pepper

–**inglesa** *ing-leh-sah* allspice

–**recién molida** *re-see-en mo-lee-dah* freshly ground black pepper

la **piña** *lah peen-yah* pineapple

las **piñatas** *lahs pee-nya-tahs* balloons or animal-shaped dolls made with clay and filled with sweets

el **piñón** *ehl peen-yon* pinenut

el **pipián verde** *ehl pee-pee-an ver-day* a **mole** made with ground spices and seeds, green tomatoes, peanuts, and served over pork

el **plátano** *ehl plat-an-oh* plantain/banana

la **platija** *lah plah-tee-ha* plaice/flounder

el **platillo** *ehl plat-ee-yoh* dish (food)

el **plato** *ehl plat-oh* plate

–**fuerte** *fwer-teh* main meal

–**principal** *prin-see-pal* main course

el **platón** *ehl plaht-on* bowl

**poblano** *po-blah-nohl* originating from the state of Puebla

el **poc chuc** *ehl pok-chuk* a thin slice of pork, cooked on a grill and served on a sizzling plate with a bitter orange sauce (Yucatáan)

el **pollo** *ehl pohl-yoh* chicken

–**a la pibil** *ah lah pee-beel* barbecued chicken

–**asado** *a-sah-do* roast chicken

–**frito** *free-toh* fried chicken

el **polvo de curry** *ehl pohl-voh deh kur-ree* curry powder

el **ponche de frutas** *ehl pon-chay deh froo-tahs* fruit punch

el **popote** *ehl po-po-te* straw

un **poquito** *oon poh-kee-toh* a little (amount); a dab

la **posada** *lah poh-sah-dah* inn

las **posadas** *lahs poh-sah-dahs* celebrations where people do a representation of the Virgin and Joseph when they were looking for an inn (**posada**) eight days before Christmas

el **postre** *ehl pos-tray* dessert

el **pozole** *ehl pos-oh-leh* a thick soup made of corn, chicken or pork, lettuce and slices of radish, eaten as a meal in itself, traditionally at Christmas. (Jalisco)

**precalentar** *preh-kal-en-tahr* to preheat

la **prensa** *lah pren-sah* food press

**preparar** *preh-pah-rahr* to prepare/make

la **preparación** *lah preh-pah-rah-see-on* preparation

el procesador de alimientos *ehl pro-seh-sah-dohr deh a-lee-men-tos* food processor

los productos congelados *lohs prod-uk-tos kon-ge-lah-dohs* frozen foods

–lácteos *lahk-tay-os* dairy products

una propina *oon-ah prop-ee-nah* tip (gratuity)

el puchero *ehl poo-cheh-roh* a stew made of chicken and vegetables

el puerro *ehl pwer-roh* leek

los puestos *lohs poo-ehs-tohs* kerbside eateries run by cooks using comales

el pulpo *ehl pul-poh* octopus
–en su tinta *ehn soo tin-tah* octopus in its own ink

el pulque *ehl pool-keh* a white, thick, sweet alcoholic drink made from the fermented sap of agave plants, especially the maguey; also used in regional recipes for sauces and stews

la pulquería *lah pool-keh-ree-ah* a bar that produces and serves pulque

## Q

las queretanas *lahs keh-reh-tah-nahs* Queretaro-style enchiladas topped with shredded lettuce and other raw vegetables

la quesadilla *lah ke-sah-dee-yah* a flour tortilla with a savoury cheese filling

el quesillo *ehl keh-see-yoh* a stringy goat's milk cheese from Oaxaca

el queso *ehl ke-soh* cheese
–añejo *ah-nye-ho* a hard, aged cheese with a sharp flavour similar to parmesan

–azul *a-sul* blue cheese

–blando *blan-doh* soft

–crema *ehl ke-soh krem-ah* cream cheese

–de soja *deh so-kah* tofu

–duro *doo-roh* hard cheese

–fresco *fres-koh* cheese made from cow's milk

–fundido *foon-dee-doh* cheese fondue

–medio duro *may-dee-oh doo-roh* semi-firm cheese

–oaxaqueño *wah-ha-kehn-yo* Oaxacan cheese, made from goat's milk *(see el quesillo)*

–requesón *rek-wes-on* cottage cheese

los quince años *lohs keen-se ah-nyos* celebration when a girl turns 15

Quisiera comprar ...
*kee-see-her-ah komp-rahr ...*
I'd like to buy ...

quitar *kee-tahr* to take away; remove

## R

el rábano *ehl rab-an-oh* radish
–picante *pee-kan-teh* horseradish

el rabo *ehl rah-boh* tail
–de buey *deh boo-ay* oxtail

el rallador *ehl ral-yah-dor* grater
rallar *ral-yahr* to grate

el ramito *ehl ra-mee-toh* sprig

la rana *lah rah-nah* frog

la ranchera *lah ran-cheh-rah* a music style similar to country music, featuring heavy bass beats and accordians

rancio *ran-see-oh* stale

los raspados *lohs ras-pad-ohs* 'scrapings', flavoured ice

la **rebanada** *lah re-bah-nah-dah* a slice

**rebanar** *re-bah-nahr* to slice

el **recado** *ehl reh-kah-doh* marinade; seasoning paste

el **recalentado** *ehl re-kal-en-tah-doh* leftovers

la **receta** *lah re-set-ah* recipe

el **recibo** *ehl re-see-boh* receipt

**recién** *re-see-en* 'recent', fresh

el **recipiente para mezclar** *ehl re-see-pee-en-the pa-rah mes-klahr* mixing bowl

la **red** *lah re-ehd* net

el **regaliz** *ehl reg-ah-lis* liquorice

**regatear** *re-gah-teh-ahr* to bargain

un **refresco** *oon re-fres-koh* soft drink

el **relleno** *ehl rel-ye-noh* stuffing/stuffed

–**negro** *neg-roh* a Yucatáan speciality made with **chiles anchos**, green pepper and **achiote**, served over shredded turkey and a hard-boiled egg

el **reposado** *ehl reh-poh-sah-doh* a tequila that has been aged two to 12 months

la **repostería** *lah reh-post-eh-ree-ah* dessert shop; dessert making

la **res** *lah res* beef

**reservar** *re-serv-ahr* to reserve (a table)

¡Rico!
*ree-soh!*
Delicious!

el **riñón** *ehl rihn-yon* kidney

el **robalo** *ehl rob-ah-loh* sea bass

**rociar** *roh-see-ahr* to sprinkle

el **rodaballo** *ehl ro-dab-ah-yoh* brill

el **rodillo** *ehl rod-ee-yoh* rolling pin

el **rogatear** *ehl reh-gaht-eh-ahr* to bargain

el **romero** *ehl ro-meh-roh* rosemary

el **ron** *ehl ron* rum

la **rosca de reyes** *lah ros-kah deh ray-yehs* served on Epiphany (6 January), a large, wreath-shaped pastry with a small china doll representing Christ baked into it. Whoever gets the piece with the doll in it throws a party on Candelmas Day (2 February).

el **roscón de Pascua** *ehl ros-kon deh pas-kwa* Easter cake

**rostizar** *rost-ee-sahr* to roast

la **rotisería** *lah roh-tee-se-ree-ah* a restaurant serving roast chicken cooked on a rotisserie

las **ruedas** *lahs roo-eh-dahs* wheel-shaped **frituras**

el **ruíbarbo** *ehl rwee-bar-doh* rhubarb

**ruidosa** *rwee-doh-sah* noisy

## S

el **sabor** *ehl sa-bor* flavour

el **sagú** *ehl sa-goo* sago

la **sal** *lah sal* salt

**salado** *sal-ah-doh* savoury

los **salbutes** *lohs sahl-boo-tays* **tortillas**, fried crisp then topped with a tower of shredded turkey or chicken, tomato, lettuce and onions

la **salchicha** *lah sal-chee-chah* frankfurter

la **salchichonería fina** *lah sal-chee-choh-neh-ree-ah fee-nah* delicatessen

**salpimentar** *sal-pee-men-tahr* to season

la **salsa** *lah sal-sah* a spicy, tomato-based sauce

–**bandera** *ban-eh-rah* 'flag sauce', named for the red of the tomato, the white of the onion and the green of the **chile**

–**borracha** *bohr-rah-chah* 'drunken sauce' made from roasted **pasilla**, **chiles**, garlic, onion, cheese and **pulque**

–**china** *chin-ah* soya sauce

–**inglesa** *in-glay-sah* Worcestershire sauce

–**picante** *pee-kan-te* hot sauce

–**roja** *roh-khah* red sauce made with plum tomatoes, onions, garlic and salt

–**tártara** *tahr-tah-rah* tartare sauce

–**verde** *ver-de* green sauce made with **tomatillos**, green **chiles** and coriander/cilantro

la **sandía** *lah sán-dee-ah* watermelon

**saltear** *sal-teer-ahr* to sauté

¡Salud!
!*sa-lud*!
Cheers/Good health!

el **salvado** *ehl sahl-vah-doh* bran

la **salvía** *lah sal-vee-ah* sage

la **sangre** *lah san-gre* blood, used to describe a meat cooked in its own blood, blood sausage or rare (underdone) meat

la **sangria** *lah san-gree-ah* refreshingly cool on a summer's day, this delightful drink derives its name from **sangre** (blood). Made with red wine, fruit juices, soda water and sliced fresh fruit, and sometimes also brandy, cognac or liqueur, served cold over ice.

–**blanco** *blahn-koh* made with white wine

la **sangrita** *lah san-gree-tah* though there are many varieties of this drink, usually served chilled

with a shot of **tequila**, typically it's a bright red, thickish mixture of crushed tomatoes (or tomato juice), orange juice, grenadine, **chile** and salt

la **sardina** *lahs sahr-di-a* sardine

el **sartén** *ehl sahr-ten* frying pan

**secado** *sek-ah-doh* dried

**secar** *se-kahr* to dry

el **segundo plato** *ehl seg-oon-doh plat-oh* second course

la **sed** *lah sed* thirst

**Semana Santa** *se-ma-nah san-tah* Easter

**sembrar** *sem-brahr* to plant

la **semilla** *lah sem-ee-yah* seed

–**de amapola** *deh a-mah-poh-lah* poppy seed

–**de apio** *deh a-pee-oh* celery seed

–**de hinojo** *deh in-ok-oh* fennel seed

–**de sesamé** *deh ses-amo* sesame seed

–**de soya** *deh sol-yah* soya bean

–**oriental** *or-ee-en-tahl* mung bean

la **semita** *lah sem-ee-tah* flat, round bread

la **sémola** *lah sem-ol-ah* semolina

el **sendecho** *ehl sen-deh-choh* a beer made with corn and flavoured with **tepozán**

**servicio a domicilio** *ehl ser-vi-see-oh ah dom-ee-see-yoh* delivery service

los **servicios** *lohs ser-vi-see-ohs* toilets

la **servilleta** *lah ser-vil-yet-ah* napkin

los **sesos** *lohs seh-sos* brains

**sidra** *see-drah* cider

la **siesta** *lah see-ehs-tah* an afternoon rest

la **silla** *lah sil-yah* chair/seat

las **sobras** *lahs so-brahs* remains (that which isn't used in a particular dish)

la **sopa** *lah so-pah* soup/chowder

  –**de coco** *lah so-pah deh koh-koh* coconut soup (Colima)

  –**de nopales** *deh no-pah-lehs* soup with cactus leaves

  –**de tortilla (sopa Azteca)** *deh tor-til-yah* a chicken broth-based soup featuring strips of leftover corn **tortillas**

  –**seca** *se-kah* 'dry soup' a rice, pasta or **tortilla**-based dish. The name may come from the fact that the dish is often made by boiling down liquid.

  –**tlalpeño** *tlahl-pehn-yoh* vegetable soup

  –**xóchitl** *soh-chee-tl* a fiery hot soup with serrano peppers on top

el **sopache** *ehl so-pah-cheh* fried taco

el **sope** *ehl so-peh* cornflour shell stuffed with refried beans then fried, served as a **botana**

los **sopes** *lohs so-pehs* **tortillas** shaped like beaver tails and topped with beans and vegetables/**antojitos** in a variety of ways

  **sucio/a** *soo-see-oh/ah* dirty

el **suero de leche** *ehl swe-roh deh lah le-chay* buttermilk

el **supermercado** *ehl su-per-mer-kah-doh* supermarket

# T

la **tabla** *lah tah-blah* cutting board

las **tablillas** *lahs tah-blee-yahs* tablets of ready-made chocolate

el **taco** *ehl ta-koh* a small, folded corn **tortill**a filled with meat, beans and other ingredients

  –**al pastor** *ahl pas-tohr* **taco** with meat cut from a roasting spit

  –**arabes** *ah-rah-behs* **taco** made with slightly thicker wheat bread

  –**de pollo** *deh pohl-yoh* chicken **taco**

  –**dorados** *doh-rah-dohs* deep fried **taco**

el **tallo** *ehl tah-yoh* shank

los **tamales** *lohs tah-mah-lays* corn dough stuffed with meat, beans, **chiles**, fruit or nothing at all, usually wrapped in banana leaves, sometimes in corn husks and then steamed in onion and chicken sauce

  –**oaxaquenos** *oh-ah-shah-keh-nohs* wrapped in banana leaves

el **tamaño** *ehl tam-ahn-yo* size

las **tangas** *lahs tan-gahs* village sittings where food is served

  **tapar** *ta-pahr* to cover

las **tapas** *lahs ta-pas* appetisers or snacks, usually served with wine

el **tapesco** *ehl tah-pes-koh* a bed of plantain leaves

  **taquear** *ta-keh-ahr* to put into a **taco** (*see* la carne para taquear)

la **taquería** *lah ta-keh-ree-ah* place that specialises in serving **tacos**

el **taquito** *ehl tah-kee-toh* a **tortilla** wrapped around meat or chicken

la **taza** *lah ta-sah* cup

el **té** *ehl té* tea

  –**de limón** *deh lee-mon* lemon tea

  –**de menta** *deh men-tah* peppermint tea

  –**herbolario** *her-boh-lah-ree-oh* herbal tea

  –**manzanilla** *man-sah-nee-yah* chamomile tea

–**negro** *neg-roh* black tea

–**sin cafeine** *des-kah-fay-nah-doh* decaffeinated tea

–**verde** *ehl té ver-day* green tea

el **técnico** *ehl tek-nee-koh* technique

el **tejate** *ehl te-ha-teh* Oaxacan recipe for chocolate that includes mamey seeds, cacao flowers and corn dough

las **tenazas** *lahs ten-ah-sahs* tongs

el **tenedor** *ehl ten-e-dor* fork

**tener** *ten-er* to have

–**hambre** *am-breh* to be hungry

**Tengo ...**
*ten-goh ...*
I have ...

el **tepesquincle** *ehl teh-pes-kwin-tlay* small pig native to Yucatán

el **tepozán** *ehl te-poh-sahn* a vegetable with curative qualities

la **ternera** *lah ter-neh-rah* veal

**terrible/de pena** *ter-ree-bleh/deh pen-ah* terrible

el **tescalate** *ehl tes-kah-lah-tay* a type of chocolate popular in Chiapas, made by grinding the cacao beans with toasted corn and **achiote**

al **tiempo** *ahl tee-ehm-poh* at room temperature

**¿Tiene usted ...?**
*tee-en-eh oos-tehd ...?*
Do you have ...?

la **tierra** *lah tee-ehr-rah* earth/land

las **tijeras** *lahs tik-her-as* scissors

el **tímalo** *ehl tee-mah-loh* grayling

la **tlayuda** *lah tlah-yoo-dah* a large, crisp **tortilla** topped with Oaxacan cheese, tomatoes and beans

el **tocino** *ehl toh-see-noh* bacon

–**de lomo** *deh loh-moh* bacon (from the back)

**tomar** *tom-ahr* to take (food)

el **tomate** *ehl to-ma-tay* green tomato

el **tomatillo** *ehl toh-mah-tee-yoh* Mexican green tomato, with the flavour of a mixture of lemon, apple and herbs

el **tomillo** *ehl to-mil-yoh* thyme

la **tonronja** *lah oon-ah tor-on-ha* grapefruit

el **to'owloche** *ehl toh-oh-loh-cheh* 'wrapped in corn leaves' – Mayan **tamale** served on festival days and made by home chefs and served to people in the street

el **topinambur** *ehl top-ee-nam-bür* Jerusalem artichoke

el **tordo** *ehl tor-doh* thrush (bird)

el **toro** *ehl to-roh* bull

los **toros cohetes** *lohs toh-rohs koh-eh-tehs* papier mâché bulls equipped with scaffolding that carries fireworks, used in the celebrations for the patron saint of El Grande, Veracruz

la **torta** *lah tor-tah* sandwich made with crusty bread

la **tortilla** *lah tor-til-yah* ubiquitous round flatbread made with corn or wheatflour, a staple in the Mexican diet for thousands of years. Used in making **tacos**, **chalupas** and **tostadas**.

la **tortillería** *lah tor-tee-yeh-ree-ah* bakery from where Mexicans buy their **tortillas** by the dozen if they don't make it themselves at home

las **tortillas de maíz** *–deh may-is* corn **tortillas**

–de trigo *deh tree-go* wheat **tortillas**

–yucatecas *yoo-kah-te-kahs* (*see* **papadzules**)

las **tostadas** *lahs tost-ah-dahs* fried thick corn dough

el **tostador** *ehl tos-tah-dohr* toaster

los **totopos** *lohs toh-toh-pohs* deep-fried wedges of stale corn **tortillas**

el **trigo** *ehl tree-goh* wheat

–integral *in-teg-ral* wholewheat

–resquebrado *ehl tree-goh res-kwe-brah-doh* cracked wheat

la **tripa** *lah tree-pah* tripe

el **tronco** *ehl tron-koh* a large, round bisection of a tree used as a cutting board

la **trucha** *lah troo-chah* trout

la **trufa** *lah troo-fah* truffle

–blanca *blan-kah* white truffle

la **tuna** *lah too-nah* prickly pear

el **tuétano** *ehl too-eh-tah-no* marrow

la **turista** *ehl/lah too-rees-tah* tourist/diarrhoea

el **turrón** *ehl too-rron* nougat

# U

las **uvas** *lahs oo-bahs* grapes

# V

la **vaca** *lah ba-ka* cow

el **vagón restaurante** *ehl vah-gon restor-an-te* dining car

la **vainilla** *lah vay-nil-yah* vanilla

el **venado** *ehl ven-ad-oh* venison/deer

el **vendador** *ehl ven-deh-dohr* seller

**vender** *ven-dehr* to sell

la **veracruzana** *lah ver-ah-kroo-sah-nah* a **salsa** of tomato, onion and green olives

la **verdulería** *lah ver-dul-ehr-ee-ah* greengrocer

las **verduras** *lahs ver-doo-rahs* mixed greens

**vertir** *ver-teer* to pour

**vegetariano** *veh-et-ar-ee-ah-noh* vegetarian

el **vapor** *ahl va-poor* steam

el **vaporcito** *ehl vah-pohr-see-toh* flat **tamales** stuffed with meat and wrapped in **plátano** leaves

**vaporizar** *va-por-ree-sahr* to steam

lah **vid** *lah vid* vine

el **vinagre** *ehl vin-ag-reh* vinegar

el **vinagre de arroz** *ehl vin-ag-reh deh a-rros* rice vinegar

un **viñedo** *oon vee-nay-doh* vineyard

el **vino** *ehl vee-noh* wine

–a frutas *ah froot-as* fruity wine

–abocado *ehl vee-no abo-kah-doh* medium-sweet wine

–blanco *blan-koh* white wine

–completamente seco *kom-plet-ah-men-the sek-oh* full wine

–de la casa *deh lah ka-sah* house wine

–de Madeira *deh ma-deh-ee-rah* Madeira

–espumoso *es-poo-moh-soh* sparkling wine

–ligeramente dulce *lee-ge-rah-men-the dul-se* lightly sweet wine

–muy seco *mu-ee sek-oh* very dry wine

–nacional *nah-see-oh-nal* domestic wine

–seco *sek-oh* dry wine

–**semi-seco** *se-mee sek-oh* semi-dry wine

–**tinto** *teen-toh* red wine

**vuelva a la vida** *vwehl-vah ah-lah-vee-dah* seafood cocktail in a tomato **salsa**

## W

el **whisky de centeno** *ehl gwis-kee deh sen-ten-oh* bourbon whisky

el **whiskey canadiense** *ehl gwis-kee kan-ah-dee-en-say* rye whisky

## X

el **xcatik** *ehl ex-kah-teek* kind of chile found in the Yucatán

## Z

la **zanahoría** *lah zan-a-or-ee-ah* carrot

el **zapote** *ehl sah-poh-te* a fruit used for making juice that has several forms and colours

la **zarzamora** *lah zahr-zah-mor-ah* dewberry/blackberry

el **zócalo** *ehl soh-kah-loh* city square

el **zorzal** *ehl sohr-sal* thrush (bird)

el **zumo** *ehl soo-moh* juice

## Photo Credits

**Greg Elms** Front & back cover, p1, p5, p8, p9, p11, p12, p16, p17, p18, p19, p20, p21, p22, p23, p24, p29, p31, p33, p34, p35, p37, p38, p40, p42, p44, p45, p47, p48, p49, p50, p51, p52, p54, p55, p56, p57, p58, p60, p62, p66, p67, p68, p69, p70, p71, p73, p74, p76, p77, p78, p81 top, bottom left, p85, p86, p97, p100, p102, p105 left, p105, p110, p112, p113, p115, p116, p117, p118, p121, p123, p124, p126, p127, p129, p130 left, p133, p134, p135, p136, p138, p139 top right, bottom left, p140, p141, p142, p143, p145, p146, p147, p148, p151, p152, p154, p156, p157, p159, p168, p171, p172, p174, p176, p177, p179.

**Bruce Geddes** p41, p81 bottom right, p108, p130 right, p139 top left, bottom right, p144.

**Beckers Entertainment, Columbia Tri Star** p91, p92.

## More World Food Titles

Brimming with cultural insight, the World Food series takes the guesswork out of new cuisines and provide the ideal guides to your own culinary adventures. The books cover everything to do with food and drink in each country – the history and evolution of the cuisine, its staples & specialities, and the kitchen philosophy of the people. You'll find definitive two-way dictionaries, menu readers and useful phrases for shopping, drunken apologies and much more.

The essential guides for travelling and non-travelling food lovers around the world, look out for the full range of World Food titles including:

**Deep South (USA),
Italy,
Morocco,
Spain,
Thailand,
Turkey,
Vietnam,
France,
Ireland &
Hong Kong.**

## Out to Eat Series

Lonely Planet's Out to Eat series takes its food seriously but offers a fresh approach with independent, unstuffy opinion on hundreds of hand-picked restaurants, bars and cafes in each city. Along with reviews, Out to Eat identifies the best culinary cul-de-sacs, describes cultural contexts of ethnic cuisines, and explains menu terms and ingredients.

Updated annually, new Out to Eat titles include:
**Melbourne, Paris, Sydney, London and San Francisco.**

## Planet Talk

Our FREE quarterly printed newsletter is full of tips from travellers and anecdotes from Lonely Planet guidebook authors. Every issue is packed with up-to-date travel news and advice, and includes:

a postcard from Lonely Planet co-founder Tony Wheeler
a swag of mail from travellers
a look at life on the road through the eyes of a Lonely Planet author
topical health advice
prizes for the best travel yarn
news about forthcoming Lonely Planet events
a complete list of Lonely Planet books and other titles

To join our mailing list, residents of the UK, Europe and Africa can email us at go@lonelyplanet.co.uk; residents of North and South America can do so at info@lonelyplanet.com; the rest of the world can email talk2us@lonelyplanet.com.au, or contact any Lonely Planet office.

# The Lonely Planet Story

Lonely Planet published its first book in 1973 in response to the numerous 'How did you do it?' questions Maureen and Tony Wheeler were asked after driving, bussing, hitching, sailing and railing their way from England to Australia. Written at a kitchen table and hand collated, trimmed and stapled, *Across Asia on the Cheap* became an instant local bestseller.

Eighteen months in South-East Asia resulted in their second guide, *South-East Asia on a Shoestring*, which they put together in a backstreet Chinese hotel in Singapore in 1975. The 'yellow bible', as it quickly became known to backpackers around the world, soon became the guide to the region. It has sold well over ¾ million copies and is now in its 10th edition, still retaining its familiar yellow cover.

Today there are over 400 titles, including travel guides, walking guides, language kits & phrasebooks, travel atlases & maps, diving guides, restaurant guides, first time travel guides, condensed guides, illustrated pictorials and travel literature. The company is the largest independent travel publisher in the world.

The emphasis continues to be on travel for independent travellers. Tony and Maureen still travel for several months of each year and play an active part in the writing, updating and quality control of Lonely Planet's guides.

They have been joined by over 120 authors and over 400 staff at our offices in Melbourne (Australia), Oakland (USA), London (UK) and Paris (France). Travellers themselves also make a valuable contribution to the guides through the feedback we receive in thousands of letters each year and on our web site.

The people at Lonely Planet strongly believe that travellers can make a positive contribution to the countries they visit, both through their appreciation of the countries' culture, wildlife and natural features, and through the money they spend. In addition, the company makes a direct contribution to the countries and regions it covers. Since 1986 a percentage of the income from each book has been donated to ventures such as famine relief in Africa; aid projects in India; agricultural projects in Central America; Greenpeace's efforts to halt French nuclear testing in the Pacific.

## Lonely Planet Offices

### Australia
PO Box 617, Hawthorn, Victoria 3122
☎ 03-9819 1877
fax 03-9819 6459
email:talk2us@lonelyplanet.com.au

### USA
150 Linden St, Oakland, CA 94607
☎ 510-893 8555  TOLL FREE: 800 275 8555
fax 510-893 8572
email: info@lonelyplanet.com

### UK
10a Spring Place, London NW5 3BH
☎ 020-7428 4800
fax 020-7428 4828
email: go@lonelyplanet.co.uk

### France
1 rue du Dahomey, 75011 Paris
☎ 01 55 25 33 00
fax 01 55 25 33 01
email: bip@lonelyplanet.fr